Information Analysis

THE COMPUTER STUDIES SERIES

Information Analysis

Janice Burn and Mike O'Neil

Series Editor: David Hatter

Paradigm

Paradigm Publishing Limited
Avenue House
131–133 Holland Park Avenue
London W11 4UT

© Janice Burn and Mike O'Neil 1987

First published 1987

British Library Cataloguing in Publication Data

Burn, Janice
   Information analysis.—(The computer
   studies series)
   1. Business—Information services
   I. Title II. O'Neil, Mike III. Series
   025′.06658   HF5351

ISBN 0-948825-50-2

Typeset by Mathematical Composition Setters Ltd, Salisbury.
Production by Deer Park Productions, Tavistock and printed in Great Britain
by Hollen Street Press Limited, Slough, Berks.

Contents

About the book

This book deals with the provision of information in today's business organisations, giving an analysis in terms of

- the information needed
- the requirements to meet that need
- specifications and procedures
- the techniques available

It is particularly suitable for students taking BTEC Higher National Certificate and Diploma courses in Computer Studies, CNAA Computer Studies degrees and a wide range of Business Studies courses.

The book reflects the emerging importance and increasing attention being given to the provision of meaningful information. Aspects of information that have until now tended to be treated separately in textbooks are integrated: the book relates 'organisations: their structure and functions' with 'essential topics in quantitative decision-making' so that the reader can establish a firm foundation for Information Systems development. Thus the book is essentially about the development of a sensible and consistent approach to effective information provision, whether the information analysis exercise be large or small, the information analyst working alone or within a team.

Much of the material in the book refers to a case study on a local authority organisation, Anyshire County Council. This is a theme with which every reader will be familiar — the operations and activities of local authorities affect all of us. Moreover, local authorities are large organisations with widespread interests: they have diverse responsibilities, from highways to education, but their various departments have many information requirements in common. For instance, population projections are useful to both the Education Department (planning for numbers of teachers and expenditure per pupil) and the Social Services Department (planning for support services to different age groups). A local authority is not necessarily concerned, as is the private sector, with products and profits; however, it does deal with services and expenditure and it strives to be efficient right across its operations in much the same way as does a private sector organisation. This discipline is reinforced by the extra problems of financial constraint currently facing local authorities.

The book begins by highlighting in Chapter 1 some of the more common types of information problems. This, together with the Anyshire County Council case study, provides the context for consideration, in Chapters 2, 3 and 4, of the 'status' of information and its provision in organisations, both generally and specifically by example. In a natural development, Chapters 5 and 6 investigate the provision of information in Anyshire's Social Services Department.

For the simple reason that much of any organisation's information is based on data of a financial nature Chapter 7 gives an insight into accounting procedures and budgetary control. In Chapters 8 and 9 the reader is introduced to some common quantitative techniques that allow the business manager to obtain a basis for decisions and to improve his/her own and the organisation's effectiveness. The final chapter of the book considers a number of factors involved in the computer-based development of information systems and puts into perspective the role of the information analyst.

Selected exercises are given in the Appendix. The reader is encouraged and advised to use whatever suitable computer software packages are applicable and available.

We sincerely hope that you will enjoy the book.

Janice Burn
Mike O'Neil

About the series

This series of books is the first which presents an integrated approach to the complete range of topics needed by students of Computer Studies who are currently on the Higher National Certificate and Diploma courses or the first two years of a degree course.

Each volume has been so designed through its approach and treatment of a particular subject area to stand alone: at the same time the books in the series together give a comprehensive and integrated view of computing with special attention devoted to applications in business and industry.

The authors are experienced teachers and practitioners of computing and are responsible for the design of computing syllabuses and courses for the Business and Technician Education Council, the British Computer Society and the Council for National Academic Awards. In addition many of them are members of the appropriate boards of studies for the three organisations. Their combined experience in computing practice covers all aspects of the subject.

The series presents a uniform and clear treatment of the subject and will fit well into the syllabuses of the great majority of undergraduate courses.

Setting the scene

1.1 Introduction

The scenario that follows describes the type of situation which might be found by interpreting the figures published in regular local government reports. It highlights difficulties in:

- accessing all information relevant to a particular issue;
- interpreting the value of information in particular situations;
- using information in an unbiased manner for particular concerns.

The situation provides a very brief introduction to the need for a full understanding of the nature and value of information. In particular, it stresses the importance of gaining a broad appreciation of the context in which the information will serve.

The extracts that you are about to read from the *Anytown Post*, Anyshire's weekly free newspaper, set the scene for a major case study which will be developed throughout the book. At this stage attention is focused on one issue only, namely the allocation of funding in local government education and social services departments.

1.2 Local press reports

1.2.1 *Anytown Post* — week ending March 7th

Anyshire Education not up to Standard

Figures published today by the Government (see Table 1.1) show an appalling level of provision for educational services across the county. The figures

Table 1.1 Government comparative statistics (actuals) — Anyshire compared with five other similar counties (B–F)

	Anyshire	B	C	D	E	F	Rank (Total = 6)	All CCs	Rank (Total = 39)	Rank change (Total = 39) over year
(1) *Population ('000) All services*	526.9	503.1	543.0	584.5	546.2	470.0	—	—	—	—
(2) Net cost per 1,000 pop(£)	286,460	332,740	314,130	291,040	287,700	310,710	6th	296,520	29th	—
Education Primary										
(3) Pupil/teacher ratio	*23.97*	22.16	23.93	23.39	24.73	23.00	5th	23.28	30th	+3
(4) Gross cost per pupil(£)	*504*	626	542	528	559	531	6th	531	36th	—
Secondary										
(5) Pupil/teacher ratio	*17.34*	17.02	16.70	16.49	17.73	17.58	4th	17.05	25th	–10
(6) Gross cost per pupil(£)	*749*	820	898	811	812	795	6th	790	36th	–4
Further education										
(7) Net cost per 1,000 pop(£)	*15,090*	16,230	18,450	19,570	16,280	19,700	6th	15,890	23rd	+10
School meals										
(8) Revenue/cost ratio(%)	*34.9*	56.0	42.3	37.6	40.4	32.9	5th	38.8	31st	–6
(9) Pupils receiving free meals as proportion of the school roll(%)	*7.7*	8.0	4.7	8.8	4.4	4.8	3rd	7.4	19th	+9

show Anyshire ranking thirty-sixth out of a league table of thirty-nine county councils, based on the amount of money councils are prepared to spend per pupil. The report suggests that a level this far below the national average can only mean that children are suffering a poor standard of teaching in inadequately provisioned schools.

Councillor Alan Herriott, Chairman of the Education Committee, was unavailable for comment. Councillor Jane Watt, spokeswoman for the opposition and herself a mother of two primary school children, said 'I intend to ask for a full statement regarding the estimated budget provision for next year. The present party in control of the County Council are now reaping the harvest of their short-sighted financial stringencies over the last four years. It is time the ratepayers of this county voted for the future of their children.'

1.2.2 *Anytown Post* — week ending March 14th

'Government figures misleading' says Education Committee Chairman
Alan Herriott said today that it was necessary to take a much broader view of educational expenditure than that suggested by the government league table. In fact, the figures produced were misleading and concealed a considerable shift in educational allocations which had proved necessary after the disastrous five years of mismanagement which preceded his party gaining power four years ago.

Mr Herriott produced a table summarising expenditure per pupil over the last six years related to the retail price index so that the effects of inflation could be clearly highlighted (see Table 1.2).

Mr Herriott pointed out that there had been a considerable increase in expenditure levels since his party gained control, and indeed that primary school education had for the first time in many years seen a real increase, this at a time when government cutbacks kept most services operating below the level of inflationary efficiency.

When asked to comment on this latest report Ms Watts said: 'If my

Table 1.2 Expenditure per pupil over last six years

Year	Expenditure per pupil index Primary	Secondary	Retail Price Index
y − 5	100	100	100
y − 4	111	110	116
y − 3	117	112	126
y − 2	132	126	142
y − 1	150	137	168
y	197	181	188

children's schooling is the result of an increase in spending on primary school education then all I can say is heaven help them when they reach secondary school!'

1.2.3 *Anytown Post* — week ending March 28th

Misguided use of educational budget

At a special meeting of ratepayers called today Jane Watts said that in order to gain a real understanding of the figures presented by Education Committee Chairman Alan Herriott and their horrendous long-term implications the ratepayers needed possession of the full facts. After much research she had prepared a table summarising the overall trends in the county and the country as a whole. It was her belief that the results would come as a shock in the light of the current budget provisions for education. Figure 1.1 shows

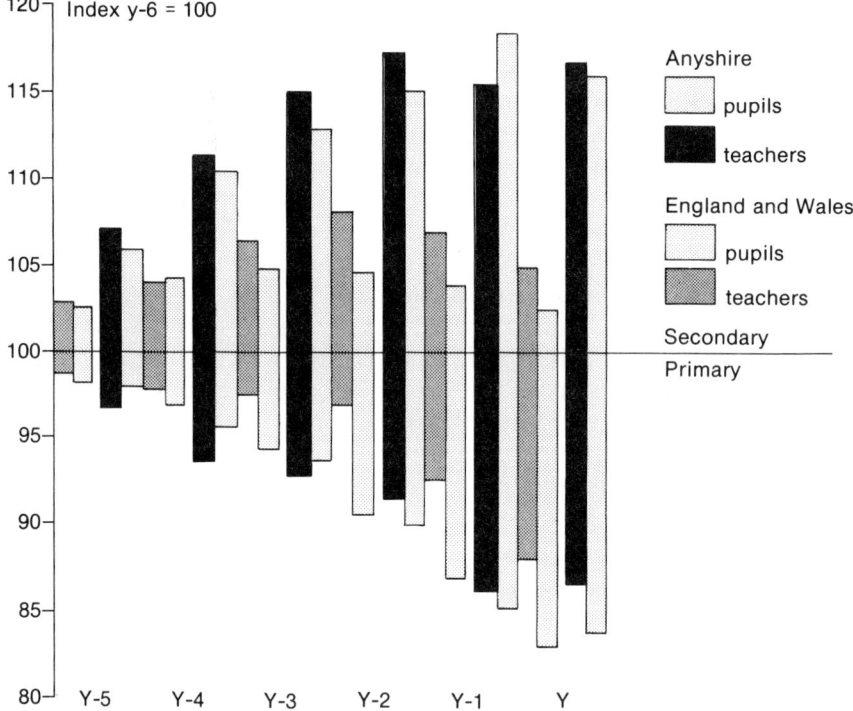

Figure 1.1 Trends in pupil/teacher numbers over last six years. A beginning has been made with improving pupil : teacher ratios compared with $y - 2/y - 1$, although these remain less good than the national average as shown. It is also now seen to be necessary as secondary pupil numbers begin to fall to base the assessment of teacher requirements on the curricula provided in schools rather than purely on pupil numbers

that the county has experienced a steep decline in the number of primary school pupils in line with trends across the country as a whole. There has, however, been an upward trend in secondary school student numbers greatly in excess of the national average which, she suggests, could have been accurately predicted some years previously.

'Surely the allocation of the educational budget should have been directed towards the groups in greatest need — secondary school children. These figures merely emphasise the failure of the present party to perceive local needs as differing from national needs and their continuing short-sighted planning and control.'

Councillor Herriott was unavailable for comment but in his absence Mark Tidy, Educational Finance Officer, confirmed: 'Indeed it is true that we have experienced falling numbers in the primary sector. However, the larger increases in expenditure are a reflection of the fact that as pupil numbers fall expenditure per pupil tends to rise, since certain fixed costs remain to be shared among fewer pupils.'

1.2.4 *Anytown Post* — week ending April 4th

Why fewer children mean higher pupil–teacher ratios

Councillor Jane Watts produced statistics at the Education Committee meeting yesterday to show that the pupil–teacher ratios in primary and secondary schools were well below the national average.

The decrease in student numbers should have led to improved ratios in primary schools but, in fact, the figures (see Table 1.3) showed little improvement on six years previous. 'It is most noticeable that the figures are worse than two years ago despite an increase in expenditure — what is the money being spent on?'

The meeting ended with a final comment from Ms Watts. 'This only proves that, as usual, we are paying far more to provide far less.'

Table 1.3 Pupil–teacher ratios for last seven years

Year	Anyshire Primary	Anyshire Secondary	England and Wales Primary	England and Wales Secondary
y − 6	24.5	17.4	23.9	17.0
y − 5	24.9	17.2	23.8	17.0
y − 4	25.1	17.3	23.6	17.1
y − 3	24.7	17.1	23.1	16.8
y − 2	24.0	16.9	22.3	16.5
y − 1	24.4	17.9	22.4	16.5
y	24.3	17.3	22.5	16.6

1.2.5 *Anytown Post*: special election edition — June

The elections this week have swept a new party into power in the County Council. Part of the swing has been attributed to the local debate on educational provision in the county and the growing awareness of the electorate for a real need to provide long-term planning for the future of their children.

Newly elected Education Committee Chairperson Jane Watts has promised an immediate injection of £2.5 million into next year's budget aimed at improving the secondary school service provision.

'It is time to take a long-term view of our planning for the future. In this era of information technology decisions should be made on the basis of the best collective information available — this means co-ordinating all sources of information available to the council and making this available to councillors and ratepayers.'

1.2.6 *Anytown Post* — October (16 months later)

Plight of elderly must take precedence

Councillor Alan Herriott spoke today of his growing concern for the elderly and, in particular, the need for directing funds away from less critical areas towards social services and help for the aged.

In his statement Councillor Herriott quoted the latest government report providing population predictions for the 15 years after the census.

'Not only does this prove conclusively that there is going to be a massive upsurge in the over 70s client group, but it also highlights a substantial drop in client groups where we are currently expending vast and increasing amounts of ratepayers' funds. In particular, the drop, already apparent in the 11–15 year old age group, will result in over-staffed and under-utilised secondary schools unless we rapidly divert some funds into more deserving areas.'

Councillor J. Watts, chairperson of the Education Committee, was asked to comment on the report — printed in full below — but was unavailable.

Extract from a government report

Client Group Projections

The types and quantities of services that need to be provided by the County Council are closely determined by the number of people who are served by the authority. Over the past ten years the total population of the county has increased by more than 12%, which is one of the highest growth rates of all English shire counties. As far as the next ten years is concerned the most noticeable factor is the way that the numbers of people in the various age groups are going to change:

of special interest are the young and elderly who constitute the major demand for county services.

It is clear that the number of children of secondary school age will fall markedly over the next ten years. However, the number of younger children is more difficult to predict since the birth rate has been erratic in recent years. Initially, the annual number of births rose after rapid falls in previous years, but in the last year the number of births has fallen again. The population projections given in Table 1.4 assume that the birth rate will gradually rise during the next ten years; thus, if current conditions prevail the projections of the 0–4 age group especially will not be achieved, and similarly the recovery in primary school numbers shown toward the end of the period will be delayed.

Of particular significance in the elderly population is the fact that the number of very old people will bear the greatest increase; it is the very old who make most demand on the social services.

Table 1.4 Population projections over ten years

Year	The young 0–4	The young 5–10	The young 11–15	Those of working age 16–59/64	The elderly 65–74	The elderly 75–79	The elderly 80 +
y − 1	35,000	47,400	44,700	312,900	43,900	14,300	13,500
y (current year)	35,500	45,700	44,500	316,800	43,600	14,600	14,000
y + 2	37,600	43,000	43,500	325,200	43,200	14,900	14,700
y + 4	39,500	43,000	41,200	333,300	42,700	15,200	15,200
y + 6	40,900	44,500	37,900	340,100	42,800	15,300	15,800
y + 8	42,200	46,900	36,000	345,500	42,900	15,200	16,200
y + 10	43,400	48,500	36,400	349,000	42,800	14,900	16,600
Change over 10 years	+24%	+2.3%	−18.6%	+11.5%	−2.5%	+4.2%	+23%

1.3 Summary

The situation described provides an example of the use of information to gain power and control. It could also be said to show the *misuse* of information since particular statistics are presented out of their original context and without full consideration of all the issues involved.

Information in itself has no value; it is only when it is used to affect opinion that we can weigh its real substance. In order to assess this worth the information recipient must develop an overall understanding of the situation and its affecting characteristics. It is also important, however, to evaluate the information in itself for its accuracy, reliability, timeliness and relevance.

The remainder of this chapter presents the full case study of Anyshire County Council. This study will be used throughout the book to provide specific examples related to information analysis. Students are not expected to assimilate all of the details contained in the case study at first reading but to refer to the study as they progress through the book. Later chapters will examine particular areas in more detail and provide further background for the case study. The main purpose of the study is to show the large quantities of information which may be collected and the need to present the information in various ways in order to match the required information flow of various groups.

In this first part of the book we will aim to present the global context for information analysis in an organisational environment and then explore the concepts of information and its relevance to particular organisational situations.

1.4 Case study: Anyshire County Council

1.4.1 Introduction

The present system of local government in England and Wales is based on two principal tiers of local authority — county councils and district councils.

Anyshire is one of 47 non-metropolitan county councils, and within the county there are 7 district councils.

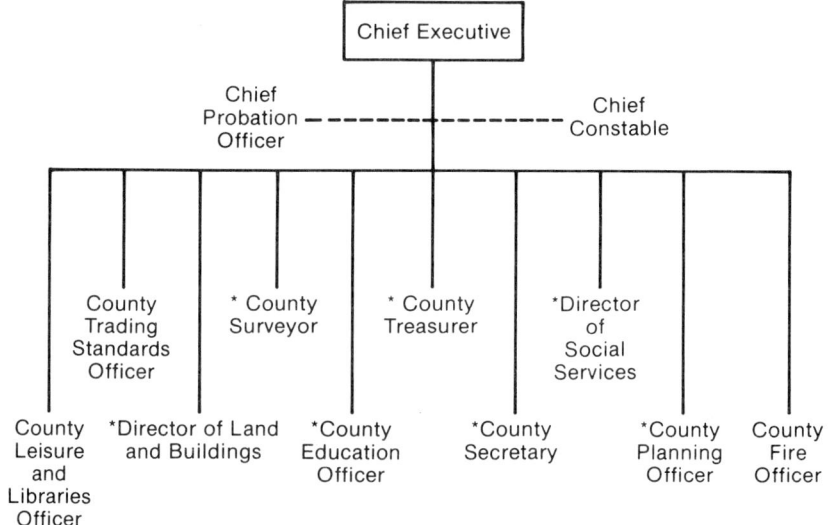

Figure 1.2 Personnel organisation

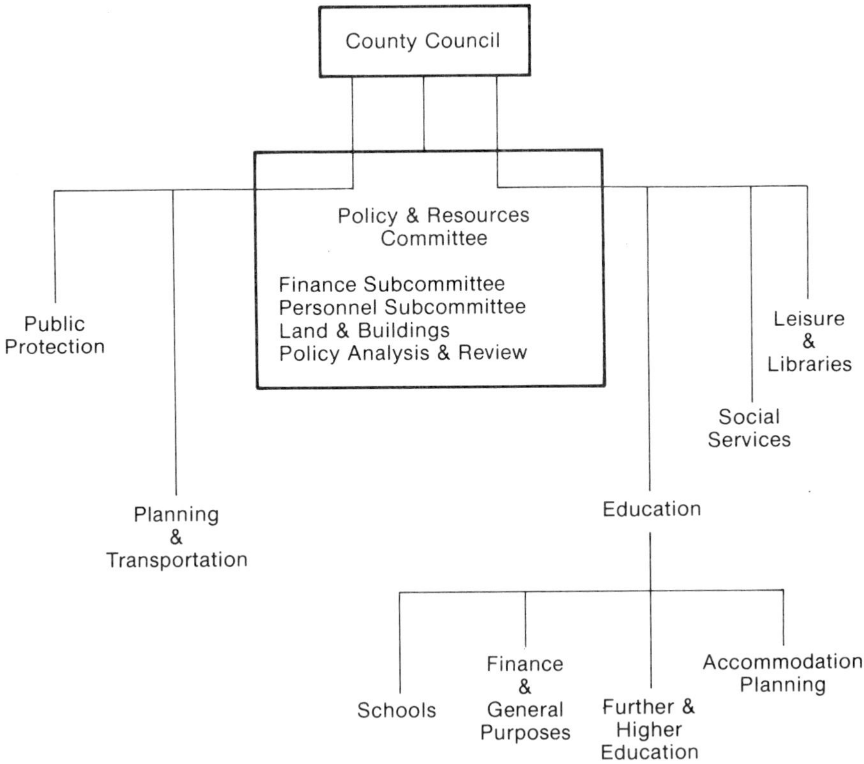

Figure 1.3 Committee organisation

The principal services provided by the county are as follows:

● Education
● Planning and transportation
● Public protection
● Social services
● Leisure and libraries

Figures 1.2 and 1.3 show the personnel and committee organisational hierarchies.

Committee structure (*general overview*)

The workings of the local authority are divided out amongst the various committees and sub-committees created. The 1972 Local Government Act enabled authorities to set up committees in which the councillors take an active part. There are three main types of committee.

(1) *Statutory and permissive.* Statutory committees may be, for example, the Education Committee or Police Committee; permissive committees are those which may be set up if the authority wishes to do so.
(2) *Standing and special.* Standing committees are set up on a permanent basis and special committees will be brought about to deal with specific short-term issues.
(3) *Service and machinery.* These types of committee will be used to administer services or will be concerned with administrative machinery such as finance and personnel.

Ultimately, the various committees are responsible to the Council. Most committees have a wide measure of delegated authority on matters which do not involve new policy, therefore increasing the speed with which decisions are made.

Party politics in local government

Party politics play a large role in the operation of local government. The involvement of party politics in local government began in the last century with the Labour movement which realised that local reforms could be brought about by having sympathetic councillors · represent their case. Therefore, candidates stood for election whilst being financed by party funds.

Since the Second World War the Conservative movement has been more openly active, and more recently other parties have also become involved.

An advantage of having party politics within local government is that authorities will be more responsive to public opinion. Some people also argue that local issues are linked to national issues and accurate planning and administration could not be executed through divergent interests at national and local level.

However, solutions to local problems may in some instances be delayed or diluted by the working of the party political system. Indeed, the Maud Committee in its findings reported that to increase the dependence of local authorities on central government, a result of the closer association of political parties at national and local level, would adversely affect the provision of services.

The council and its various committees

The council, made up of county councillors, is elected every four years. It is the ultimate decision-making body within any local authority. The way in which the decision-making role is exercised differs widely from authority to authority.

In some authorities the full council considers the minutes and reports of every committee meeting, and in others virtually nothing comes before the full council unless members specifically ask for a particular item to be placed upon the agenda.

The main differences are procedural, as in both cases members receive all the relevant information. They do, however, choose which items to discuss at the meeting. The council will usually reserve for itself the most important wide-reaching policy decisions and will request the various sub-committees to advise and report upon these matters.

The constitution of the various committees and sub-committees must reflect the political influences of the county council so that the wishes of the ruling party will not be frustrated.

The Local Government Act 1972 prescribes the procedural arrangements relating to the meetings of the county council and its allied committees. The minutes of the various committees must be available for inspection by the electorate and the 1972 Act states that the press and public will be allowed to attend the full council meeting, although they can be excluded from parts if it is considered to be in the public interest.

Delegation of powers and duties to committees and sub-committees

Policy and Resources Committee
The duties of the Policy and Resources Committee are as follows.

(1) To guide the county council in the formulation of its corporate plan of objectives and priorities, and for this purpose to recommend to the council such forward programmes and other steps as may be necessary to achieve those objectives, either in whole or in part, during specific time spans. For this purpose to consider the broad social and economic needs of the authority and methods of comprehensive importance to the area including the contents of the structure plans. To advise the council generally as to its financial and economic policies. Thirty county coun-cillors are appointed to serve on this committee.

(2) To review the effectiveness of all the council's work and the standards and levels of service provided. To identify the need for new services and to keep under review the necessity for existing ones.

(3) To submit to the council concurrent reports with the programme com-mittees upon new policies or changes in policy formulated by such com-mittees, particularly those which may have significant impact upon the corporate plan or the resources of the council.

(4) To be responsible for allocating and controlling the financial manpower and land resources of the council.

(5) To ensure that the organisation and management processes of the council are designed to make the most effective contribution to the

achievement of the council's objectives. To keep them under review in the light of changing circumstances, making recommendations as necessary for change in either committee or departmental structure, or the distribution of function and responsibilities.

(6) To be concerned, together with the appropriate programme committee, in the appointment of heads of departments and any deputies.

Sub-committees of the Policy and Resources Committee

(1) Finance Sub-committee
The duties of the Finance Sub-committee are to keep under review and advise the Policy and Resources Committee on all aspects of policy in relation to the council's services and the achievement of the overall objectives, and to examine and advise the Policy and Resources Committee upon the revenue and capital estimates of programme committees.

(2) Personnel and Management Services Sub-committee
The duties of the Personnel and Management Services Sub-committee are to keep under review and advise the Policy and Resources Committee on all aspects of the manpower needs of the council for the effective discharge of its functions and achievement of its objectives, on the manpower implications of any proposed new policies or significant alterations to existing policies, on policies relating to the conditions of service and welfare of the employees, and on the retirement training and effective utilisation of staff at all levels. It shall also advise on the promotion of good industrial relations between the council and all employees, including effective communication and joint consultation with employees, and procedures for resolving disputes and on proposals for any alteration in departmental establishments, grading of posts, salaries or conditions of service of officers.

(3) Land and Buildings Sub-committee
The duties of the Land and Buildings Sub-committee are to keep under review and advise the Policy and Resources Committee on all aspects of the land needs of the council for the effective discharge of its functions and the achievement of its objectives, including the implications in relation to land resources and needs of any proposed new policies or significant alterations to existing policies. Further duties include to keep under review and advise the Policy and Resources Committee on the development and effective and economic use of the county council land and buildings, to secure co-ordination of the county council's activities in relation to the acquisition and disposal of land, to recommend the acquisition of land and buildings in advance of requirements when this is likely to be a financial advantage to the council and consistent with their plans and objectives, to recommend

the disposal of properties which are surplus to the council's requirements and to advise the Policy and Resources Committee on the building, acquisition, management, allocation and furnishing of office accommodation.

Education Committee
The duties of the Education Committee are to advise the county council on all aspects of the council's functions as local education authority. Thirty county councillors are appointed to serve on this committee.

Social Services Committee
The duties of the Social Services Committee are to advise the county council on all aspects of its functions as social services authority. Twenty-five county councillors are appointed to serve on this committee.

Planning and Transportation Committee
The duties of the Planning and Transportation Committee are to advise the county council on all aspects of its functions relating to town and county planning including the preparation and review of the county structure plan and to advise the county council on all aspects of its function relating to highways, transport, road traffic regulations, and road safety. Thirty county councillors are appointed to serve on this committee.

The General Services Committee
The duties of the General Services Committee are to advise the county council on all aspects of its functions under legislation relating to consumer and public protection, smallholdings and land drainage, refuse disposal and other miscellaneous matters referred to it by the council. Twenty-five county councillors are appointed to serve on this committee.

Leisure and Libraries Committee
The duties of the Leisure and Libraries Committee are to advise the county council on the provision and promotion of recreational, cultural and leisure services for the community, on the development of tourism in the county, on the provision of entertainment and on assistance to the arts, including museums and galleries, and for those purposes to foster and maintain co-ordination and co-operation with the Education Committee, other local authorities, development corporations and appropriate national, regional and local organisations and voluntary bodies. Twenty-five county councillors are appointed to serve on this committee.

Police Committee
The Police Committee, appointed in accordance with section 2 of the Police Act 1964, is the police authority for the county. The duty of the committee is to secure the maintenance of an adequate and efficient police force for

the county and exercise for that purpose the powers conferred on a police authority by the Police Act of 1964. Sixteen county councillors are appointed to serve on this committee.

1.4.2 Profile of Anyshire

The current population is 542,000 which represents an increase of 11.5 per cent over the last decade. This shows a sizeable increase in comparison to population gains across the rest of England and Wales as shown in Figure 1.4 but is also high when compared within the classification of other non-metropolitan counties. The growth rate is, however, slowing down and the pattern in geographical terms has been uneven with urban areas growing faster than rural areas — 13.3 per cent and 10.8 per cent respectively — although variations within these groups are considerable.

Underlying the increasing numbers there are fundamental changes occurring in the characteristics of the population which are altering the pattern of demand for public and private services.

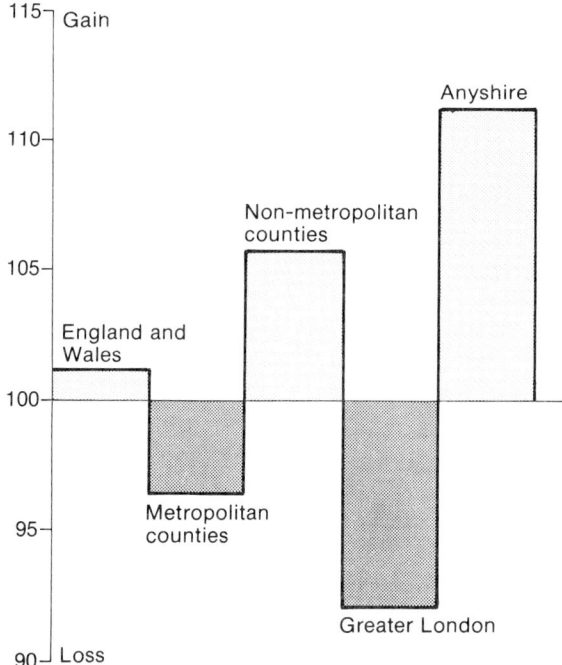

Figure 1.4 Anyshire population changes over last decade

Age of population

The current population could be described as 'young' but in the process of ageing. Figure 1.5 shows projections over a 15 year period which suggest

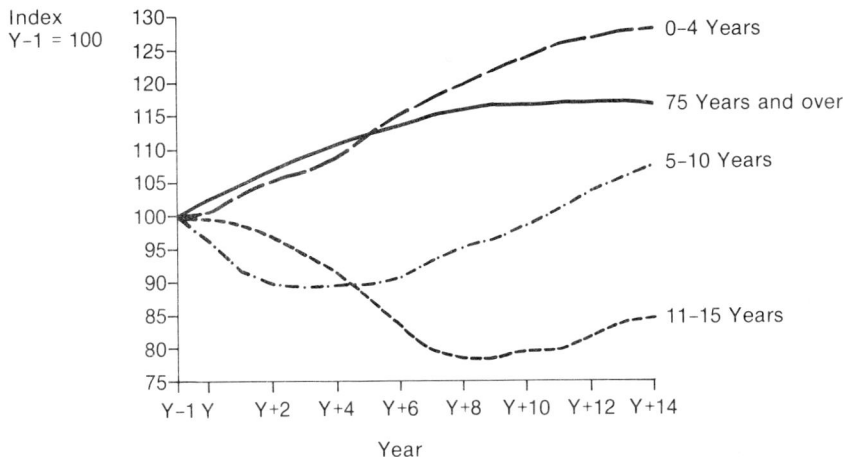

Figure 1.5   Anyshire projected population structure over 15 year period

dramatic increases in the population groups 0–4 years old and 75 years old and over, but a real decline in the 11–15 year olds.

The general pattern across all age groups (not shown in Figure 1.5) indicates a projected decline in real terms for the 10–20 age groups and relative declines for all other groups apart from the 20–29 year olds and the two groups already highlighted.

Employment

The general employment figures reflect an increase in unemployment over the last 10 years but conceal a rise in the number of full-time students and higher economic activity amongst married women as shown in Table 1.5.

Table 1.5 Economic activity

% men aged 16–64 years	Year		% women aged 16–59 years	Year	
	y − 11	y − 1		y − 11	y − 1
In employment	92.4	81.5	In employment	55.7	57.8
Out of employment	3.3	10.3	Out of employment	2.1	4.3
Economically inactive	4.3	8.2	Economically inactive	42.1	37.9
of which, full-time			of which, full-time		
students	(2.8)	(4.9)	students	(2.7)	(5.0)
			Married and		
			economically active	52.5	59.3

Households and types

There are 189,700 households in the county representing a 20 per cent increase over the last decade. Married couples with children under 16 account for only a quarter of all households and only 14.3 per cent of households contain one or more children under 5 years. One person, pensioner households have increased from 19,000 to 25,800 and over 44,000 households comprise exclusively persons of pensionable age.

Car ownership increased as shown in Figure 1.6 but there are still over 65,600 households without access to a car.

Other statistics include:

● 59.5 per cent of households are owner-occupiers
● 32.1 per cent of households are council rented
● 8.4 per cent of households are privately rented

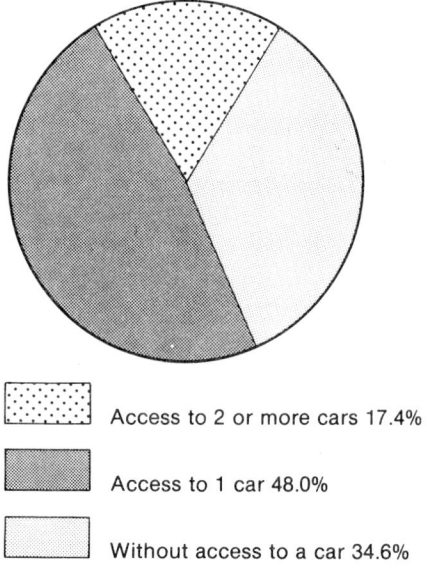

☐ Access to 2 or more cars 17.4%

☐ Access to 1 car 48.0%

☐ Without access to a car 34.6%

Figure 1.6   Car ownership during last year

1.4.3 Budgets and manpower

The current budget is £243.6 million of which:

● 41 per cent is raised from rates
● 40.7 per cent comes from grants from central government
● 18.3 per cent is raised from fees and other charges (by the county council)

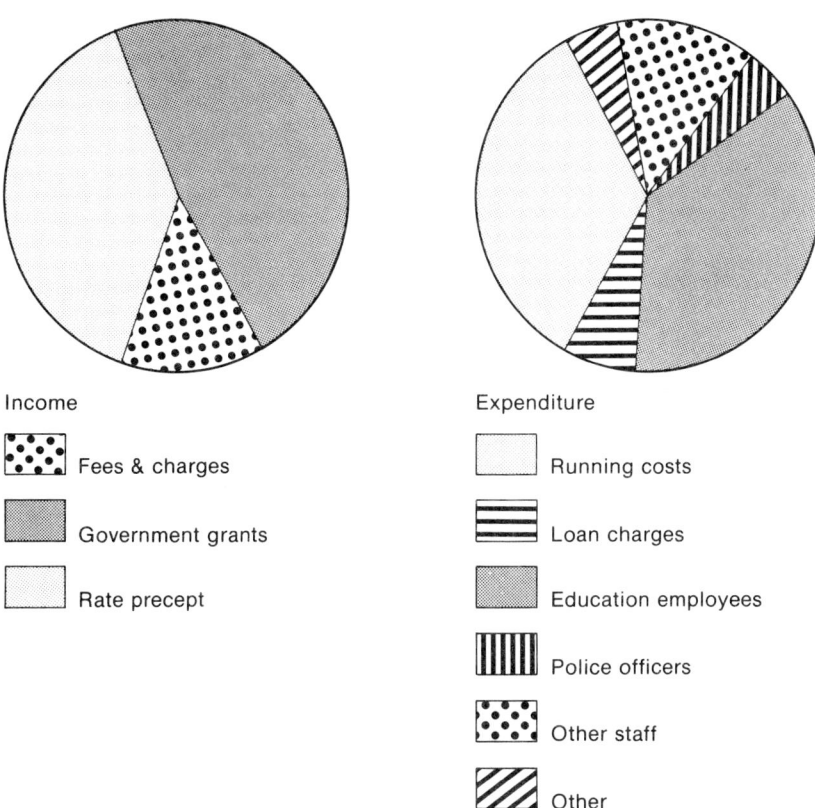

Income

▨ Fees & charges

▨ Government grants

▢ Rate precept

Expenditure

▢ Running costs

▤ Loan charges

▨ Education employees

▥ Police officers

▨ Other staff

▨ Other

Figure 1.7   Income and expenditure of the County Council during last year

Table 1.6 Number of employees on the county council payroll, March this year (full-time equivalent)

	Non-manual	Manual	Total	Change over 1 year
Central Services	420.5	36.5	457.0	+ 3.0
Education: teachers, lecturers	6344.5	—	6344.5	+ 173.5
other	1499.5	2414.5	3914.0	+ 211.0
Fire	253.5	12.0	265.5	+ 2.5
Highways & Transportation	279.5	244.0	523.5	− 0.5
Leisure & Libraries	262.0	16.0	278.0	+ 8.0
Planning	35.0	—	35.0	− 1.0
Police	1262.5	66.0	1328.5	+ 12.0
Probation & Courts	177.0	13.0	190.0	+ 1.5
Social Services	912.5	874.5	1790.0	+ 117.0
Trading Standards	31.0	1.0	32.0	—
Total	11480.5	3677.5	15158.0	+ 527.0

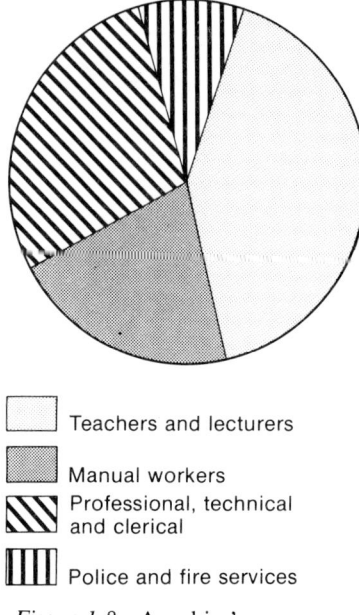

Teachers and lecturers

Manual workers

Professional, technical and clerical

Police and fire services

Figure 1.8   Anyshire's manpower

Income and expenditure breakdowns are shown in Figure 1.7 for the previous year.

The county council is a labour intensive organisation with over 15,000 employees distributed as shown in Figure 1.8. Over 75 per cent of all employees are engaged in the direct provision of services with less than 10

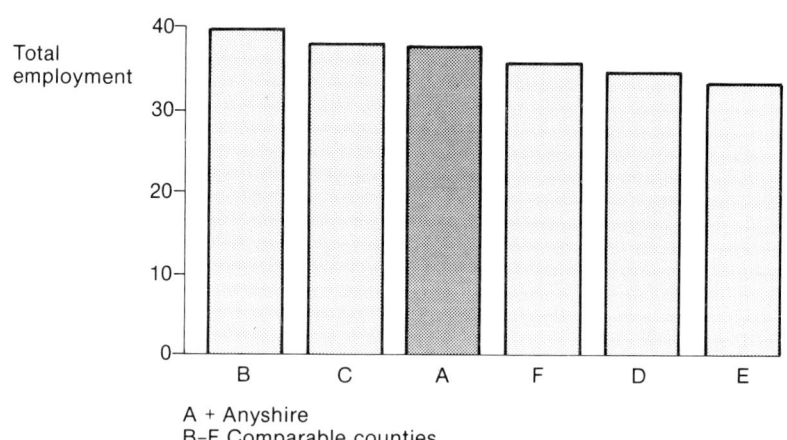

A + Anyshire
B–F Comparable counties

Figure 1.9   Total number employed by the County Council per 100,000 population rose from 35.9 in March last year. The position with regard to other comparable counties is shown

per cent engaged in purely clerical and administrative work. The restoration of the budget in the last year led to an increase in staff resources and an employment level within the county as shown in Table 1.6 and Figure 1.9.

1.4.4 Services (in order of expenditure)

Education

Education is provided for approximately 97,000 pupils, 16,000 F.E. students, and 20,000 adult education enrolments. Trends in pupil–teacher numbers over the last six years, as shown in Figure 1.1, indicate a steep decline in the number of primary school pupils, a halt in the upward trend in secondary schools and the beginning of an overall annual decline.

The pupil–teacher ratios are not as high as the national average at present and expenditure per pupil, while rising, has not kept pace with inflation over the last ten years.

Highways

The county council is responsible for the upkeep of 3,441 kilometres of roads in the county. In addition, it maintains 254 kilometres of motorways and trunk roads on behalf of the Department of Transport. Subsidies are provided for essential public transport facilities. Street lighting is also maintained.

Waste disposal services are provided with 9 county council and 48 private landfill sites disposing of 750,000 tonnes of waste per year. Twelve waste recycling centres are also in operation.

A breakdown of road accident figures over the last year is provided in Figure 1.10.

Social services

The county council has 935 children in care. Of these 66 per cent are placed in the community, not in residential establishments.

The county council also cares for:

  1,133 elderly people in residential care;
     89 mentally handicapped;
    641 handicapped at training centres;
  5,000 elderly or handicapped with domestic help;
270,000 meals on wheels to be served.

The annual rate of referrals, that is number of problems referred for

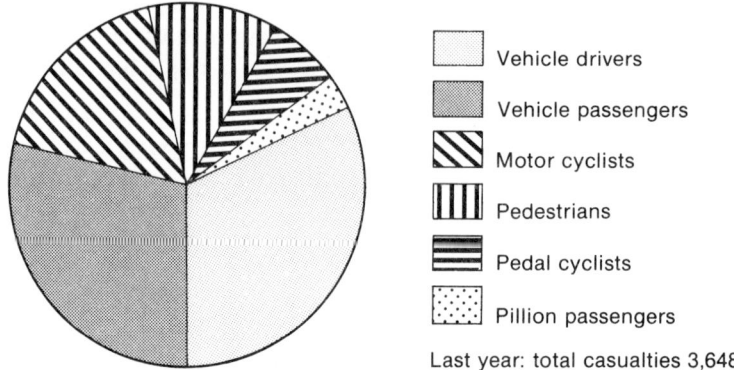

Vehicle drivers

Vehicle passengers

Motor cyclists

Pedestrians

Pedal cyclists

Pillion passengers

Last year: total casualties 3,648

Figure 1.10   Casualties as a result of road traffic accidents last year

help, is around 21,000, and the breakdown of expenditure shows:

33 per cent are children and young people;
22 per cent are chronically ill, sick and handicapped;
45 per cent are elderly.

Police

About 18,000 emergency 999 calls for assistance are received at Police Headquarters Operations Centre each year.

Of 30,800 reported crimes approximately 40 per cent were cleared up last year.

A communications interface provides a link to the Police National Computer system.

Fire

Each year the Fire Brigade turns out to about 5,000 emergency incidents and carries out about 8,000 prevention inspections.

The 21 stations in Anyshire operate as one of the cheapest and most cost effective units in the country, where as a whole fire losses presently amount to over £450 million.

Leisure and libraries

Over 1.25 million books are available for loan and over 6 million issues are made in any year. Leisure services are assisted by grants to local community and sports groups and combine to around £100,000 per year.

1.4.5 Central services

There are four main departments as follows.

(1) *Chief executive's department*
Main functions are as follows:

- overall responsibility for all paid staff and policy advice to the council and committees
- personnel function
- research and policy planning
- employment promotion

(2) *County secretary's department*
Main functions are as follows:

- administration of committees
- provision of legal services
- administration of council accommodation
- operation of central stores and negotiations or contracts
- printing services
- management services
- emergency planning
- registration of births, marriages and deaths
- county council elections

(3) *County treasurer's department*
Main functions are as follows:

- provision of financial advice to the county council
- control of the preparation of revenue and capital budgets
- financial planning and evaluation
- internal audits
- computer services
- management of loans and investments
- payment of salaries and accounts

(4) *Land and buildings department*
Main duties:

- design and supervision of construction work
- building and plant maintenance
- acquisition and disposal of property
- management of land holdings

Table 1.7 Income and expenditure over last year by service area

	Gross expenditure	Income	Net expenditure
	£	£	£
Education			
Nursery/primary education	28,229,900	121,000	28,108,900
Secondary education	49,471,400	820,500	48,650,900
Special education	5,885,200	189,800	5,695,400
Administration & inspection	3,854,800	20,800	3,834,000
Further education/teacher training	26,341,300	11,484,200	14,857,100
Youth & community	1,097,100	124,300	972,800
Meals	6,358,300	2,274,800	4,083,500
Other	7,609,500	3,574,300	4,035,200
Fire service	3,524,400	172,500	3,351,900
Trading standards	432,200	30,800	401,400
Waste disposal	1,673,200	182,500	1,490,700
Leisure & libraries (with archives)	2,852,000	169,000	2,683,000
Planning	690,700	22,800	667,900
Highways	22,730,500	10,936,100	11,794,400
Central services	1,978,300	1,394,000	584,300
Police	17,973,600	9,754,800	8,218,800
Social services			
Children & young people	6,880,800	1,474,200	5,406,600
Sick & handicapped	4,587,200	982,800	3,604,400
Elderly	9,383,000	2,010,300	7,372,700
Other services			
Magistrates courts	200,600	—	200,600
Probation & after care	226,800	—	226,800
Land drainage precept	1,113,700	—	1,113,700
Other	3,020,000	4,788,100	CR 1,768,100
Contributions to			
Repairs and renewals fund	4,720,000	800,000	3,920,000
Insurance fund	250,000	—	250,000
Total	£211,084,500	£51,327,600	£159,756,900

* Figures have been rounded to the nearest £100

Table 1.8 Net expenditure* by service area over three years

	Year before last $(y - 2)$ Actuals	Last year $(y - 1)$ Approved estimate	Last year $(y - 1)$ Actuals	This year (y) Original estimate
Education	£	£	£	£
Nursery/primary education	25,681,700	25,793,000	28,108,900	29,000,200
Secondary education	44,121,200	45,088,200	48,650,900	50,353,100
Special education	5,252,900	5,191,000	5,695,400	5,955,500
Administration & inspection	3,060,800	3,550,900	3,834,000	4,302,200
Further ed/teacher training	12,378,200	12,581,300	14,857,100	15,540,200
Youth & community	892,400	811,000	972,800	982,000
Meals	4,395,900	3,901,400	4,083,500	4,277,500
Other	3,421,200	3,949,800	4,035,200	4,822,900
Fire service	3,125,800	3,018,600	3,351,900	3,516,100
Trading standards	396,200	401,300	401,400	426,200
Waste disposal	1,402,300	1,408,200	1,490,700	1,418,300
Leisure & libraries (with archives)	2,640,400	2,506,000	2,683,000	2,854,900
Planning	624,600	754,800	667,900	806,000
Highways	11,612,100	10,738,300	11,794,400	12,851,500
Central services	80,700	485,700	584,300	716,300
Police	6,978,500	7,897,900	8,218,800	9,345,700
Social services				
Children & young people	4,709,100	4,915,300	5,406,600	5,899,900
Sick & handicapped	3,139,400	3,276,800	3,604,400	3,933,200
Elderly	6,421,500	6,702,600	7,372,700	8,045,300
Other services				
Magistrates courts	177,100	164,400	200,600	197,600
Probation & after care	186,800	201,100	226,800	236,800
Land drainage precept	954,600	956,900	1,113,700	1,120,600
Other	CR 1,472,200	CR 469,200	CR 1,768,100	CR 782,700
Contributions to				
Repairs and renewals fund	—	—	3,920,000	—
Insurance fund	—	—	250,000	—
Provision for contingency sum for pay and price increases	—	10,800,000	—	10,500,000
Total	£140,181,200	£154,625,300	£159,756,900	£176,319,300

*Figures have been rounded to the nearest £100

Table 1.9 Comparative statistics (year before last (y – 2)) actuals — Anyshire compared with five other similar counties (B–F)

	Anyshire	B	C	D	E	F	Rank (Total = 6)	All CCs	Rank (Total = 39)	Rank change over year
Population('000)	526.9	503.1	543.0	584.5	546.2	470.0	—	—	—	—
All services										
Net cost per 1,000 pop(£)	286,460	332,740	314,130	291,040	287,700	310,710	6th	296,520	29th	—
Education										
Primary										
Pupil/teacher ratio	23.97	22.16	23.93	23.39	24.73	23.00	5th	23.28	30th	+ 3
Gross cost per pupil(£)	504	626	542	528	559	531	6th	531	36th	—
Secondary										
Pupil/teacher ratio	17.34	17.02	16.70	16.49	17.73	17.58	4th	17.05	25th	– 10
Gross cost per pupil(£)	749	820	898	811	812	795	6th	790	36th	– 4
Further education										
Net cost per 1,000 pop.(£)	15,090	16,230	18,450	19,570	16,280	19,700	6th	15,890	23rd	+ 10
School meals										
Revenue/cost ratio(%)	34.9	36.0	42.3	37.6	40.4	32.9	5th	38.8	31st	– 6
Pupils receiving free meals as proportion of the school roll(%)	7.7	8.0	4.7	8.8	4.4	4.8	3rd	7.4	19th	+ 9
Social services										
Children in care										
As proportion of population aged under 18(%)	0.66	0.97	0.71	0.57	0.63	0.48	3rd	0.69	16th	– 4
Gross cost per child(£)	4,282	3,190	2,453	3,749	3,469	3,599	1st	3,214	5th	+ 1
Care of the elderly										
Supported residents as proportion of pop. aged 75 + (%)	2.91	4.03	3.13	4.08	—	4.17	5th	3.53	35th	—
Gross cost per resident/week(£)	72.97	80.40	78.13	73.22	83.51	64.66	5th	72.54	18th	– 2
Home helps										
Contact hours per 1,000 aged 65 +	7,435	11,158	9,275	9,791	12,214	15,226	6th	9,889	33rd	– 5

Indicator									+/−
Manpower									
Social work staff per 1,000 pop.	*0.45*	0.43	0.43	0.37	0.41	0.42	0.39 1st	0.43 12th	+16
Admin employees per 1,000 pop.	*0.32*	0.23	0.23	0.24	0.23	0.32	0.33 2nd	0.31 13th	− 8
Whole service									
Net cost per 1,000 pop.(£)	*27,080*	33,190	24,230	25,830	28,510		25,060 3rd	28,070 18th	+ 8
Highways									
Maintenance cost per km- Principal roads(£)	*6,267*	6,498	4,229	5,481	4,404		4,330 2nd	5,058 9th	+12
Maintenance cost per km- Non-principal roads(£)	*1,475*	2,288	1,895	1,607	1,333		2,197 5th	1,808 25th	+ 1
Net cost per 1,000 pop.(£)	*22,290*	17,750	19,980	21,340	19,000		22,540 2nd	22,230 13th	+ 7
Police									
Serious offences per 1,000 pop.	*47.90*	56.02	41.83	50.97	41.83		31.08 3rd	43.01 8th	—
Pop. per police officer	*555*	529	602	538	602		518 3rd	495 3rd	− 1
Net exp per 1,000 pop(£)	*26,140*	29,240	24,730	26,710	24,730		26,960 4th	28,750 33rd	—
Fire									
Full-time uniformed staff per 1,000 population	*0.42*	0.60	0.45	0.46	0.40		0.66 5th	0.57 33rd	+ 1
Part-time uniformed staff per 1,000 population	*0.37*	0.26	0.43	0.48	0.53		0.34 4th	0.39 22nd	− 3
Net cost per 1,000 population(£)	*5,930*	7,800	6,760	6,680	6,410		8,060 6th	7,590 38th	+ 1
Refuse disposal									
Net cost per 1,000 population(£)	*2,660*	1,220	2,570	—	1,670		2,360 1st	2,780 18th	+ 8
Employees per 1,000 population	*0.06*	0.07	0.08	—	0.04		0.07 4th	0.09 29th	+ 2
Trading standards									
Net cost per 1,000 population(£)	*752*	753	626	936	613		1,181 4th	791 28th	− 2
Employees per 1,000 population	*0.06*	0.07	0.07	0.09	0.05		0.11 4th	— 24th	—
Libraries									
Net cost per 1,000 population(£)	*4,390*	5,610	4,990	4,860	4,330		4,170 4th	4,470 21st	+11
Employees per 1,000 population	*0.42*	0.58	0.49	0.42	0.38		0.46 4th	0.45 27th	−12
Planning									
Net cost per 1,000 population(£)	*1,190*	1,730	1,310	1,300	570		1,910 5th	1,640 34th	−12
Employees per 1,000 population	*0.07*	0.13	0.09	0.09	0.09		0.13 6th	0.10 38th	− 7
Recreation									
Net cost per 1,000 population(£)	*90*	260	230	10	160		220 5th	340 34th	—

General developments and resources

In recent years the major emphasis of central services has been to introduce new technology into the administration of the work of the authority and the development of better management information systems. Anyshire County Council have a sizeable investment in computer hardware.

The central provision runs major applications such as salaries, rates and budget accounting, as well as providing services for the county council service areas such as the following:

- a further education awards system
- automatic library lending system
- transportation accounting system
- highways database
- social services records for residential homes
- gun licensing system for the police

There are links to the mainframe distributed throughout the other departments but there are also around two hundred stand-alone microcomputers which are in use for a variety of applications. The total staff involved in computing number 51 and are organised in project teams. All departments now operate word processors and the link-up of these to the mainframe system allows easier development of management information systems.

One advantage of having a group of central departments, other than the more efficient provision of common services, is that it enables the authority to respond to issues or problems facing the community as a whole which may not fall within the jurisdiction of any one particular department. The establishment of a network of terminals within departments together with the development of new computer applications provides both officers and councillors with management information which is more reliable, more easily accessible and more up to date.

1.4.6 Further details

Tables 1.7, 1.8 and 1.9 provide a breakdown of budget expenditures and some comparative statistics with other counties on spending.

Introduction to organisations

2.1 Introduction

An organisation is a changing and on-going system in which people and resources interact in some ordered manner to accomplish common goals. The organisation could be a private commercial business such as Marks and Spencer PLC, a government agency such as a local authority or indeed anyone from a multiplicity of other such groups. In financial terms it could represent an investment spanning millions of pounds of shareholders' funds down to the weekly church collections. Probably the only thing that we can truthfully say that they will have in common is that they will all be different and all have differing needs for information processing. How then does the information analyst react in the organisational environment?

This chapter attempts to provide the reader with a framework which can be used to examine organisations, identify their structures and explore their functional activities. From this it will be possible to derive the information flows which help to co-ordinate such activities towards the attainment of the strategic organisational objectives. Finally, the chapter will discuss the role of information systems and introduce the reader to ways by which computer systems can help organisations to respond to changing needs as effectively as possible.

2.2 Definition of the organisation

All organisations can be viewed as highly complex systems of interacting variables with an open-ended list of factors which may affect the organisational effectiveness. At a very simplistic level, however, we have defined the organisation as an interaction of people and resources in some structured manner to accomplish certain goals.

Figure 2.1 provides a useful framework to examine the effect of change since all these variables are highly interdependent and a change in any one will probably result in compensatory or retaliatory changes in others. For example, a technological change providing new tools will affect the tasks which have to be performed and the people who perform them. As a result the structure of the organisation may have to adapt and indeed a shift in organisational purpose may result.

The interactions among these variables is essentially a system of communications and work flow. It is likely therefore that a computer system which provides information improving the system of communications and/or affecting the system of work flow will have the effect of changing the structure, policies, personnel and tasks within the organisation. Given that this is so it is obviously important for the information analyst to develop this global framework and arrive at a more precise understanding of the nature of organisations.

The first step is to define the purpose of the organisation — in other words someone needs to consider the question 'What business are we in?' — meaning what is the product/service, the client and the scope — or 'Why does the organisation exist?' Such a definition must be agreed and accepted by all the people associated with the organisation in order to identify a rational set of corporate objectives. This is normally, therefore, a highly creative activity which may have very far reaching and dramatic results. It is also likely that definitions which may prove successful at one point in time will be less appropriate at another, and so it should be viewed as a dynamic rather than a static decision-making process.

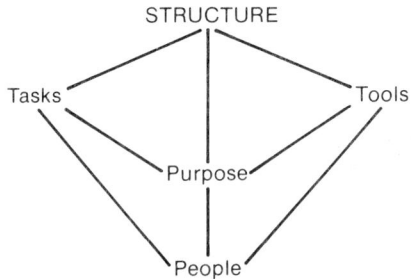

Figure 2.1 A framework for organisations

Consider the evolutions of some of the major businesses in the world to-day. It is highly probable that they bear little relation to the original companies from which they spawned. By seizing market opportunities they will have developed into wider or even different definitions of their business. This process is not, however, restricted to competitive market situations; organisations which start life as one man protests may snowball into large revolutionary movements or complex charity trusts. Legislation can also act as a major stimulus to the way organisations see themselves, particularly in the public sector where redefinitions of scope, client and service are frequently initiated by parliamentary decree. An important factor in this on-going process of definition must be the flexibility of the organisation to respond to change and this is closely tied to the quality and availability of information which the organisation can use.

Arriving at the definition of a business is not as simple as it might appear. If you were asked to define the purpose of IBM you might, after some thought, suggest that it is 'to manufacture and sell computer systems at the maximum achievable profit', a fairly good definition of the company in terms of the products or services which it supplies. However, it could also be defined in terms of the market it serves. In this case the definition would be 'to serve the needs of organisations throughout the world for information technology systems support for the maximum achievable profit'. Again this is a perfectly reasonable definition, but basically it serves no purpose other than to explain to the completely uninitiated what type of business IBM operates.

To assist management within IBM to arrive at an understanding of corporate strategy such global definitions need to be broken down to specific groupings at three levels.

(1) *Who is being served?* The classification to be used here could be geographic, demographic, on the basis of industry groupings, etc. IBM could meaningfully classify by particular types of installation — retailing, education, banking, public institutions, etc. — but also by country or size of business as subsets within these groupings.

(2) *What need is being satisfied?* Sometimes products are multi-functional in that they serve clusters of related needs, but in other cases the business serves multiple customer functions but with separate products. IBM provides hardware and software to improve information services within organisations, both with separate and multi-functional products, and covering a wide variety of functions within the customer organisation — computing, reprographics, office services, typing, word processing, and so on.

(3) *How are the needs being satisfied?* This relates to the technology which is being used or services and products provided. IBM offer a wide range of machines and support services — personal computers, mainframe

computers, office equipment, software packages, systems support services, etc.

A new or smaller computing company is likely to have a very much more restrictive definition of its business such as 'to supply a range of microcomputers and supporting software to educational institutions to be used to teach students to program'. Such definitions allow organisations to develop strategic plans for the future and, in the private sector, to define profitable markets in competitive areas.

It also enables them to identify their information needs within a certain range. For example, if IBM do not currently operate in Russia, and furthermore have no plans to do so, then information pertinent to the expected market for mainframe computing in Russia over the next five years will have no real value to the organisation. Similarly, a company which has restricted its market area to education will want information relevant to the growth in student population over the next five years and all such relevant information on educational policies, as well as specific information related to the microcomputing market.

Public corporations must similarly define their role, and in the case of Anyshire County Council this will relate directly to 'providing an acceptable level of services (as defined by the Local Authorities Act) to the residents of the county in the most cost effective manner and to the greatest possible well-being of those in need'. While there is no direct profit motive as with private organisations there is still a major overriding concern on the most effective utilisation of cash flows and, as such, cost justification will still be required for any new project or information system.

Within Anyshire County Council we have already examined one service area regarding its information needs. Certainly a major concern of all services will relate to population growth, and changes in this will vary the demand for many services. It is therefore vital that Anyshire should receive up-to-date information not only on population movements but also on the nature of the population with regard to age, income, health, employment, etc. This information will thus allow each of the service areas within the council to redefine its strategic objectives within the corporate objectives defined by the council's policy committee.

The definition of the business also has an obvious effect on the other major variables within the organisational framework. Structure, tasks, people and tools are all implicitly dependent on the defined purpose of the organisation. A typical example is shown by the organisation of IBM in the 1970s when they used product and market as part of their business definition. The company structure required product managers responsible for major product lines, such as IBM 360/370 etc., and market managers with responsibility for each of the major customer groups, such as hospitals, banks, educational institutions, etc., to which the products were sold.

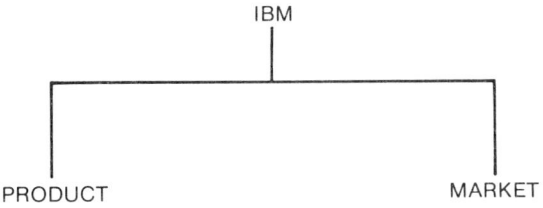

Figure 2.2   A global structure

Figure 2.2 shows the global structure of the organisation. Within each sub-structure, a separate set of functional areas were defined which required certain people to perform different tasks using appropriate tools.

Functional decisions are thus affected by the scope of the organisation's activities and by the segmentation criteria chosen. Similarly the selection of new products, decisions to expand into new markets and product abandonment will all be influenced by the earlier definition of the scope of the business and have an effect on the functions such as research and development, roles, distribution and manufacturing. This automatically implies direct effects on people, tasks and tools. For instance, in the case of local authorities, central government plays a large part in defining scope, often causing considerable disruptions in a relatively short space of time.

2.3 Organisational structures

The structure of an organisation really relates to the system of communications, authority or other roles, control and work flow. Different organisations will therefore have different structures related to such characteristics as:

- size
- age
- ownership
- objectives
- technology
- environment
- people

It is obvious that a very small company comprised of highly professional personnel in a technological industry may require a very different structure from a large, old-established chain of retail stores. The differences in work flow, authority, control and communications systems would require appropriately different means of information dispersal throughout each organisation. Structure is, in fact, all about the dissemination of information within an organisation, and an examination of the structure will show not only the required flow but also the appropriate content, detail and frequency required at each hierarchical level of the organisation.

Structures are not, however, rigidly correct for a particular definition of an organisation. It is possible to identify certain types of structure which may seem more appropriate to particular organisational profiles. It is also implicit that structures may change as organisational profiles change. It is also true, however, that the most anomalous combinations sometimes work despite the unanimous incredulity of management and organisational analysts.

It is sadly also often the case that organisations are unaware of the disparity between their operational structure and their real needs. The information analyst may find himself in a position of compromise, working to provide the best possible information system for an organisation where the basic structure itself inhibits the realisation of the most effective information flows. However, although not everyone can create the ideal organisation or influence structural directions, the identification of information needs may provide the motivation for change within the organisation. Undoubtedly the provision of an effective computerised information system can have a major impact on organisational design and control, as we shall discuss at the end of this chapter.

For the purposes of this book we can usefully identify four types of structure which we will describe as:

- bureaucratic
- project-oriented
- control-centred
- individualistic

2.3.1 Bureaucratic

Figure 2.3 shows a typical organisational structure for a bureaucracy with horizontal segregation — usually based on functional management: production, finance, marketing, purchasing, personnel, etc. Work is controlled by procedures for roles, communications and settlement of disputes, and anyone joining this type of organisation will have well-defined responsibilities and an agreed line of control. A typical organisation using this structure will be large in a stable market with programmable work procedures.

Unfortunately, the very term chosen to describe this structure, bureaucratic, is synonymous with sluggish, over-restrictive, red-taped, boring, no-initiative organisations — a term in fact most often used to describe government procedures! It is true that bureaucracy can stifle, but it can also stimulate by providing clear lines of communication and regular information flows. A large number of organisations adopt some form of bureaucratic structure and for many it is the only viable operational mode.

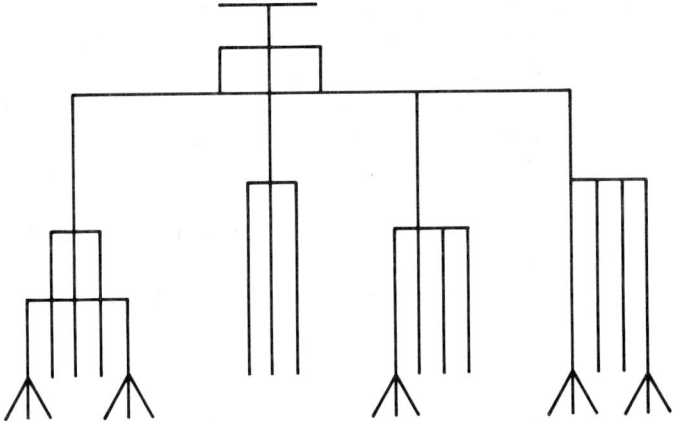

Figure 2.3   A bureaucratic structure

In Anyshire County Council there is evidence of a global bureaucratic structure with obvious definitions of authority, communication and control. There will, therefore, be a predefined information flow to facilitate the operation of committees and the management of functional areas. Within the organisation, however, service groups may operate with a different but more appropriate structural form.

2.3.2 Project-oriented

The second type of structure described is project-oriented and is often represented by the matrix structure shown in Figure 2.4. The whole emphasis here is on getting the job done and bringing appropriate people and resources together at appropriate levels for specific tasks.

This structural form still enjoys an 'in-reputation' with organisational psychologists and is also the one preferred by most middle and junior management with the emphasis on groups, expert power, rewards for

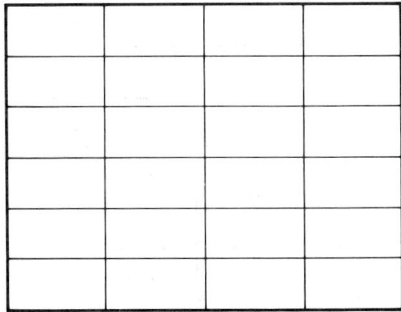

Figure 2.4   A matrix structure

results and merging individual and group objectives. It is very much the appropriate structure for flexibility and change but as a result presents a real problem for control. This frequently means that we only find this structure subsumed within an essentially bureaucratic structure — product groups of marketing departments, data processing departments, new venture sections of banks. Some highly creative, reactive and integrated organisations such as advertising agencies or computing and management consultancies thrive on this structure and will generally continue to flourish as long as resources are available without rationing procedures. Once bargaining for resource allocations becomes necessary it is normally accompanied by demands for stricter control of results and the structure moves towards one which gives greater centralisation of power.

In Anyshire County Council the Social Services Department is an unusual combination where signs of all four structural types are apparent. Essentially, however, the structure is project-oriented and displays the matrix form to considerable extent as shown in Figure 2.5.

Within the overall definition of objectives four policy groups have been identified: children, the elderly, the handicapped, and administration. The whole area has, however, also been segregated geographically and divisional heads appointed for each geographic region. Within each region there will be a certain structure enabling the teams of social service workers to complete their tasks as appropriate to that local region. All of these workers will also, however, be members of one of the policy groups and be brought together as part of that project team at certain times of the month. Effectively everyone in the group has at least two roles, and sometimes more, but each role identifies their level of responsibility within a certain project grouping.

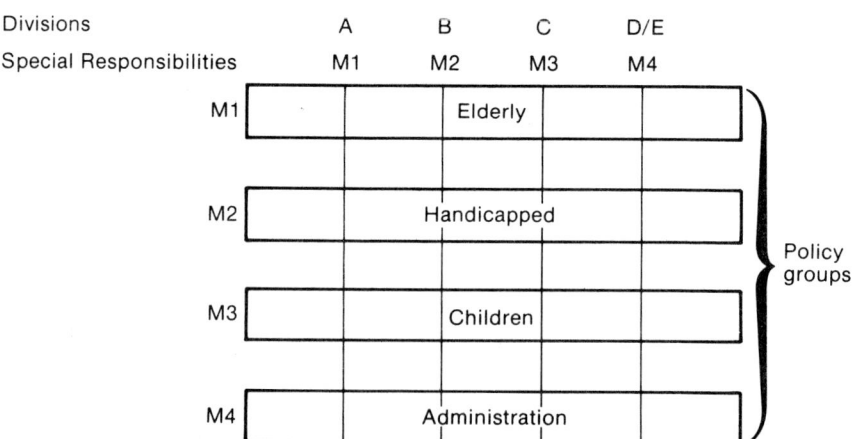

Figure 2.5   A specific matrix structure

2.3.3 Control-centred

Control-centralisation is often representative of small entrepreneurial organisations and is described in Figure 2.6. The structure revolves around a central power source, often a key figure who may have developed the organisation from scratch. All decisions in the organisation are made by the key individual or by a small political group who surround the central source. As a result the quality of the individual is the key to success and many such structures fail when the succession issue is unresolved.

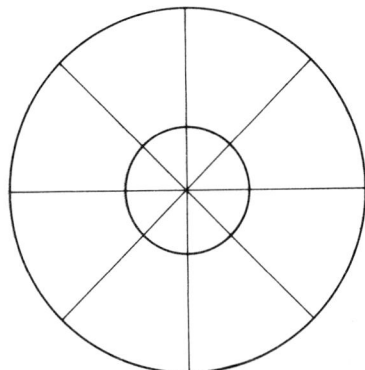

Figure 2.6 A control-centred structure

Family businesses are typical of this structure, but size can be a major problem and is normally only successfully resolved by building several such structures which can be linked together but with each unit having maximum independence. Such a structure can provide very fast-moving channels of communication while preserving autonomous work units and have all the benefits of centralised authority within the distributed organisation as a whole. In many cases, however, the answer for survival has been to impose highly bureaucratic structures on all the extremities whilst maintaining the superimposed centralised structure. This normally only results in the worst of both worlds but it is amazingly easy to identify this hybrid in today's organisational world.

In Anyshire County Council a highly probable base for control-centralisation is within the committee structure. Local authority committees have sufficient invested power to determine their own structures and as such often gravitate towards a central source of power within the group. An appreciation of group dynamics and an understanding of power bases should be an essential study for any aspiring local councillor — and is also of considerable assistance to an information analyst!

2.3.4 Individualistic

This last type of structure is not really a form at all since it is represented by a group of individuals, and at best can only be shown diagrammatically as in Figure 2.7. This grouping enables individuals 'to do their own thing better' and was much beloved in the sixties and early seventies. It works successfully for all sorts of groups — co-operatives, small professional partnerships such as barristers, architects, computer consultancies and, of course, most commonly for social groups. It is also true to say that many individuals wish to be in this form of organisation but may find themselves in another. Typical of this is the oft parodied academic who may merely be attempting to justify individual eccentricities whilst perpetuating the myth of academic freedom! It is also typical of specialists in organisations such as senior consultants in hospitals or design architects in local authority planning departments.

In Anyshire County Council several small pockets will exist harbouring this structure, possibly in the planning department or educational groups and certainly in social services. Most ground-level workers in social services respond well to the belief that this is the only viable structure for their department and with disgust to their manager's belief that greater formal structure is required to control the jobs effectively.

A certain paradox within this type of structure, however, is the fact that all information should be available to all the group members, and the moment any one individual abdicates responsibility for analysing the information they are effectively placing power in the hands of another member of the group, hence changing the very structure they desire.

The beginning of this section provided a list of factors which influence the organisation's structural needs. It should now be obvious that a multiplicity of such combinations can exist and as a result any organisation may find itself, on examination, being pushed toward at least two and perhaps three different structural preferences. Within the organisation, too, there will

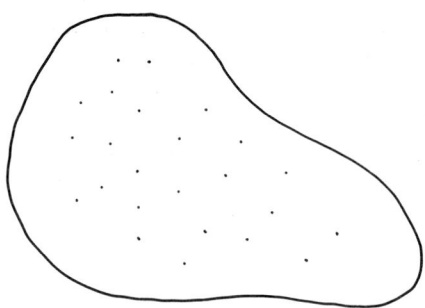

Figure 2.7 An 'open' structure

be different personal inclinations and influences and any imposition of a certain style could cause serious friction. The solution is most likely to be found in a set of differentiated structures which then require overall integration possibly by a separate structure.

Anyshire County Council is typical of such an organisation, and it will be possible to find examples of all four structural forms and combinations existing within the overall group. Each structure will impose different information requirements and this means that the information analyst cannot look at the global organisation chart and design an information system on this basis alone. He will have to conduct detailed examinations at lower organisational levels — that is to say service and operational levels within Anyshire — and for each identify the particular information flows. The main problem will be to ensure the integration of such information to provide co-ordinating management and committees with meaningful results. This problem relies on the approach which the analyst adopts to the design of information systems and will be considered in Section 2.4 below.

2.4 Functional responsibilities

One of the basic reasons for the existence of organisations would seem to be that they allow a co-ordinated division of labour between tasks and between persons carrying out these tasks. The nature of the division of labour within organisations, both between individuals and between departments or sections, is clearly of importance both for task accomplishment and for the maintenance of organisational control. One important issue is: how is the division of labour effected?

The most common answer is by function, but it can, as noted earlier, be based on products, geography or types of customer, or indeed by a complex mixture of all simultaneously. The logic implied in this division is quite simply that by subdividing tasks those tasks can be carried out more effectively by being done better, faster or cheaper.

Some typical examples of labour division should help to clarify these concepts. Figure 2.8 shows organisation A with a functional division of labour. These functions incorporate a lateral split between functions which contribute directly, such as manufacturing and sales, and those which are there primarily to assist co-ordination and control, such as finance and information services. Two of the divisions show examples of further segmentation by product line and by geographical area but all sub-groups are coordinated by the centralised functional areas.

Figures 2.9 and 2.10 show a complete decentralisation of structure with product and area used as the primary segmentation and each division maintaining separate functional support. Obviously the mode of division affects the information flow requirements of the organisation.

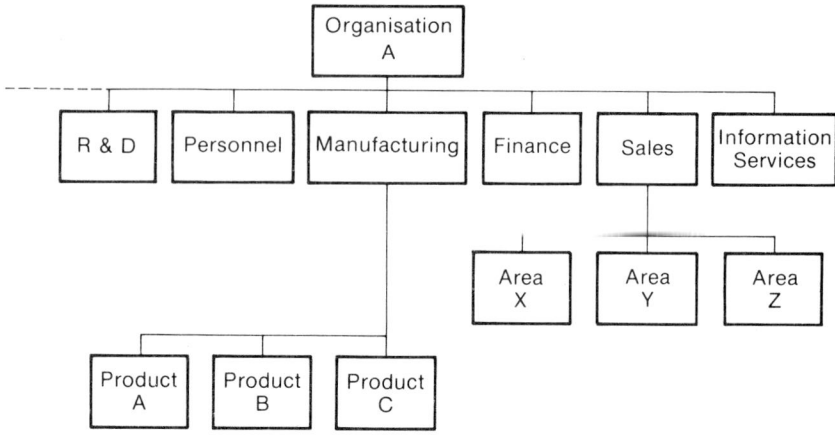

Figure 2.8 A structure with functional divisions

In the centralised structure of Figure 2.8 far more standardised procedures will be imposed at lower levels to help provide uniform data sources and integrated information. In a decentralised organisation, such as in Figures 2.9 and 2.10, each sub-division can maintain its own information system and co-ordination is generally only applied to a subset which is required by higher management levels acting as integrators. Both of these have obvious problems since in one case too much rigidity and standardisation will hinder effective communication and in the other too little standardisation will inhibit real integration across the organisation and promote a diversity of separate information systems.

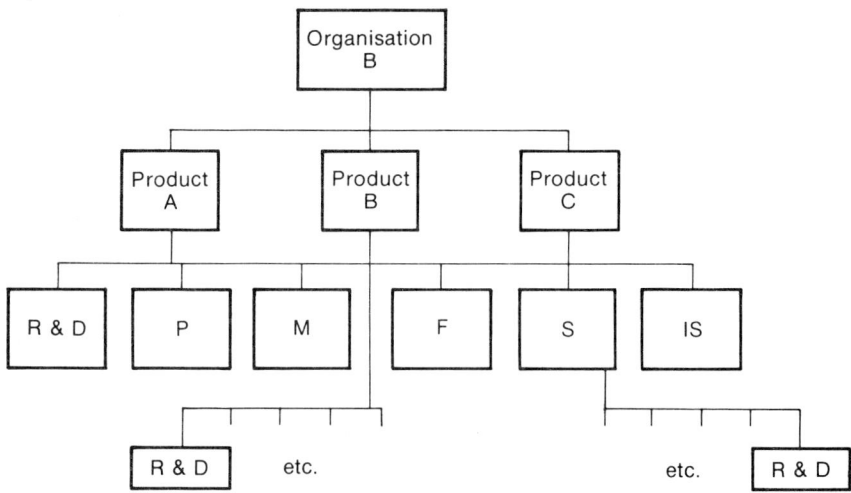

Figure 2.9 Structure by production

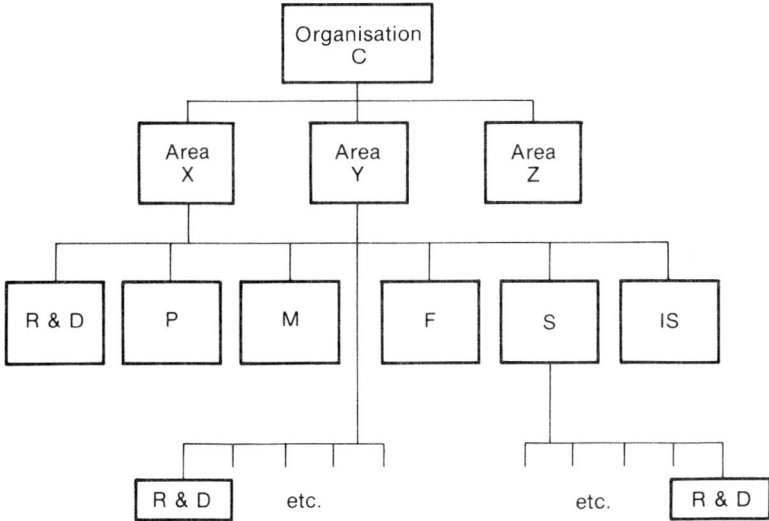

Figure 2.10   Structure by geographic area

A particular development which has exacerbated this problem in recent years is the wholesale introduction of microcomputers into organisational life. The positive effects are obvious but tend to obscure the potential for creating an information tragedy for the organisation. As we have already seen stored data is a valuable resource for any organisation and its value depends on its relevance, accuracy and accessibility. In Anyshire County Council many people will collect and use information relevant to their particular service area, and a centralised automated system will allow this information to be shared by other service groups (see Figure 2.11).

It may be, however, that one service group, say education, is dissatisfied with the performance of the system. Receiving no response from the data processing department to requests for improvements they acquire a personal computer and create a highly satisfactory local storage and retrieval scheme for themselves. This now raises the danger that the data will no longer be submitted to the central system, or if it is it may not be to the same quality since it is no longer being used by that service department. The result is a decrease in the quality of information for everyone in the organisation.

This is not solely an issue of centralised versus decentralised technology — it is primarily about organisational co-ordination. It requires not only easy-to-use personalised local schemes but also a requirements analysis to identify everyone else who uses the data so methods may be devised to translate the information from the local storage scheme into a form usable by others and accessible through a distributed network of computer systems.

Divisions of labour do not apply solely to tasks but also between the

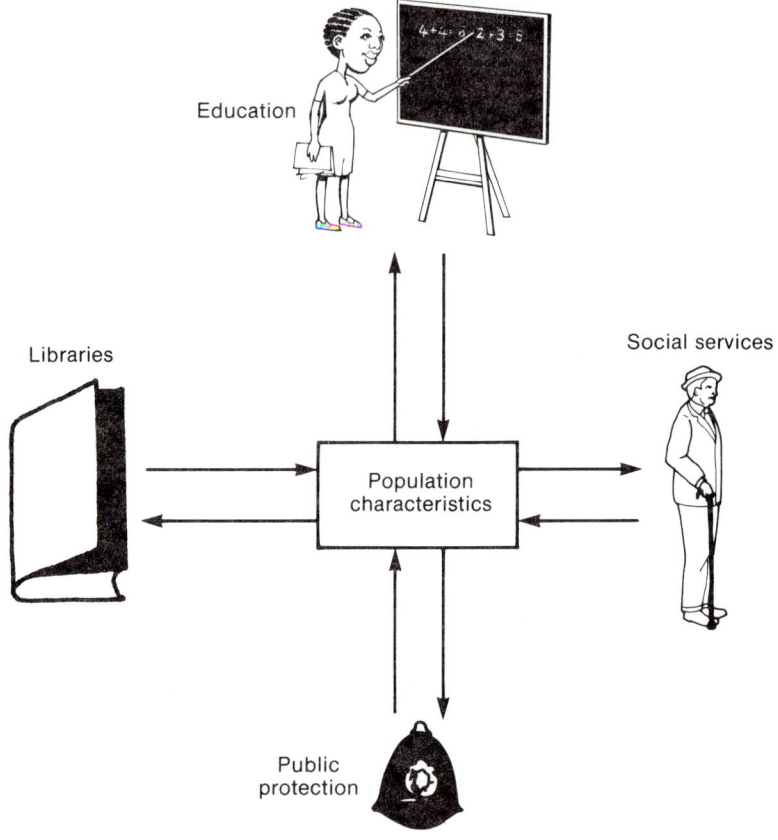

Figure 2.11 A shared system

actual carrying out of the task and the control of the task. In other words, in most organisations there is some division between operators, supervisors and managers translated into a hierarchy for planning, co-ordination and control of directly productive work. The hierarchical levels are most commonly identified as:

Strategic ↑ long term
Tactical
Operational ↓ short term

spanning short- and long-term planning.

Decisions which are made at these levels differ not only with regard to time but also as to how specific they are. Each level will make decisions to assist in the following:

> Planning
> Co-ordination
> Control
> Maintenance of the organisational activities

and also the   Motivation of the workforce

At *operational* level these decisions are for specific situations and can usually be judged against specific rules. Hence in a manufacturing organisation the decision whether or not to start the production schedule for an order relates directly to the availability of resources and the priority of the order on the day in question. The information needed by operational management is therefore quite specific and required daily.

At *tactical* level management is more concerned with resource deployment in the medium term and will need to know the order fulfilment record over a weekly or monthly period, the coming monthly sales figures and the likely stock position. The information is still fairly specific but will be more predictive than at operational level.

At *strategic* level plans have to be made affecting the long-term future of the organisation and hence information requirements will be much less well-defined and also include far more external sources. The information will be historically comparative, such as this year's sales figures against last year's, but also of greater use predictively, concerning likely influences over future years. At this level the information system will model organisational management to provide effective decision support.

In Chapter 1 of this book we have already seen examples of short-term and long-term planning based on information which has not been properly integrated into the overall information system and hence providing ineffective support to decision making.

One further concern which relates to functional responsibilities and the levels at which decisions are made arises from a consideration of the span of control utilised by the organisation. Figure 2.12 is typical of a highly structured organisation with many hierarchical levels and fairly short control spans between each level. Information flows upwards in a controlled manner and may be sifted, aggregated, summarised or added to at each level. Figure 2.13 illustrates a very broad span of control with information going from a wide variety of sources to centralised authorities where it must be co-ordinated before it is transmitted upwards through the hierarchy.

In other words, the span of control identifies whether the major problem for the gathering of information is one of vertical co-ordination or horizontal co-ordination and this should be reflected by the way in which information is presented at each level.

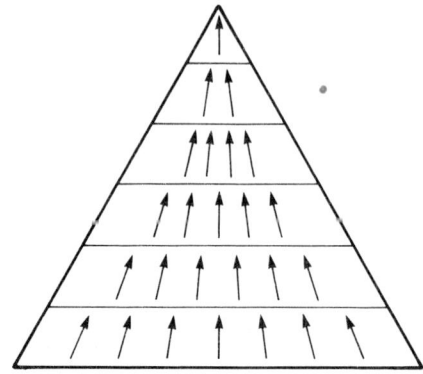

Figure 2.12   A highly structured organisation

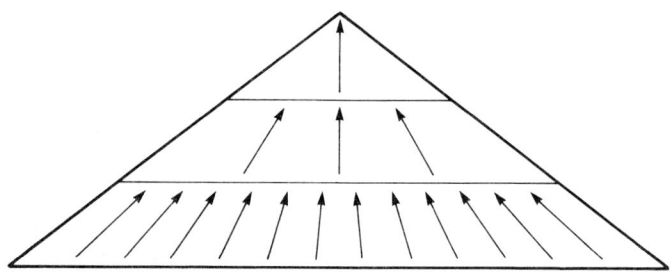

Figure 2.13   A broadly structured organisation

2.5 Information systems in organisations

The very nature of our definition of organisations implies that there will be a required flow of information and that this will be both horizontal — between different functional areas or other groupings — and vertical — between different hierarchical levels of management. This helps us to classify the types of information systems which can be developed.

2.5.1 Operational

In every organisation there will be a need for a regular flow of 'bread and butter' type information. This is the basic facts and figures which must be shared between functional areas and other operational divisions in order to get the day-to-day running of the organisation underway. Many such systems deal with accounting operations such as payroll, invoicing, order processing, etc. Computer-based systems will normally mirror the clerical activities giving benefits of accuracy and speed over the old system.

2.5.2 Planning and control

In order to assist management within an organisation there needs to be performance reports. These basically compare expected performance against actual and may relate to sales figures, production schedules, costs, profits and so on. Every organisation will have a certain meaningful time span. A growing retail company would request weekly sales figures, a car manufacturer might be more concerned with monthly sales or production units whereas a local authority might only require yearly or half-yearly comparisons.

Computer-based systems will summarise information normally derived from operational systems and present this in a comparative manner. Ideally such reports would not only summarise but present information graphically so that comparisons could be made at a glance. These systems assist management to make more effective use of their time by providing them with a basis for planning and control.

2.5.3 Decision support

In order to make decisions most managers have to be predictive. That is they have to make enlightened guesses on the basis of the information available to them. They may therefore set targets for the next five years on the basis of what has happened in the last five years or what they believe concerning their competitors' intended actions or in anticipation of a world recession, or any combination of these and more.

A computer-based system which can help in this area must therefore be able to access all information which might be relevant to the decision-making process but further it should then be able to predict decisions and the probable consequence of such.

Ideally therefore all organisations should adopt a top–down development approach to systems. That is to say they should define their needs at decision support level so that all systems, even at operational level, can feed through information into the overall management information system. As we have said previously in this chapter, effective stand-alone systems can actually be detrimental to the organisation as a whole unless planned with integration in mind.

So far in this chapter we have concentrated on the formal side of organisations and identifiable information flows. Possibly a more important aspect is that which we will classify as the informal channels of communication. Information is not passed solely through hierarchical levels; it is also shared by expert groups, status groups and friendship groups. In any situation where the formal structure is perceived by the employees to hinder communication informal structures will grow in importance and there will be some situations where organisation charts purportedly mirroring information flows bear no relation to actual practice — 'Oh yes, I know that's what it says in the policy document but this is the way we really do it.'

An information system is a model of the way an organisation really works, not the way we would like it to work. The system is therefore only as good as the analyst's understanding of the organisation's information flow and needs of the people involved. For any system to work properly it also needs the commitment of the users and this implies some understanding of the motivational factors which affect human behaviour. Many computerised information systems have failed because they have been perceived as threatening by their intended users. For example:

(1) A system which produces figures monitoring sales performance by sales staff can be seen as a weapon in the hands of the sales manager rather than a useful guide to improve individual performance.
(2) An automated stock control system can be seen as a threat to replace jobs in the store-room and accounts office.
(3) A system monitoring progress of cases through social services can be seen as a device to monitor social service workers rather than their clients.

It would be foolish to deny that a computerised information system will have an effect on people's jobs. The very purpose of such a system is to improve the organisational effectiveness and undoubtedly this will have a direct effect on people within the organisation, their roles and tasks they must perform. What is important is that the affected personnel participate in the analysis and understand and approve of the overall objectives which the information system intends to satisfy.

User participation implies a particular design philosophy for system development and while a full discussion lies outside the scope of this text an overview will help place future chapters in perspective. The recommended approach is described in Figure 2.14 and is sometimes referred to as the 'socio-technical' approach since it aims to adapt to particular organisational needs by exploring the organisation, the people within the organisation and the appropriate levels of technology. The major emphasis in the design process is at the early stages of development since it is clearly at this stage that the objectives are set and the framework is defined for the model. Research has shown that 60 per cent of all errors occurring in computer-based information systems result from lack of understanding at the early stage of the project.

Goals should be developed and made explicit for each of the major design variables:

(1) *Organisational factors* such as:
● management and work roles

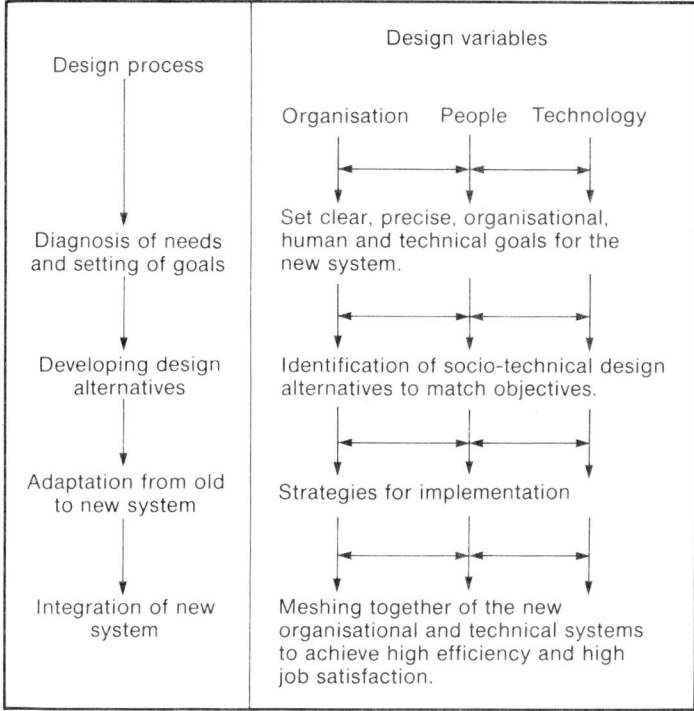

Figure 2.14   A 'socio-technical' approach to system development

● organisational structures
● relations within the organisation and with the outside world
● job design and work practice

(2) *Human requirements* such as
● need for job satisfaction
● motivation
● positive expectations

(3) *Technology* which meets organisational and human objectives such as being:
● flexible
● adaptive to changing user environments
● with high quality user/system interactions

The involvement of users in the design process therefore becomes a dual process since it helps to ensure the creation of acceptable and well functioning organisational structures and also ensures the likely success of the information system due to a clear understanding of the objectives.

2.6 Summary

This chapter has dealt with the main features of organisations which concern the information analyst. In particular it has emphasised the constant interaction of organisational variables and the major role which information systems can play.

At this stage it must be emphasised that the introduction of computer-based information systems using appropriate Information technology tools will bring about a major change in the organisation. Such systems will not only replace personnel in the operations area but will also have a powerful effect on the role of management, possibly reducing the need for middle management and extending the role of senior management into the external relations field. It is also likely that given time functional areas can be consolidated into a central information services area where control is exercised over all data input in the organisation.

Faced with such changes it becomes obvious that the control of information is a significant, if not the most significant, source of power in an organisation. As such the role of information analysis is to ensure that this power is based on the most relevant, meaningful and accurate information available to the organisation and hence used to co-ordinate and control decision-making to greatest effect.

CHAPTER 3

Fundamentals of information provision

3.1 Introduction

Information analysis, or even information processing, is a current in-phrase not only in society and the media at large but across all types of business organisation. The opening chapter highlighted the fact that information, if not considered in context with other relevant factors, can be misrepresented. Clearly, to some extent, such situations will always exist in the use of information.

However, the provision of pertinent information and the knowledge that can be gained from it is seen as a resource growing in importance. These days it is often considered to be as important a resource to an organisation's successful operation as are, say, the raw materials, machines and tools of a manufacturing company. No longer is it sufficient just to process data to provide information. The information made available must be of sufficient quality to satisfy the requirements of the person, committee or board making the request. To this end, this chapter considers the interrelationship of data, its use and the general information needs within organisations.

3.2 Data and information

3.2.1 What is data?

A dictionary definition of data is 'raw facts'. In the context of a business environment this is taken to mean a collection of unprocessed facts

Mr Smith's national insurance number is YZ-72-88-43-C
There are 4 children under the age of 16 in the family
The VAT % rate is 15

Figure 3.1 Data statements

associated with a particular activity. At a primitive level, these facts or data use groups of characters in the form of a message or statement usually with a coded or numerical attachment as illustrated in Figure 3.1.

To give order to data, facts are categorised by two components, namely *data name* and *data item*. A *data name* is the designation given to a class of data. Examples of data names from Figure 3.1 would be 'national insurance number' and 'VAT % rate'. Note that these are not values but names given to the set of values associated with the data. The *data items* are the specific or actual values for the data named, for example 'YZ-72-88-43-C' for national insurance number and '15' for VAT % rate.

3.2.2 What is information?

Data becomes information once facts have been processed or data names and data items are grouped together in some way. As previously described in the case study at the end of Chapter 1, an organisation is a complex set of management systems. Thus data and information can and do take many forms according to how they relate to the different elements and functions of an organisation.

Often different information requirements are based on an analysis of data common to more than one subsystem. Such situations clearly require the data to be consistent across all subsystems. Accordingly, the way in which data is represented is important and organisation standards need to be adopted. For data items such as national insurance numbers, as is implied, there are nationally adopted formats. For organisation generated data items and data names such uniformity is also necessary no matter what the environment. For example, in a manufacturing organisation data items for raw material part numbers in the production system must be consistent with those in the company's stock control system. In the case of Anyshire County Council Education Department, compiling a student record system across the county's colleges, it is essential to adopt an agreed format for, say, student registration numbers in order that record systems of the individual colleges can be consolidated into one complete system.

3.2.3 Data representation

National insurance numbers, raw material part numbers and student registration numbers are illustrations of data items that are in a coded format according to some pre-specified arrangement of letters, digits and perhaps other, special symbols. Data items in this form would be used for referencing purposes in an organisation's business systems in that other data items will naturally relate to them. For instance, a raw material part number would have associated with it a unit cost and a stockholding.

Data items for information analysis are those given wholly in numerical form, and processing such data items in a variety of ways is fundamental to most organisations' daily functions. From its original form, data may be processed through a number of intermediate stages until the purpose of an analysis is achieved. This may be to satisfy a particular operational need of an organisation or, perhaps, it may be a long-term strategic planning calculation. No matter what the purpose, the reason for the analysis will be to provide information in order that a recommendation or decision becomes a valued judgement made on a sound and firm basis.

3.2.4 Information provision

While the two terms 'data' and 'information' are clearly related their meanings should certainly not be confused. *Information analysis* is an analysis of data presented in a way that makes it significant and relevant, giving potentially useful knowledge to the recipient.

The provision of information as data processed in an inappropriate or misleading manner can, at the very least, be time consuming to sort through in order to achieve a correct insight. With data being produced in abundance in all areas of an organisation it may be considered efficient to have data amassed in reports for a manager's or officer's perusal and digestion. However, indigestion will be the only outcome if a report does not highlight pertinent information and key pieces of data.

For effective use of any organisation's manpower resource, requested information must be easily identifiable. The need to have meaningful information available across all levels of management is imperative as organisations strive to improve their service or product. Applications of work study, budgetary control, project planning, etc., are now well accepted within management for the importance to their organisation's operations and development. While these fields are areas for detailed study in their own right, this book aims to cover some fundamental requirements as they relate to information analysis in general.

3.3 Data sources within organisations

3.3.1 Internal and external data

Information used by an organisation in connection with its business activities and in the solution to its problems can be prepared from internally generated data or can come from sources external to the organisation. Intuitively, most people can generally contemplate the nature and sources of data from within their own organisation or environment. So, before examining more closely sources of *internal data* and ways to collect it, let us consider first likely *external data* sources.

Organisations from both the private and public sectors are obliged to submit annual and other reports to appropriate bodies. Thus information that has been produced and consolidated internally within one organisation could become external data for the purposes of providing specific information to another organisation. For a private sector organisation the annual report would not only cover broad issues concerning the company's operational policies but it would also include a summary of their accounts. A competitor then has available certain data on which to base a comparison. Accounting comparisons could be made with regard to turnover, profit before and after taxation, earnings and dividends per share and capital expenditure. Annual growth factors for such items could also be determined from the figures available.

3.3.2 Primary and secondary data

The above information would be considered *primary data* to the recipient organisation because it comes from the source where it was originally compiled. There are numerous sources carrying economic and business data; often they contain both primary and secondary data, a *secondary data* source being one in which the data is collected from other publications and organisations.

Generally the only way to decide which are good sources of data is to research all publications related to the topic under investigation and use them. It is always advisable to consider carefully the use of secondary data. It is already less likely to be as reliable as primary data and numbers could be rounded, combined or adjusted so losing some of the original accuracy. Also, the explanatory notes that usually accompany primary data are often omitted from secondary data sources.

3.3.3 Anyshire County Council: external primary data sources

For the above reasons, if no other, it is advisable to confine any information analysis to the use of primary data. It is perhaps fortunate, therefore, that the nature of the case study central to this text is such that much of the information available to Anyshire County Council is primary data, even that from external sources.

CIPFA (the Chartered Institute of Public Finance and Accountancy) publish a series of yearly reports giving financial details of first the estimated and then the actual spending of local authorities. These details of expenditure and income are prepared under set headings on a common price basis, this being that used for determining a county council's annual rate support grant. The reports, although concise, are comprehensive, each one covering an area of a county council's responsibility (education, personal social services, etc.).

A second external source of primary data that is particularly useful to local authorities is the series of county reports from OPCS (the Office of Population Censuses and Surveys). These are publications available through the Government Statistical Service and are prepared following the national census, the last two being in 1971 and 1981. Each county report gives information on data collected via the national census forms. As well as a number of general tables there are tables giving information on aspects concerning a county's demographic characteristics, economic classifications, housing and amenities, and household composition. The 1981 OPCS reports are a significant improvement on those of 1971 as searches for particular information can be more easily made with the availability of keyword searching.

These two external data sources are those most often referred to by local authorities. Primarily, this is because they allow direct comparisons to be made between county councils and, for future planning purposes, certain patterns and trends can be readily identified. The OPCS reports are also a valued source of data to private organisations. For instance, they contain information that would clearly be of use to a company mounting a marketing or promotion campaign. Also, knowledge of particular census and population data could indeed influence decisions regarding the location of a company's new operations in a county or district.

The nature of the data within any organisation reflects and is dependent upon the type of its business. However, irrespective of its business activities, the prime goal of data collection is to obtain information about organisational functioning, efficiency and effectiveness. Private and public sector organisations clearly differ in their aims but many of their operational procedures follow the same principles and guidelines. Private organisations are governed by the need to secure a profit which is the difference between price and cost or income and expenditure. However, public sector organisations operate not dissimilarly in that they endeavour to achieve the best obtainable balance of income and expenditure according to their terms of reference.

3.4 Information needs of organisations

3.4.1 The information analysis process

The specification and collection of data together with the resultant data analyses are fundamental on-going functions of organisations to enable

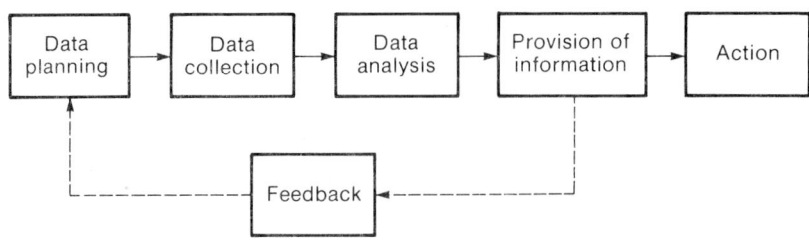

Figure 3.2   Information analysis cycle

them to maintain their operations on a successful basis. This includes their need to plan for future developments. Situations can change over periods of time and information that is obtained, interpreted, analysed and fed back to relevant individuals or groups often leads to a continuation of this sequence. The overall cycle of information analysis is shown in Figure 3.2.

This overall process of information analysis is a sequence of data-related activities. The outcome is the provision of information to satisfy some organisation requirement and to influence the basis on which action may be taken. While there will be many different ways of using data within organisations, the cycle readily identifies the various stages of the process

Table 3.1 Data activities of information analysis cycle

Stage	*Activity*
Data planning:	To clearly understand the data to be collected and analysed, and the nature of the information to be provided; to formulate plans for data collection.
Data collection:	The planned collection of primary and secondary data from internal and external sources.
Data analysis:	The application of appropriate quantitative techniques.
Provision of information:	Presentation of information in a meaningful and usable form.
Action:	Decision or recommendation based on the knowledge gained from the information.
Feedback:	Output information leading to change or improvement.

that are fundamental to all of them. The activities of these stages are described in Table 3.1.

The discussion in the remainder of this chapter considers the general information needs of organisations and the issues for consideration in the planning and data collection stages of the cycle. The next chapter introduces some statistical methods of data analysis together with a section on presentation of information. Feedback and its importance to information systems is considered where relevant in later chapters.

3.4.2 Information needs

Invariably books on statistics and quantitative methods for business concentrate solely on particular methods without directly relating the analysis techniques to the information needs of the organisation. The use in this book of case material will alleviate this situation by deliberately first identifying certain information requirements of Anyshire County Council and secondly considering the approaches necessary to achieve those requirements by the use of well established techniques. In line with this approach we now give some general guidelines to follow to ensure a quality endproduct.

First of all information excludes the routine day-to-day paperwork of an organisation that enables, for example, orders to be processed or people to be paid. A set of despatched invoices is not information in itself. Information in this context would be a management report giving, say, the monthly summary figures of income against payments outstanding (and for how long) in order that a comparison can be made with the position at the end of the previous month. An information analysis may be needed to satisfy a specific one-off requirement.

Often, however, reporting information is required at regular intervals, the frequency of the reports increasing the lower the management level. The senior officers of Anyshire County Council are required to report to the various elected members' committees on an annual and quarterly basis. They, in turn, analyse the operations of their own departments monthly with section heads producing weekly data on request.

3.4.3 Guidelines to follow

It is important that any information analysis should meet its full requirements. Accordingly, the person or group responsible for the information analysis needs to consider, at the outset, a number of factors in order that the quality of the resultant information is apparent to the recipient. Such criteria can be used not only to appraise the quality of the information itself but also to determine whether some feedback information is desirable. The criteria are reflected in the following questions:

Is the information:
- *well-presented*, facilitating an easy assimilation of the content?
- *relevant*, giving a valid view of the circumstances?
- *accurate*, resulting in a valid outcome?
- *significant*, highlighting any particular factors or trends?
- *comprehensive*, giving a balanced viewpoint?
- *timely*, enabling necessary action or decisions to be taken?

Invariably the most immediate aim of any data collection exercise is to obtain information about the functioning of an organisation. Basically, is it effective and efficient? Data is used to create a picture of that part of the organisation's activities under analysis from which judgements are made on how well that activity is going or if problems or difficulties exist in its operation.

While this book is not directly concerned with ways in which the acquisition of information can bring about a change in the structure of an organisation, clearly the provision of information, especially if from multiple sources, can be used to build up an overall picture of organisational functioning. Accordingly, the information analysis process can often lead to constructive change in an organisation, and data collection can serve a number of purposes in this area. For example, a questionnaire could be used to obtain information from employees on issues in the organisation that concern them. This approach not only indicates to employees that change is possible but also that the organisation is willing to take into account their views.

It has been stated that any data collection exercise helps build a functional picture of an organisation's activity or activities. It may be that the resultant provision of information produces a complete picture in itself. However, more often than not, the information may provide a single perspective of a larger picture involving the relationships of many other pieces of information.

This situation was seen in Chapter 1 when some information from Anyshire County Council was judged solely in its own context. You will recall that different views of county council and government educational statistics were produced and considered at face value only. As a result, political change occurred, one reason being that the reality of the interrelationship of the educational statistics with other information was not realised. The effect of increasing one county council budget heading together with the implied decrease in another was only seen when the plight of the elderly in the community was identified at a later time.

While, in this instance, political influences were ultimately apparent it does at least highlight the situation whereby two activities were viewed independently without regard to their albeit indirect relationship within the organisation and in ignorance of longer-term projections. Thus data collection activities can and should be used to establish the process of relationship-building across sections and departments of an organisation.

3.5 Planning to use data

Often it is the case that specific plans are made for the collection of data without due regard to the expectations and the information needs of the organisation. The importance of adequately preparing for data collection and the following phases of the information analysis cycle has been touched upon earlier. This section reinforces what has already been mentioned as it is imperative that it is very clear what data is to be collected, what is to be done with it and why it is being collected in the first place. It is all too easy to say 'Let's collect the data, analyse it and see what we come up with. Then we'll decide what to do with it.' Unless adequate plans are made, poor preparation will lead to unforeseen consequences. In addition the planning itself may raise issues for further prior consideration.

3.5.1 Plan early

Why is early and thorough planning so important? One prime reason that is apparent irrespective of the nature of the data application can readily be identified. Simply the collection, analysis and provision of information to individuals or groups of people means that a number of decisions must be made in good time. It is necessary to decide on the data itself, which sources it can be obtained from or which collection techniques to employ, which data analysis techniques can and should be used and the forms in which the information is to be presented. It is likely that every decision has some consequence on a following activity. For example, the decision to, say, perform interviews rather than use questionnaires to obtain certain data has consequences of cost and time needed for gathering the data as well as the time needed for its analysis.

There are also other reasons for in-depth planning. One factor is that unless it is firmly established at the outset who will receive available information, a manager may be reluctant to circulate, on a wide basis, the results from a sensitive data analysis if they reflect poorly on the functioning of his/her department. Further, where feedback is an essential part of the information analysis cycle, constructive change cannot be brought about if the wrong data is collected or if incorrect analyses are performed.

3.5.2 The activities of planning

In planning, there are four basic areas in which decisions need to be made. First, it is necessary to have the goals of the information analysis agreed and to determine the procedures to be employed. The second area involves the planning for data collection, that is what kind of data to collect and the strategies for its collection. Next the various issues of data analysis need to be considered. Included here would be an analysis of the commitment of resources required to support a recommendation or alternative. Finally, should a feedback element be an inherent aspect in the exercise, the on-going effects of functional changes will need to be evaluated and assessed.

The degree of formality that needs to be applied to each of these areas is clearly dependent on the nature, range and size of the information analysis application. The larger the exercise the more detail and formality is required throughout. Invariably, the degree to which detail and formality is required is mirrored by the accustomed reporting procedures in operation across the different managerial levels of an organisation.

3.5.3 Aims and objectives

The first decisions to be made are related to the specification of the analysis goals and procedures. The main reason for the exercise should be given and the overall aims of the analysis stated. The objectives to be achieved should be recorded both in general terms, for example 'to improve the effectiveness of the education service of Anyshire County Council', and via more specific terms such as 'to calculate projected pupil numbers for existing primary and secondary schools during the next five year period'. It should be clear who has commissioned the analysis and to whom the ensuing report is addressed. It is also important here to include who is granted access to the report as often confidentiality of information is an important factor to consider.

The project leader will need to develop a project plan and schedule man-power and duties according to an agreed timescale — this aspect will be discussed further later in the book. The data elements to be considered at this stage are: what kind of data is to be collected or which sources are to be explored? The procedures and facilities for data analysis need to be investigated as to their suitability. Other resources to be assessed and accounted for at the outset are:

(1) computer time and other logistical support;
(2) time for meetings and other indirect support; and
(3) time for training sessions and other managerial support.

The level to which this assessment has to be detailed will naturally depend upon the complexity of the project.

3.5.4 Initial planning

Once the scope of the project has been fully identified using the above guidelines, the planning process can continue with a more detailed development, and the next phase is to plan what data to collect and how this is to be done. In most reasonably sized information analysis projects the possible range and volume of data that might be used for diagnostic and/or functional change purposes can be quite high. However, the selection of which data to collect and which to ignore should be apparent having earlier specified all the issues under consideration.

It must be remembered though that sometimes data collection can prove expensive and so the collection of irrelevant or trivial data must be avoided. For this very reason many departments in organisations now employ personnel who have a specialist knowledge of information analysis techniques. This, in conjunction with their knowledge of the workings of their department, makes them almost indispensable! However, for, say, computing or work study personnel undergoing an information analysis project in conjunction with another department, it is imperative that at least a basic understanding of the department's work and operations is obtained together with knowledge of any interaction with other departments related to the project.

With either situation it can be useful to undertake a small investigation first so that an initial response can be evaluated to decide if that data used is indeed relevant to the goals of the whole information analysis exercise. In this context it is always helpful to gain some feedback at this stage from people in the organisation who are highly knowledgeable of a particular system and environment as it may be that perhaps the jargon or coding system used in a questionnaire seems ambiguous. Such involvement between the project and departmental personnel will invariably help in the interpretation of initial data collected and govern the approach to be taken for further data collection. Particular techniques of data collection will be discussed in the next section.

The detailed concerns of how to use data — basically the stages of data analysis and ways in which information is presented — are discussed in the next chapter. It is important to note here, however, that the processes involved with using data need to be planned in advance. Certainly this does not mean that an outcome is to be pre-empted. Obviously, this should not be the case if, say, a database internal evaluation is taking place within an organisation as this could lead to disastrous effects, wrong expectations, and a non-beneficial situation for employees, especially if functional changes and reorganisation are a possible outcome. What is meant is that at the data planning stage of the information analysis cycle it is necessary to determine what type of investigations are to be performed with the data, by whom, and whether or not the computing and associated resources are readily available to make the necessary analyses.

In addition, the mode and format for the presentation of the data as information needs to be considered at this stage. For instance, will the information be provided in written reports, via meetings or through a combination of both? With a written report, how much data will be provided within it, and will it be raw or processed, detailed or summarised, etc.? If meetings and training sessions are to be part of the information provision, how many meetings should be organised, who will run them, what form should they take? All these possibilities need to be addressed with plans made in good time in order to ascertain properly the overall resources and personnel commitments necessary to support the successful completion of the project.

3.5.5 Planning for evaluation

As has been said, feedback can be an essential part of the information analysis cycle in certain applications, e.g. the functional reorganisation of activities with a business operation. However, even for more straightforward applications it is often necessary to have the results emanating from an information analysis exercise evaluated. So, whereas the particular issues of feedback as an inherent part of the cycle will be discussed later, some general pointers concerning evaluation of an information analysis should be considered at the planning stage, as it may be appropriate to qualify an analysis's recommendation that it should be subject to an ongoing evaluation. One reason for this is that the data used in the analysis may have been incomplete or even subjective. So from a practical point of view a systematic evaluation of an outcome is useful.

If nothing more an organisation would certainly wish to perform a cost-benefit analysis. It is obvious that such an analysis would undoubtedly be a requirement for a large proportion of Anyshire County Council's operations since a local authority is continually trying to match its services against its income in the most effective and efficient manner possible. Evaluation allows individuals and organisations the facility to determine what has gone well and what has not and to learn, perhaps, what further recommendations would be desirable or possible. One specific reason why evaluation should be planned early in an information analysis exercise is that objective evaluation requires the identification of criteria *before* rather than *after*. For example, a local authority's refuse collection system may have been reorganised as part of an exercise. Unless evaluation criteria have been established initially it may be impossible later to obtain some accurate previous data on what might be deemed relevant criteria, e.g. productivity, employee accidents, absenteeism.

At the planning stage it should also be established whether or not it would be beneficial first to see a changed system working as a pilot project with a control group as a way to evaluate a new system against an old one. Finally, there must be the questions of who would do the evaluation, would it be independently supervised, who will get the results and who will act on the results of the evaluation?

3.6 Data collection

Previously in this chapter the existence and suitability of external sources for data has been examined, albeit briefly. For data analyses where the use of such data is required the sources available to an organisation are usually well known, as is knowledge of whether the data, acquired from an external source, is primary or secondary. If such data sources are not able to provide the data necessary for analysis then, before going ahead with the collection of fresh data, all possible internal sources should be explored to see if suitable data is available.

In many organisations much data is recorded in written form and thus available. In business, however, data can become out of date in relatively short periods of time and so data of this type must always be examined carefully for such items and investigated thoroughly before use. This is necessary for two reasons. First, the data may not be fully compatible and adjustments may be needed in order to make it approximately comparable. Secondly, sometimes the reliability of available data may be questionable. If data consists of estimated figures their accuracy may not be measurable and so to use this unreliable data would be worthless.

Having researched through and exhausted all possible sources for the data needed without finding it, then data will have to be collected. Methods for the collection of raw data will now be discussed. While there are many different ways of collecting raw data, the techniques fit into one of three main categories. These are by *questionnaire*, by *interview* and by *observation*, and in considering the approaches to be taken for the application of each of these techniques their advantages and limitations will be outlined.

3.6.1 Data collection by questionnaire

A *questionnaire* is a list of questions circulated to respondents in a printed form. Essentially it is a 'distance' form of obtaining data, highly dependent upon the respondents completing and returning their questionnaires. Generally, however, questionnaires have been found to be an economical means of data collection primarily because they achieve simultaneous responses from many people. Thus a large amount of data can be obtained quickly.

The form of a questionnaire either gives space for the respondent to fill in his/her answers or is of a fixed response type whereby it allows for a selection to be made from a choice of possible answers which have been predetermined as alternatives. Questionnaires of this latter type are the most used as the questions can be expressed objectively. The answers to the questions become easily quantifiable and so are very useful for analysis.

What is an important consideration with all kinds of data collection but particularly important with the design of questionnaires is that the words and terms used in the questions should not be ambiguous so that the responses can be freely and accurately made.

The scope of a questionnaire should clearly reflect the goals of the information analysis. For instance, a questionnaire might be designed to focus on one particular issue whereas another might be used to ascertain broader issues and feelings within an organisation.

Examples of fixed response type questionnaires

The examples shown below demonstrate the variety of use of the fixed response type of questionnaire and cover some questions that might appear on a questionnaire sent to data processing managers of a number of different types of organisation.

1. Tick the manufacturer of your main hardware and to which industrial sector you belong

IBM	Engineering
DEC	Process industry
ICL	Retail and distribution
Univac	Public utilities
Honeywell	Finance
Data General	Education/research
HP	Public administration
Phillips	Service bureau
Burroughs	Other
Other	

2. Place, in order of concern, the issues currently worrying you

Meeting project deadlines ☐
Maintaining existing programs ☐
Recruiting ☐
Predicting future technology ☐

3. How do you expect the following to vary in your organisation over the next twelve months? Ring as appropriate.

	Increase	Stay approx. same	Decrease
(i) Amount spent on hardware	(1)	(2)	(3)
(ii) Amount spent on software	(1)	(2)	(3)
(iii) No. of operating, data entry and control staff	(1)	(2)	(3)
(iv) No. of analysts and programmers	(1)	(2)	(3)

Advantages and disadvantages

There are a number of advantages of using the fixed-response type of questionnaire that can be readily identified. First, from the nature of the above examples it is seen that the expected responses to the questions are of a form that can be easily categorised, summarised or further quantified. The cost of administering a questionnaire is generally relatively low once it has been developed. A questionnaire is an easy way of sampling large groups, and with skilful design a large amount of data covering a number of issues can be obtained within a single questionnaire.

Many of the problems that occur with questionnaires arise from their design. In this context it is particularly important for designers to pay attention to certain inherent characteristics of questionnaires. By definition the structure of a questionnaire is predetermined and so is not adaptive and cannot be changed if some questions are found to be inappropriate to a proportion of respondents. While this sometimes cannot be wholly avoided, by researching the likely respondent groups the situation whereby respondents are unable to give answers to certain questions can be avoided or at the very least optimised to a minimum. Investigative research at the design stage may also throw up new areas in which respondents have much information to offer.

The validity of the information provided by questionnaires is often open to interpretation. As with any sort of data analysis the results obtained can be no more accurate than the data itself. With fixed response questionnaires the data has to be considered limited in the sense that the format of these questionnaires only allows the respondent to choose from those alternatives listed.

3.6.2 Data collection by interview

An *interview* is a more direct way of collecting data than a questionnaire. By its very nature it is also more powerful and flexible. Depending on the information goals of the exercise, interviews can be conducted in different ways.

One extreme is the unstructured interview in which the questions asked would only give guidance to the range of possible answers and the respondent would be encouraged to answer stressing the aspects of the issue under consideration which he/she feels important. This type of interview would tend to start with general questions, developing its ultimate direction according to the respondent's answers; it is thus adaptive.

At the other end of the spectrum, there is the structured, fixed response type of interview. This is similar to questionnaires of this type whereby the questions are predetermined along with a number of possible responses. While basically it is an orally administered questionnaire it further allows the interviewer to ask relevant supplementary questions, particularly when extreme positive or negative answers have been given.

Interviews can vary in structure between these two types. The form an interview should take will be governed by the information goals, and for a specific respondent group by how much they are to be constrained in their answering.

Client-centred data collection

Anyshire County Council operate as the local authority for social services. The case-load of social workers covers children and young people, the elderly, chronically ill and the handicapped, and so much of their field work is client-centred. In these circumstances, interviews would form the basis of many data gathering exercises.

Social workers are a good illustration but it is implicit in conducting any interview that the interviewer has a good understanding of the factors and problems which might be significant in the appraisal of the data. It is clearly necessary to be precise in specifying the data to collect and to plan soundly the questions to ask as the more structured the interview the more quantifiable data will be yielded for further analysis.

Advantages and disadvantages

Much of what has been said about the design and use of questionnaires can be applied to the interview as a collection device. However, interviews can be time-consuming and thus a costly means of data collection, so their appropriateness to a situation should always be closely examined at the outset.

Potential problems that can arise can normally be avoided by using experienced interviewers. For instance, interviewers should never adapt an interview in a manner that is likely to encourage or discourage certain responses, as many biases shown by an interviewer may then be reflected in the data that is recorded.

3.6.3 Data collection by observation

A third common way of collecting data is by *observation*. Observation is used when data about behaviour or patterns of work is required. The basic strength of this approach is that data is collected directly from an activity as it occurs and is studied. In this sense, the approach is valuable because it removes any possible bias from the respondent. But, even with this in mind, in order to collect meaningful and useful data it is essential that the observation exercise is structured by adequate preplanning. Decisions need to be made concerning what to observe, how to observe, when and where to observe and what to record.

One obvious advantage of this approach is that well documented observational data is highly valid. However, to be fully effective, reliance on a trained observer of the activities is imperative. As with interviewing, observational work is time-consuming and costly, and so should be used sparingly as a means of data collection. Often, for these reasons, they are used for back-up purposes and as validity checks for more extensive data collected via questionnaires. Also, they are particularly useful when the respondent group is small.

3.7 Summary

The argument and discussion that has been presented so far is that information is an important factor in governing and assessing the operations of any organisation. From this central viewpoint the chapter has considered what is understood by data and its use in the process of providing meaningful information, terming this process the *information analysis* cycle. A broad view was taken and the stages of the cycle were identified and considered with respect to the general information needs of organisations.

The provision of information is all about the collection and use of data. However, without a clear idea of why data is being collected it is difficult to decide what kind of data is to be collected and how to collect it. Accordingly, these aspects associated with preplanning that have been stressed in this chapter.

In any organisation there is an enormous amount of data collected in the normal course of activities and is available stored in various written documents, records and computer files. Such sources of data can be particularly valuable to a data collector along with those external primary sources relating directly to the organisation's fields of activity.

The techniques associated with questionnaires, interviews and observations that are used to gather data in organisations assume that data has not already been collected or acquired and must be obtained. The choice of data collection method is an important one and the advantages and limitations of each method must be weighed against one another before one is chosen, or to avoid potential problems use can be made of multiple data sources.

People are constantly requiring information to help them make decisions and to support recommendations to higher management levels, and organisational structures perform the function of transmitting information between people and across departments. Thus information is a key factor in the understanding of how organisations work. Given this relationship, this chapter has built on the content of Chapter 2 and laid the foundations for the rest of the book.

CHAPTER 4

Statistics and information

4.1 Introduction

As we have suggested, all types of organisation routinely apply methods to collect, present, analyse and interpret quantitative data. It is this area of study that is called 'statistics' today and numerous theories and well tested methods have evolved.

The previous chapter looked at techniques for the collection of data by a careful and systematic approach. From now on, it will be assumed that the data collected has been gathered in a manner that assures its accuracy and reliability. However, before any data analysis can be applied it is invariably necessary to assemble and present the data so that its general characteristics become evident. The first main section of this chapter examines ways to fulfil this objective in order to achieve an effective communication of the data and information at hand.

Virtually any book on 'statistics' will show that there is an abundance of well documented methods available to solve a wide range of business problems. It is certainly not an intention of this book to duplicate unnecessarily a coverage of these methods. However, there are some basic information requirements common to many organisations of all types that require an introduction to particular statistical methods.

These basic requirements are threefold and are outlined as follows. First, a common requirement is to obtain some more detailed characteristics of the data. How large or small are the data items? What is the average value of the data items? How does the data vary within its range of values? The answers to these and similar questions are found by computing a number of fundamental statistical measures. Secondly, it is often necessary to obtain estimates and projections from data in order to assess trends or the general way in which the figures are moving. The third of the common requirements is to obtain a measure of comparison between two data sets, that is determining the relationship between different variables or data names.

Statistics is a conglomerate subject of study covering many complex issues. However, the three requirements identified above cover a large proportion of the general needs of statistical analysis in business. The chapter discusses each of these requirements in turn. An all round knowledge of these analysis tools will also give a firm foundation for learning more advanced techniques.

4.2 Data organisation and presentation of information

Before information can be presented, whatever form is chosen, data has to be 'organised' in order that it can provide the basis for a meaningful analysis. We know that it is common for people to visualise the world of 'statistics' just as collections of figures rather than the techniques or methods of data analysis. Also, we are all aware that people often say that anything can be read into 'statistics'. So apart from the methods themselves we have to be concerned with how information might be misrepresented, this being so even when reliable data has been used and the information has been well presented. This aspect forms the concluding section in this chapter. However, here at the outset, it is to be realised that unless data is organised properly, information resulting from a data analysis can easily be distorted.

Much of the information presented in the case study of Chapter 1 is of a general nature since the intention was to give an overall picture of the size and workings of Anyshire County Council. Such an overall picture clearly can only be gained by presenting information about the different county council operations in those summarised formats. In now looking at some of the presentation formats in more detail we will also analyse why those particular formats were the ones used.

4.2.1 Organisation of data

Clearly, some raw data needs to be available in order first to organise that data and then present it in a suitable format.

Road traffic accidents in Anyshire: casualty data

Figure 1.10 summarised a year's casualties as a result of road traffic accidents within the county's boundary. This figure is reproduced in Figure 4.1. Its format is commonly known as a *pie chart* as it is circular, resembling a pie, and is cut up into slices. From the key it is readily seen that each slice represents a category with the size of the slice indicating the proportion that that category is as a fraction of the total number of casualties.

For each traffic incident which is reported to and investigated by Anyshire police it is necessary for a Traffic Accident Report Form to be completed. An extract from this form is shown in Figure 4.2. The extract relates to the casualty's age and to an identifiable category to which the casualty must belong. For the purposes of this exercise the reader should assume that a Report Form has been completed for each accident casualty. The categories have been identified as those most useful for the purposes of providing information on traffic casualties within the county. This information is also required by all authorities with policing responsibilities so that a global picture of road traffic casualty statistics can be built up and seen from a national viewpoint.

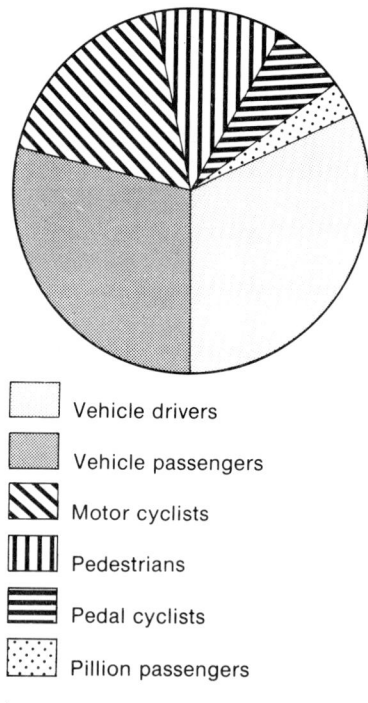

☐ Vehicle drivers

▦ Vehicle passengers

◥ Motor cyclists

▥ Pedestrians

▤ Pedal cyclists

▨ Pillion passengers

Last year: total casualties 3,648

Figure 4.1 Pie chart showing casualties by category of road traffic accident

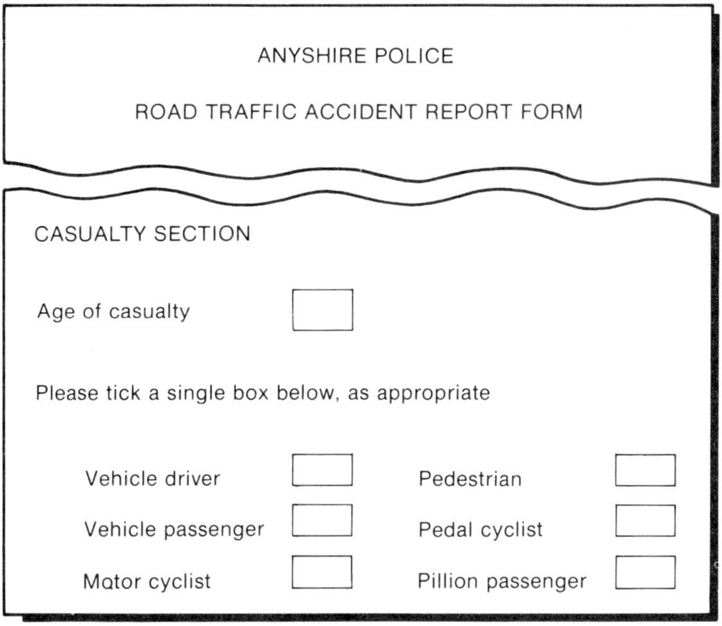
ANYSHIRE POLICE

ROAD TRAFFIC ACCIDENT REPORT FORM

CASUALTY SECTION

Age of casualty

Please tick a single box below, as appropriate

Vehicle driver
Pedestrian
Vehicle passenger
Pedal cyclist
Motor cyclist
Pillion passenger

Figure 4.2 Anyshire Police: Road Traffic Accident Report Form

Categorising data: frequency distribution table

The main object of the analysis here is to summarise the numbers in the six casualty categories and to present the information in a format which allows an easy visual assimilation of the proportions in each category. But, clearly, there may be other information that might be required for other purposes so the first step ought to be to organise the data in the form of a table which (i) summarises the results from all 3,648 report forms and (ii) reflects the numbers within each of the boxes in the casualty section against the age of the casualty.

Obviously, it would be too cumbersome to leave age in the table as single years as if the age range across all the report forms was 0–80 years then this would require either 80 columns or 80 rows in the table. In such instances it is necessary to subdivide the age range into specific age range classes. A convenient and reasonable size for an age range class for this set of data would be 10 years. Thus the data from all the report forms can be categorised and set out as in Table 4.1.

'Age', 'No. of vehicle drivers', 'No. of vehicle passengers', etc., are what were referred to as data names in the last chapter. They are also often referred to as *variables* because within each category the numbers *vary*. A table like this, where different values of a variable, here 'age', have been combined into a single class, is known as a *frequency distribution*. This

Table 4.1 Frequency distribution table of road traffic accident casualties data

Age	Vehicle driver	Vehicle passenger	Motor cyclist	Pedestrian	Pedal cyclist	Pillion passenger	Total
				Number of casualties			
0–9	0	47	0	46	57	3	153
10–19	172	102	157	73	79	30	613
20–29	360	240	372	48	28	27	1,075
30–39	295	258	103	40	19	14	729
40–49	187	231	55	46	16	6	541
50–59	101	80	26	61	10	1	279
60–69	39	32	5	83	3	0	162
70+	11	23	2	59	1	0	96
Total	1,165	1,013	720	456	213	81	3,648

form of tabular presentation is very common in many areas of statistical analysis.

Even a table of the size of Table 4.1 can give us quite a lot of useful information. Whereas the presumed initial requirement is to ascertain the proportions of casualties in the listed categories, we will see later how the same data is used to provide us with some information about the ages of casualties in road traffic accidents in Anyshire.

As it stands this table is quite compact. However, if for instance a requirement on the report form had been to record the sex of the casualty then each of the six casualty categories would need to have been split into two to record the numbers of males and females in each category, and there would be twice as many columns of numbers appearing in the table. The impact of the numbers to the eye would be lost and perhaps a confused picture would become apparent.

As a general rule, it is advisable not to have too much data organised into one table. For clarity's sake it is often better to have two or more tables than one complex one.

4.2.2 Presentation of information

Pie charts

The summary information required on casualties, i.e. what fraction of the whole in each casualty category, is easily found from the column totals within the table. It is usual to provide such information in percentage form, as in Table 4.2.

A pie chart can then be used to show pictorially the size of each component slice relative to the total. Here, there are six slices and the information

Table 4.2   Road traffic accident casualty data: casualty category percentages

Casualty category	No. of casualties	% of total[*]
Vehicle driver	1,165	31.9
Vehicle passenger	1,013	27.8
Motor cyclist	720	19.7
Pedestrian	456	12.5
Pedal cyclist	213	5.8
Pillion passenger	81	2.2
Total	3,648	99.9

[*] *Note* each percentage has been calculated correct to one decimal place, so their sum may not necessarily add up exactly to 100%.

is transmitted to the viewer easily and quickly. Obviously, with many slices in the pie the effect may not be the same.

With today's computing facilities, pie charts can be prepared using packages readily available, especially on microcomputer systems. Little knowledge of computing is necessary. Simple instructions to the computer will draw the pie chart direct from data stored in tabular form, as in Table 4.2. The pie chart in Figure 4.3 was drawn using a spreadsheet package with a business graphics facility.

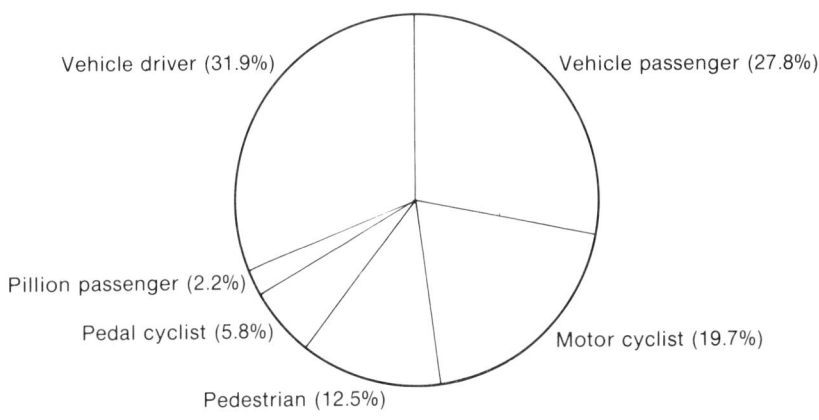

Figure 4.3

4.2.3 Information requirements and mode of presentation

As has been stated, the information conveyed by the above pie chart shows the relative size of each data item — the different numbers of casualties —

```
                        ANYSHIRE POLICE


Internal memorandum                      Date: 17th January 19..


From: (Superior)                         To: (Subordinate)


Subject: Last year's road traffic accident casualties


Use last year's road traffic accident report forms to provide me
with a summary of casualties according to the categories on the
report form. This year I also want them shown in a nice diagrammatic
format to present to the members of the Police Committee.
```

Figure 4.4   Police memorandum: road traffic accident casualties

of the total number of casualties. It was presumed that this was the information requested. But was it what was required? Obviously, there's no real
way of confirming this, one way or the other, by what has been written so
far. However, having looked at the effect of one format of data presentation, the pie chart, let us go back and examine the 'information requirement' more closely.

The original memo (see Figure 4.4) would seem to be a request from a
superior to a subordinate for a straightforward task. It is an annual exercise
and the summary is always produced in the same tabular format, that of
Table 4.3. As for the diagram to go alongside the figures, the superior liked
the suggestion for a pie chart.

However, the Police Committee members didn't really want a view of the
relative number of vehicle drivers etc. to the total casualty number. The
information was alright as it stood, but their preferred view was a represent-

Table 4.3 Anyshire police: last year's
road traffic accident casualty figures

Casualty category	No. of casualties
Vehicle driver	1,165
Vehicle passenger	1,013
Motor cyclist	720
Pedestrian	456
Pedal cyclist	213
Pillion passenger	81
Total	3,648

ation of the numbers in each casualty category relative to each other. Of course, they hadn't said this at the outset. Nevertheless, the subordinate as the person given the responsibility for the information analysis had failed to ascertain the true requirements.

Although a simple example of communication failure it serves to illustrate the importance of all that has been put forward on these matters already in Chapter 3.

Histograms

The *histogram* or *bar chart* is a common technique for presenting data. Some variations of the basic form have, in fact, already been seen in Chapter 1. (The reader is referred back to section 1.4 and Fig. 1.4 of the case study.) It is a histogram that conveys the actual information requirement in the above case. In a histogram the lengths of the bars are proportional to the size of the particular data items. The histogram in Figure 4.5 is computer drawn for the data in question; the scaling on the vertical axis is produced automatically from the data values.

A variation is the 'stacked' bar chart. In this format, the components of a total are stacked one above another. With a single list of data values, the information it conveys is similar to that of the pie chart as it shows the percentage that each component data item forms of the total.

You will recall that the Casualty Section of the Traffic Accident Report Form recorded the casualty's age and that the data was originally summarised within age bands (see Table 4.1). Below, Figures 4.6 and 4.7 show two

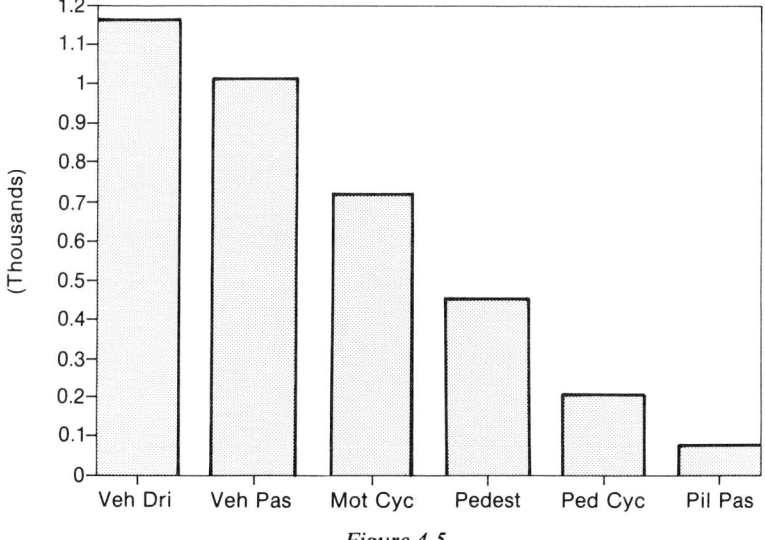

Figure 4.5

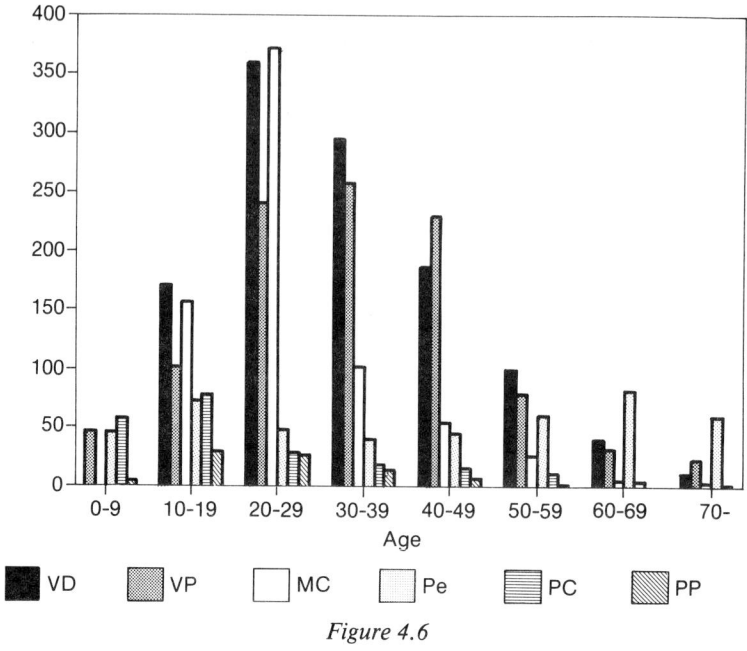

Figure 4.6

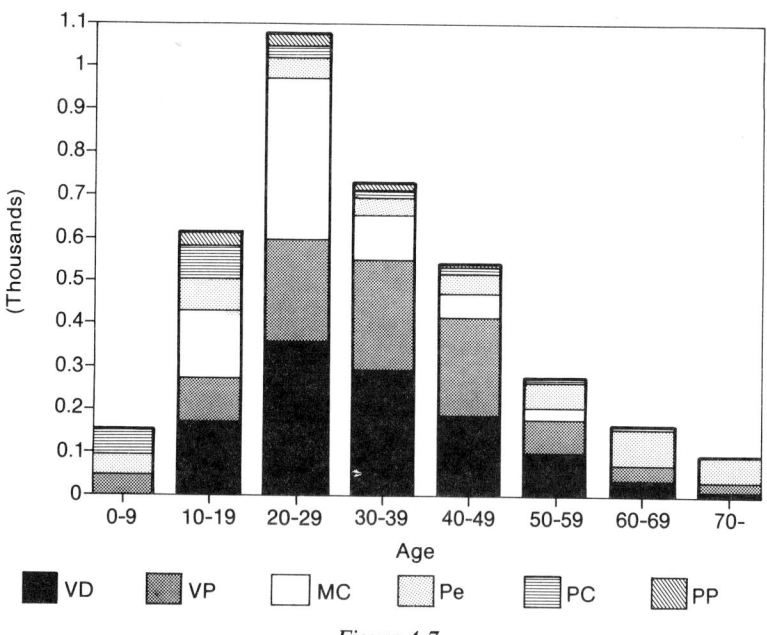

Figure 4.7

different ways of presenting that data in histogram form. The heights of the 'stacked' bars shown in Figure 4.7 represent the casualty totals in each of the age bands. A further pictorial representation may be formed by drawing lines connecting the tops of these bars. The outcome in Figure 4.8 is the *frequency polygon*. It is a particular form of what is self-evidently a *line-graph*.

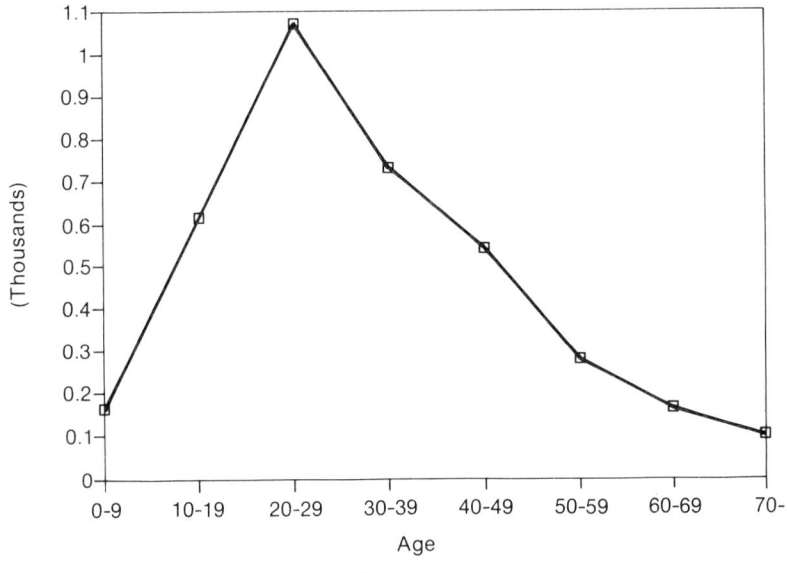

Figure 4.8

Assumptions

A frequency distribution table combines raw data values into classes, the size of each class being predetermined. By doing this we are making an assumption that the data items in the frequency distribution table are a proper representation of all the raw data values that went into the different classes. While this may be a reasonable assumption to make, nevertheless it is still an assumption and must be regarded as such. For example, there are 153 casualties aged under 10 and 766 casualties under 20, and there is an unwritten assumption from the data presented in this way that the casualties are more or less evenly distributed across these age ranges. However, it could be that all last year's casualties were aged between, say, 8 and 12 years, in which case the assumption is completely false. However, the larger the amount of raw data available the more reasonable such an assumption would likely to be.

4.3 Using statistics to describe the characteristics of data

In the ensuing discussion at the Police Committee, the statement was also welcomed that the total of road traffic accident casualties had stayed at the level of the previous year, and that the increases that had been seen for a number of years had been halted. However, it was suggested by one member, and accepted by the Committee, that as further monitoring of the figures next year's report should include details about the average age of casualties so that yearly comparisons can be made. When this information was passed back to the superior in charge of the traffic section he requested the same subordinate to get on to this straightaway.

4.3.1 Measures of 'average'

The word 'average' and its basic meaning will be familiar to all readers, but in the context of 'statistics' there are a number of different types of average. The three main types are the *arithmetic mean*, the *median* and the *mode*. In turn, we will look at the interpretation of each of these averages in relation to the data on the road traffic accident casualties and, in doing so, consider how appropriate they are to the additional details now requested by the Police Committee.

Arithmetic mean

The *arithmetic mean* is defined as 'the sum of the numbers divided by the number of numbers'. In all, there were 3,648 road traffic accident casualties last year. Thus, the arithmetic mean of the casualties' age is found by totalling up all 3,648 ages and dividing the result by 3,648, this being the number of numbers in the sum.

It is usual, however, to express this calculation mathematically in general terms as:

$$\text{Arithmetic mean} = \frac{\sum_{i=1}^{i=n} x_i}{n} \tag{4.1}$$

Should the symbols in equation (4.1) be unfamiliar to the reader they may be explained as follows:

- n represents the number of numbers, here 3,648;
- $x_1, x_2, x_3, \ldots x_n$ represents the set of numbers themselves, here the ages of the casualties, so x_i is just any member of the set;
- Σ is the Greek capital letter 'sigma'; and
- $\sum_{i=1}^{i=n} x_i$ represents the sum of all members of the set, starting at x_1, the first, and finishing at x_n, the last.

Thus

$$\frac{\sum_{i=1}^{i=n} x_i}{n} = \frac{(x_1 + x_2 + x_3 + \ldots + x_n)}{n}$$

and the dots represent all the other members of the set.

Commonly, the arithmetic mean is written:

$$\bar{x} = \frac{\sum_{i=1}^{i=n} x_i}{n}$$

and otherwise known as 'x-bar'.

In order to obtain the arithmetic mean of age of casualties, from what has been stated it is necessary to return to the raw data and the ages of all 3,648 casualties as found on the road traffic accident report forms. Doing this, and performing the calculation as described, the average age of casualties last year was found to be 33.12, or 33.1 when rounded to one decimal place.

While this gives the precise arithmetic mean, clearly it is unwieldy to have to go back to the raw data having first summarised it as required in a frequency table. The mean is a measure representative of the magnitude of the data items. As such a precise value is often not vital to the information required, and a value computed from the data in the frequency distribution table is sufficient. It gives an estimate of the arithmetic mean as would be calculated from the raw data.

The grouped data, available from Table 4.1, is presented in Table 4.4 as an extended frequency distribution table. The assumption made is that the ages of casualties within an age band is evenly distributed such that the age midpoint is representative of those casualties — a point previously covered.

The 'grouped data' arithmetic mean is a revision of the formula given in

Table 4.4 Extended frequency distribution table

Age	No. of casualties f_i	Age midpoint x_i	$f_i x_i$
0–9	153	5	765
10–19	613	15	9,195
20–29	1,075	25	26,875
30–39	729	35	25,515
40–49	541	45	24,345
50–59	279	55	15,345
60–69	162	65	10,530
70+	96	75	7,200
	3,648		119,770

equation (4.1) and is expressed as

$$\bar{x} = \frac{\sum_{i=1}^{i=n} f_i x_i}{\sum_{i=1}^{i=n} f_i} \qquad (4.2)$$

where
- x_i refers to a class midpoint value;
- f_i represents the class frequency; and
- $\sum_{i=1}^{i=n} f_i$ equals n the total number of data items.

Applying the formula of equation (4.2) gives:

$$\bar{x} = \frac{119\,770}{3648}$$

$$= 32.83 \text{ years}$$

$$(= 32.8 \text{ rounded to one decimal place})$$

Median

The *median* is defined as 'the middle number of a group of numbers arranged in ascending order'. This figure divides the numbers so ordered into two equal groups. In the case of an even number of numbers the median is taken to be the average (or arithmetic mean) of the two numbers in the centre.

Again, in basic terms, to calculate the median age of casualties it is necessary to go back to the raw data, put the ages in ascending order, and determine the middle one according to the definition. However, an estimate of this measure is easily calculable from the grouped data frequency distribution table by constructing a cumulative frequency table (see Table 4.5) and from that drawing the *cumulative frequency graph*, otherwise known as the *ogive*, shown in Figure 4.9.

Table 4.5 Cumulative frequency table

Age		Cumulative number of casualties	
Under	10	153	
	20	766	(153 + 613)
	30	1,841	(766 + 1,075)
	40	2,570	(1,841 + 729)
	50	3,111	(2,570 + 541)
	60	3,390	(3,111 + 279)
	70	3,552	(3,390 + 162)
All ages		3,648	(3,552 + 96)

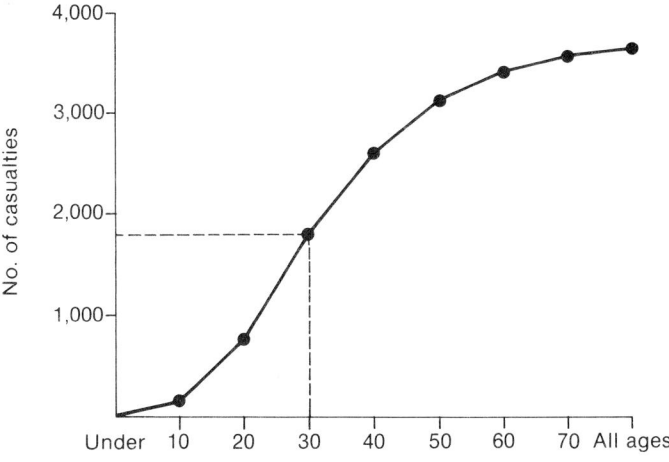

Figure 4.9   Ogive or cumulative frequency graph

With a total of 3,648 casualties, the median age is found from the age of the 1,824th casualty. Reading off this age from the cumulative frequency graph, the median age is estimated at just under 30 years.

Estimating the median in this way from the graph is sufficient for most purposes. However, a more accurate estimate can be determined by calculating what proportion the 1,824th casualty is in the age band it falls, that is 20–30 years. The 1,824th casualty is the $(1,824 - 766) = 1,058$th of the 1,075 in the 20–30 age band. Thus, using proportional parts, the estimate for the median is:

$$20 \text{ (lower age of band)} + \frac{1,058}{1,075} \times 10 \text{ (years in age band)}$$

$$= 29.8 \text{ years (rounding to one decimal place)}$$

Mode

The *mode* is defined as 'the data item or value that occurs most often'. If in the casualty figures the age 21 appeared more times than any other age, then 21 years would be the modal age of this group. As such this may be a significant age with regard to a particular factor, say, age of motor cyclist casualties. However, the mode is not necessarily a representative measure across a group, especially as the modal value can differ considerably from the measures found for arithmetic mean and median. In fact, the mode should be used as an average only when it is a highly predominant data item.

Modes are sometimes calculated from grouped data frequency distributions but any estimates are worthless as there is no comparable definition

(a)

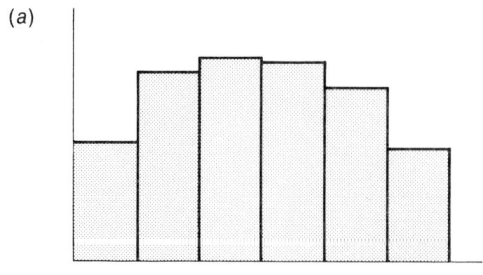

A 'normal' type of
frequency distribution.
The 'most' representative
measure is arithmetic
mean.

(b)

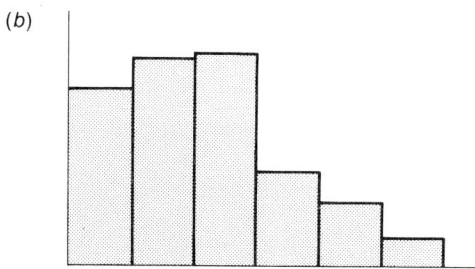

Here the frequency distribution
is more varied than the
'normal' of (a) and the
median is probably the
'best' measure.

(c)

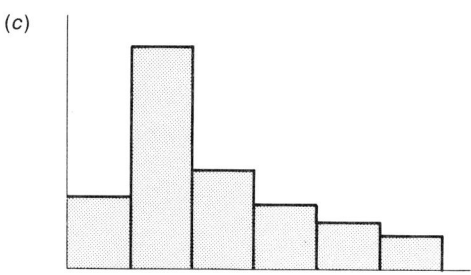

In this distribution where one
class is much larger than
any of the others the mode
becomes a representative
measure.

(d)

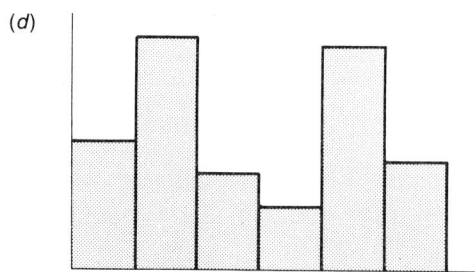

This is essentially a
bi-modal distribution and
it illustrates the situation
where no one of the measures
would be truly representative
as an 'average'.

Figure 4.10   Choosing the best measure of average

in such cases. With the data in question, the calculation of a mode is certainly meaningless.

In general terms it is not possible to establish set rules as to which 'average' is 'best' for particular frequency distributions as these themselves can vary so much. However, Figure 4.10 and accompanying comments will prove useful to the reader.

4.3.2 Measures of variation

The arithmetic mean, median and mode are 'averages' used as measures to describe the general magnitude of a group of data items or values. However, our investigation with the use of averages would not be complete without including some information on how the data itself might vary across its range of data values. It is necessary to consider measures of variation to see how well an average represents the data group.

The mode, as we have seen, is perhaps not a true measure of average. It is more of an attribute of the data in that it is the data value that occurs most often, and so the variation, dispersion or spread of the data around the mode as a computational measure does not have any real significance. We will thus confine the discussion in the remainder of this section to the establishment of measures of variation related to the arithmetic mean and the median.

Quartile values

The median, as the middle value, is easily found whether it be directly from ungrouped data or estimated from grouped data on a cumulative frequency graph. The median splits the data into two equal parts.

The data can be similarly split into *four* equal parts and, doing so, the numbers separating the divisions are called 'quartiles', so that one quarter of the numbers are less than the first quartile and so on. The measure of variation associated with this is that one half of the data items will fall between the first and third quartile values and is called the *interquartile* or *middle range*.

Accordingly, we can consider this measure using as an example the road traffic accident casualty data. In order to determine the quartile values exactly it is necessary again, as with the median previously, to put in order by age all 3,648 data items and find the ages of the 912th, 1,824th and 2,736th items in the list. The 912th and 2,736th items would give as ages the first and third quartiles, respectively, and hence the interquartile range for the data.

We can estimate this range from a cumulative frequency graph as given in Figure 4.11 to find that the middle 50 per cent of all the road accident

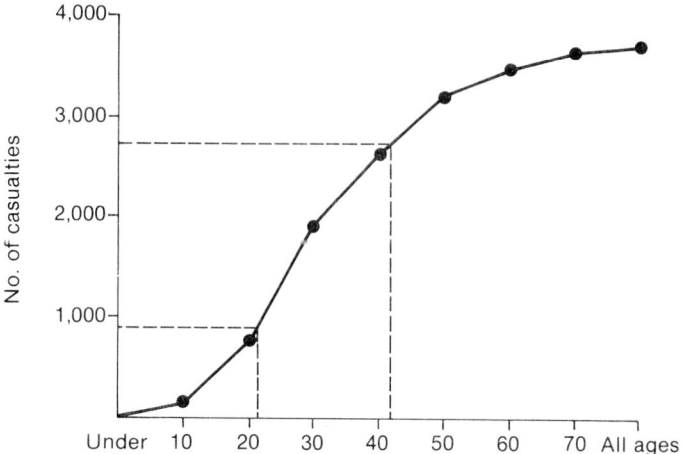

Figure 4.11 Cumulative frequency graph: quartile estimates

traffic casualties last year were in the age range $21\frac{3}{4}$–$42\frac{1}{2}$. The reader can, of course, obtain slightly better estimates for the first and third quartile ages by following, with adjustments, the mathematical calculation for the median seen earlier in this section.

Standard deviation

A sensible and convenient measure of variation around the arithmetic mean is what is generally known as *the standard deviation*. The first step in establishing a formula for the standard deviation is to calculate the average of the square of the deviations of each data value from the previously calculated arithmetic mean. This is termed the *variance* of the distribution and is expressed mathematically by equation (4.3) as follows:

$$\text{Variance} = \frac{\sum_{i=1}^{i=n}(x_i - \bar{x})^2}{n} \qquad (4.3)$$

As the variance is measured in squares of the data units it is clearly more appropriate to take the square root of this measure so that it is compatible with the units of the arithmetic mean to which it relates. Accordingly, the square root of the variance is taken. It is termed the *standard deviation* and the Greek letter σ (small sigma) is used to represent it in equations, thus:

$$\sigma = \sqrt{\left(\frac{\sum_{i=1}^{i=n}(x_i - \bar{x})^2}{n}\right)} \qquad (4.4)$$

However, the application of equation (4.4) is not the usual way in which standard deviations are found. In fact, it is more usual, because it is quicker, to calculate a standard deviation by applying the following mathematically equivalent formula:

$$\sigma = \sqrt{\left(\frac{\sum_{i=1}^{i=n} x_i^2}{n} - \bar{x}^2 \right)} \qquad (4.5)$$

Clearly, the calculation of a standard deviation can be a lengthy process when there are a large number of data items. In addition to the calculation of the arithmetic mean, the sum of the squares of the data values, $\sum_{i=1}^{n} x_i^2$, has to be found in order that equation (4.5) can be applied. For instance, with our road traffic casualty data it would first be necessary to square 3,648 age values to find the sum required, and so on. Fortunately, however, equation (4.5) is easily revised to enable the standard deviation of 'grouped data' to be calculated. The formula is

$$\sigma = \sqrt{\left(\frac{\sum_{i=1}^{i=n} f_i x_i^2}{n} - \bar{x}^2 \right)} \qquad (4.6)$$

where again:
- x_i refers to a class midpoint value;
- f_i represents the class frequency

To be in a position to determine the standard deviation from the road traffic casualty data it is an easy matter to extend the frequency distribution table (Table 4.4) that was used to calculate the arithmetic mean as shown in Table 4.6. The calculation for the standard deviation is thus:

$$\sigma = \sqrt{\left(\frac{4,870,600}{3,648} - (32.83)^2 \right)}$$

$$= 16.04 \text{ years}$$

While this sort of calculation is a quick and easy one with a calculator, sometimes, as here, the numbers involved can become very large. In order

Table 4.6 Extended frequency distribution table

Age	No of casualties f_i	Age midpoint x_i	$f_i x_i$	$f_i x_i^2$
0–9	153	5	765	3,825
10–19	613	15	9,195	137,925
20–29	1,075	25	26,875	671,875
30–39	729	35	25,515	893,025
40–49	541	45	24,345	1,095,525
50–59	279	55	15,345	843,975
60–69	162	65	10,530	684,450
70+	96	75	7,200	540,000
Totals	3,648		119,770	4,870,600

to keep the size of the numbers handled to a reasonable size, the calculation can be approached in an alternative manner by considering an 'assumed' mean.

The reader will find this approach well documented in most books on statistics, but with the software and packages now generally available on all ranges of computers there is no need to try to simplify the calculations. For instance, using a spreadsheet package on a microcomputer, the basic data is held in tabular form, formulae are input to represent the products, mean and standard deviation, and then the totals and results are automatically calculated. Accordingly, the reader would be well advised to investigate the availability and use of such packages, especially as often they can be integrated with other software, e.g. business graphics, a wordprocessor, a report generator and a database.

4.4 Analysing trends in data

The opening chapter of the book brought together, albeit in a political commentary, a number of separate items of information related to the functions and workings of Anyshire County Council. That chapter highlighted the need to piece together items of information over a period of time to show that they are interdependent. The arguments first of all called for a large cash injection into the secondary school service. This was then followed by a report advocating the plight of the elderly.

While the arguments for a big increase in the secondary school budget seemed plausible at the time, it was relatively only a short-term need, and the greater need, it later transpired, was seen to be in another area. Political opinion clouded the first issue as clearly the allocation of resources to the education service, as well as that to social services in support of the elderly, has to match, in the longer term, the projections of the different client group populations.

Some details of these population projections presented in Chapter 1, section 1.7 and the case study, are reproduced in Table 4.7 and Figure 4.12 as they represent the result of an analysis of trends in data.

The collation of this population data results from an exercise based on data from the last census, known population figures and certain trends in the variables affecting population change. The major variables involved are the birth rate, itself dependent on the young adult population and the number of marriages taking place, the general movement of families in and out of the county, the death rate and, of course, the age of death.

The inclusion of these and other variables naturally complicates the predictions. Thus the information provided has to be qualified, particularly with regard to the analysis of birth rate which has been erratic over the last decade. Taking long-term cyclic factors into account it is assumed that the

Table 4.7 Population trends in Anyshire

		The young			Those of working age	The elderly		
		0–4	5–10	11–15	16–59/64	65–74	75–79	80 +
Year	y − 1, census	35,000	47,400	44,700	312,900	43,900	14,300	13,500
	y	35,500	45,700	44,500	316,800	43,600	14,600	14,000
	y + 2	37,600	43,000	43,500	325,200	43,200	14,900	14,700
	y + 4	39,500	43,000	41,200	333,300	42,700	15,200	15,200
	y + 6	40,900	44,500	37,900	340,100	42,800	15,300	15,800
	y + 8	42,200	46,900	36,000	345,500	42,900	15,200	16,200
	y + 10	43,400	48,500	36,400	349,000	42,800	14,900	16,600
change	y − 1 to y + 10	+ 24%	+ 2.3%	− 18.6%	+ 11.5%	− 2.5%	+ 4.2%	+ 23%

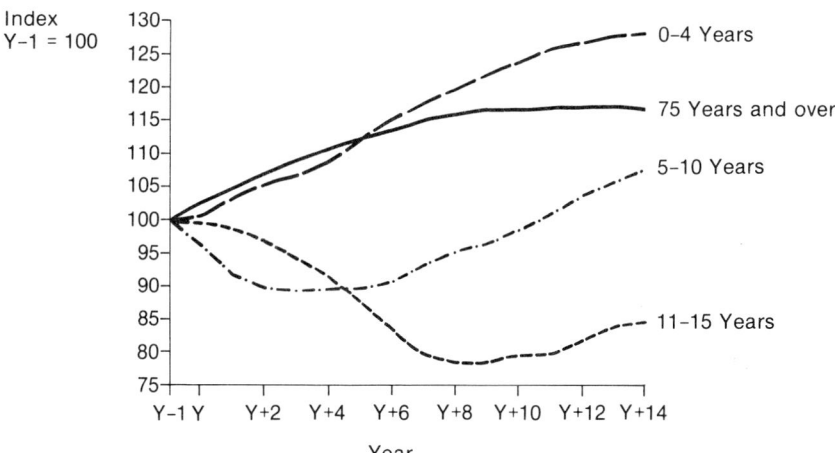

Figure 4.12 Indexed population trends in Anyshire

birth rate will gradually rise over the next decade. With this and the other factors built into the projections the information produced becomes the most reliable available.

Time series analysis

To be able to analyse trends in data in order to produce these sorts of projection it is necessary to consider how data has behaved in the past. The discovery of past patterns together with the expectation that growth and change will mostly continue at similar rates allow us to determine projections and make predictions related to future needs. Ways in which trends can be established are introduced using some past data comprising of recent quarterly figures for the number of registered births within Anyshire. An analysis such as this whereby data is given in time periods and forecasts are made is called a *time series analysis*.

The need to predict future patterns of a business operation is an important element within the decision-making process of an organisation. For any service or product the demands on that service or projected sales of the product need to be identified in order that there can be an adequate supply for that service or that there are sufficient numbers of the product available to meet the projected sales. There are likely to be many variables or parameters involved in a time series analysis some of which may need to be specifically allowed for, e.g. technological change. Usually, however, the data at hand together with other information perhaps on population, price and productivity changes can be analysed to give worthwhile results and allow meaningful decisions to be made.

The time periods of data may be given in years, quarters, months, weeks, days or even hours and will be dependent on the nature of the application. The past data we are considering at these various points in time is the *time series* itself. Often time series data will appear to fluctuate but it will still be possible to determine a trend from the data when taken as a whole.

A common fluctuation is the seasonal variation found in many types of data. For example, the amount and cost of imports and exports always fluctuate quarter by quarter. Also, the employment figures the government issue monthly are always adjusted to take account of seasonal variations.

A further factor sometimes apparent from time series data may be a cyclical fluctuation that does not, say, form a set pattern but matches a period of economic boom, increase in consumer expenditure or even a recession or strike.

There may well be other residual influences affecting the pattern of data in the time series, but unless any can be specifically accounted for it is generally reasonable to ignore them by assuming some influences will increase the figures and some will reduce them, so tending to cancel each other out.

Trend analysis: moving averages

As stated, the data we wish to use to illustrate some of the factors involved in a trend analysis relates to a set of quarterly figures of registered live births in Anyshire. The data in Table 4.8 is compiled from birth registrations across all districts in the county and is now used to ascertain what trend is apparent. Our use of this data will serve to illustrate some of the approaches that can be taken in a trend analysis. However, it should be noted it would be usual for similar trend analyses to be performed on the data applicable to each district as well as to the county itself. First of all, it is always useful to draw a line graph representing the data through each of the time periods. This is shown in Figure 4.13.

Table 4.8 Births registered in Anyshire

Year	1st Qtr.	2nd Qtr.	3rd Qtr.	4th Qtr.
y − 3	1,851	1,913	1,966	1,849
y − 2	1,799	1,833	1,887	1,673
y − 1	1,752	1,816	1,802	1,729
y	1,671	1,790		

Sometimes a linear or indeed curved trend is apparent directly from the line graph. Also, there may be cases where this is so when the odd unaccountable fluctuation is ignored. Clearly, this is not the situation with this data and there is a notable seasonal variation with more births during the summer months of each year. To take this variation into account and to analyse the overall trend it is necessary to identify a yearly measure. The most obvious yearly measure is the yearly total of births. However, from the data available above this will only provide us with three yearly totals which is not really sufficient in order to determine a trend. For the above, and other data given as quarterly figures whether these be seasonal variations or not, a good all-purpose measure is the *moving average.*

The method of calculating a moving average is straightforward. If the data is given as quarterly figures, the method is to consider, in a sequence, data values from four successive quarters grouped together. An average is then found for each group by summing the four values and dividing the total by four. The effect is to obtain a yearly average that is moving along quarter by quarter.

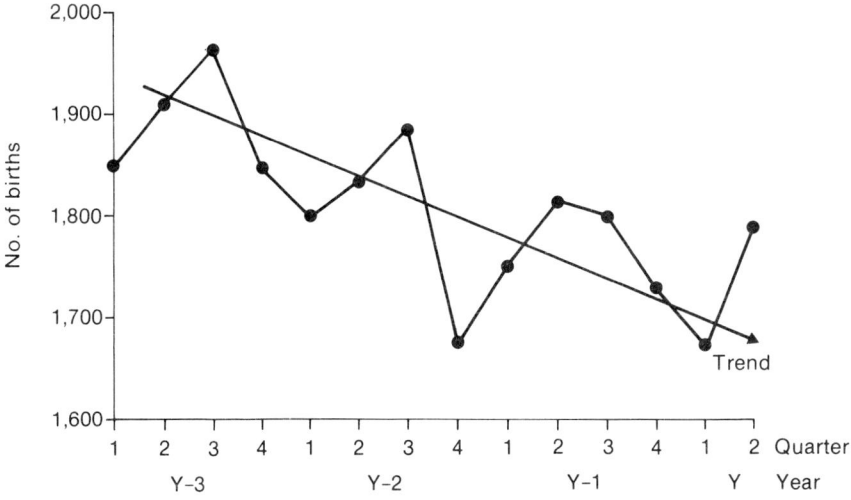

Figure 4.13 Line graph of births registration data

We will now demonstrate this method with the data under consideration. Taking the data values in quarterly order, starting at year y − 3, the successive figures are:

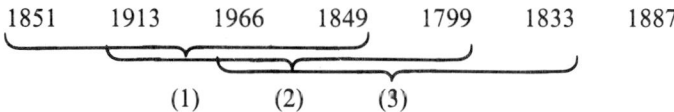

| 1851 | 1913 | 1966 | 1849 | 1799 | 1833 | 1887 |

(1)   (2)   (3)

The data values for the first four quarters, group (1), are averaged to give (1,851 + 1,913 + 1,966 + 1,844)/4 = 1,894.75. Group (2) is obtained by dropping the first number in group (1), that is 1,851, and bringing in the data value from the next quarter, namely 1,799. The group (2) average is thus (1,913 + 1,966 + 1,849 + 1,799)/4 = 1,881.75. This procedure is repeated all the way through the data for as many averages as can be calculated. This

Table 4.9 Moving averages for births registration

Year	Qtr.	Births	Centred 4 Qtr. moving average
y − 3	1	1,851	
	2	1,913	
			1,894.75
	3	1,966	
			1,881.75
	4	1,849	
			1,861.75
y − 2	1	1,799	
			1,842
	2	1,833	
			1,798
	3	1,887	
			1,786.25
	4	1,673	
			1,782
y − 1	1	1,752	
			1,760.75
	2	1,816	
			1,774.75
	3	1,802	
			1,754
	4	1,729	
			1,748
y	1	1,671	
	2	1,790	

'moving average' then establishes the trend for the data and the results are given in Table 4.9.

It can be readily seen that the data values in the 'moving average' column of Table 4.9 are relatively much more stable than the quarterly data values themselves. Thus, it is certainly more meaningful to use these values to indicate the trend or general manner in which the figures are moving. The reader should note that each moving average value is given centralised within the range of the calculated values.

While the method has been illustrated using quarterly data values, clearly the concept can be extended and the method used for any time series. For example, with yearly data it might be appropriate to determine a five-year moving average or, if sufficient data was available, even a ten-year moving average.

The concept can also be extended to calculate further averages, for instance another moving average that is the average of two successive averages. The figures in Table 4.10 illustrate this. The values in the 'Modified moving average' column give averages of successive pairs of values in the 'Centred 4-Qtr. moving average' column. These values are 'new trend' figures for the respective quarters. The right-hand column in Table 4.10 gives the deviations between the actual and the new trend values. These deviations are further analysed to calculate average quarterly deviations and seasonal variations as follows:

	Quarter 1	2	3	4
Deviations			+ 77.75	− 22.75
	− 52.875	+ 13	+ 94.875	− 111.125
	− 19.375	+ 48.25	+ 37.375	− 22.25
Average deviation	− 36.125	+ 30.625	+ 70	− 53.042 (Sum = + 12.458)
Adjustment = − (sum/4)	− 3.115	− 3.115	− 3.115	− 3.115
Seasonal variation (rounded)	− 39	+ 28	+ 67	− 55

These seasonal variations are the likely quarterly upswings and downswings in relation to the trend. Thus, if an accurate trend line can be determined then it is possible to make reasonable projections based on these calculated seasonal variations. An approach for this, called *regression analysis*, is considered in the next section.

'Births registration' data may not be wholly applicable to a moving average analysis because it can be a little erratic by its very nature. Generally, however, the above analysis is particularly useful for data that displays a significant seasonal variation or regular fluctuation.

Table 4.10 Extended trend analysis table

Year	Qtr.	Births (actual)	Centred 4-quarter moving average	Modified moving average (new trend)	Deviation (actual – new trend)
y − 3	1	1,851			
	2	1,913	1,894.75		
	3	1,966	1,881.75	1,888.25	+ 77.75
	4	1,849	1,861.75	1,871.75	− 22.75
y − 2	1	1,799	1,842	1,851.875	− 52.875
	2	1,833	1,798	1,820	+ 13
	3	1,887	1,786.25	1,792.125	+ 94.875
	4	1,673	1,782	1,784.125	− 111.125
y − 1	1	1,752	1,760.75	1,771.375	− 19.375
	2	1,816	1,774.75	1,767.75	+ 48.25
	3	1,802	1,754	1,764.625	+ 37.375
	4	1,729	1,748	1,751.25	− 22.25
y	1	1,671			
	2	1,790			

4.5 Assessing relationships between data variables

A common and all-important information requirement is the comparison of one set of data with another. In fact, the very first issue in the political debate of Chapter 1 was an instance of such a comparison. The countrywide figures on educational spending showed Anyshire to be 36th out of 39 in the national league tables for spending on pupils in both the primary and secondary sectors of education.

4.5.1 A basis for comparison: index numbers

Clearly, in order to be in a position to make comparisons it is necessary to judge the data from a common viewpoint or angle. In the case of those education comparisons made in Chapter 1 the common denominator is the amount of the gross cost per pupil for each county council and the figures allow spending comparisons to be made directly between the county councils year by year.

However, if a comparison between, say, two data sets is required over a period of years then such a direct comparison is insufficient. Although we may be comparing 'like' data the base point of each set of data may be different and any difference needs to be accounted for before a proper comparison can be made.

A convenient means of 'standardising' data, so allowing comparisons over a period of time, is to relate the values within each set of data to an index of 100 at the initial time-period.

Example 1

To see more closely how this is achieved, let us consider the spending in terms of gross cost per pupil by Anyshire over the previous six year period. The actual amounts are shown in Table 4.11, given to the nearest pound.

The technique is to set, for each list of data values, an index number of 100 at the initial time-period, here year $y - 5$, and then to revise all the other data values in the list to this number in a manner that their relationship remains unaltered. This is achieved by dividing each and every number in the 'primary' list by 256, multiplying the results by 100. Those in the 'secondary' list are divided by 414 and multiplied by 100. Table 4.12 shows the outcome of this, rounding the results, termed *index numbers*, to the nearest integer.

Table 4.11

	Expenditure per pupil (£)	
Year	Primary	Secondary
$y - 5$	256	414
$y - 4$	284	455
$y - 3$	299	463
$y - 2$	338	521
$y - 1$	384	567
y	504	749

Table 4.12

	Expenditure per pupil index	
Year	Primary	Secondary
$y - 5$	100	100
$y - 4$	111	110
$y - 3$	117	112
$y - 2$	132	126
$y - 1$	150	137
y	197	181

These index numbers are, therefore, expressly percentages of the initial time-period data values. They measure the change in a variable over time in a manner which is widely understood, that is as a percentage. In the above example, expenditure per pupil in year y is 97 per cent in the primary sector and 81 per cent in the secondary sector over what it was five years previously. For comparison purposes, over a period of time this information is, perhaps, more meaningful, if 'improvement' of level of provision is being considered rather than a direct comparison of the yearly expenditure per pupil figures from the various county councils.

Example 2

As a further illustration of the use of index numbers let us suppose there is a requirement to compare the live birth trends of Anyshire with those of England and Wales generally. The results from the calculation of the

Table 4.13 Comparative trend analysis

Year	Qtr.	Anyshire births	Anyshire modified moving average	Anyshire index	England and Wales index
y − 3	1	1,851			
	2	1,913			
	3	1,966	1,888.25	100	100
	4	1,849	1,871.75	99.1	99.5
y − 2	1	1,799	1,851.875	98.1	99.0
	2	1,833	1,820	96.4	98.6
	3	1,887	1,792.125	94.9	98.1
	4	1,673	1,784.125	94.5	98.0
y − 1	1	1,752	1,771.375	93.8	97.7
	2	1,816	1,767.75	93.6	97.3
	3	1,802	1,764.625	93.5	97.4
	4	1,729	1,751.25	92.7	97.2
y	1	1,671			
	2	1,790			

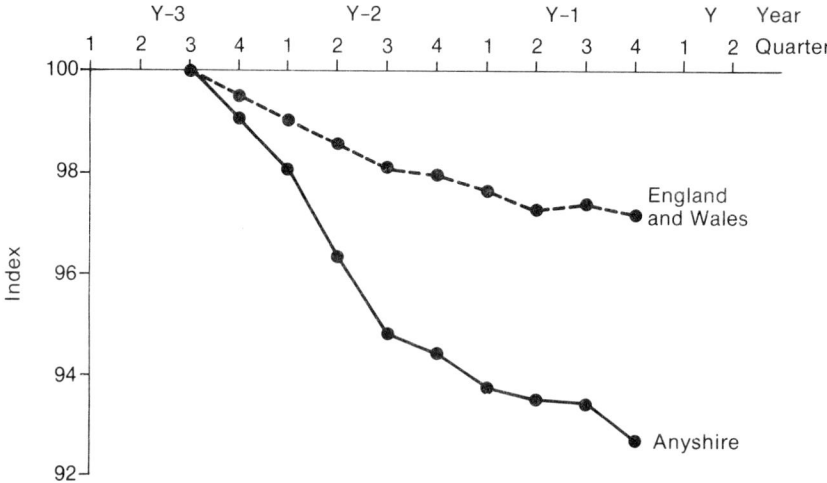

Figure 4.14 Line graphs displaying comparative trend analysis results

moving average of Anyshire's quarterly live births are set out in Table 4.10 at the end of the last section. We know from above that if the requirement is to present information comparing separate sets of data over a period of time then it is meaningful to relate the two data sets using the index number approach. Results from the application of the approach to this data are shown in Table 4.13. Given, also, are the available index numbers relating to the moving average of quarterly births in England and Wales over the same period. The line graphs showing these results in a visually comparable form are presented in Figure 4.14.

Representation of data sets using index numbers in this way allows a number of different comparisons to be made at the same time. The reader should, in fact, recall an instance of this from the beginning of section 4.3, where in Figure 4.12 four sets of data were compared together in one diagram.

4.5.2 General use of index numbers

These examples have shown us how index numbers can be used to enable us to record and compare changes in data over a period of time. Their use is widespread nowadays, especially within the economic and business environments of organisations where they are used for comparing changes in prices, income, expenditure, production and sales, etc. While there are varied forms of index, the underlying concept is as indicated.

One index which is known to us all is the *Retail Price Index* (RPI), or cost of living index. It is an index which endeavours to represent as a measure our cost/standard of living. Along with any price index the RPI measures, as a single summary figure, an aggregate of average prices of several commodities and services. With such a measure it is necessary to select a fully representative range of commodities and services, and also to ensure that the proportion of each to the whole is weighted according to our expenditure patterns. Sample surveys of our spending habits are studied and analysed for changes so that all data included in determining the measure is kept up to date. For instance, the amount of tobacco consumed per person per month is slowly reducing and now forms a much lower proportion of the average person's spending. This and other changing factors must be reflected in the RPI measure itself.

The Retail Price Index has become the standard measure of inflation, and as such allows comparisons to be made to see how costs, prices and income are varying with respect to each other. To some extent this can be achieved with the use of index numbers and making appropriate comparisons. However, it is possible to take this one step further and obtain a quantitative measure for the 'closeness' of the relationship between variables and data sets. The technique that is employed is called *correlation analysis*.

4.5.3 Correlation analysis

Another issue in the educational spending debate of Chapter 1 was whether or not the increases in expenditure per pupil had kept up with inflation during recent years. The figures, in terms of index numbers, have already been presented in this section, but we now append to them the RPI figures for the same time period with the intention of determining how close the increases in expenditure in the primary and secondary sectors have followed the increase in the RPI over the six-year period. The data is given in Table 4.14.

The measure of closeness of the relationship between two variables is called the *correlation coefficient*. It is really a measure of the linear relationship between the two variables. To put it another way: how similar are the rates of increase of the variables?

A convenient definition for the correlation coefficient is found in terms of the variances of the data variables. Supposing the two variables to be x and y then, from earlier in the chapter, their respective variances are:

$$\sigma_x^2 = \frac{1}{n} \sum_{i=1}^{i=n} x_i^2 - \bar{x}^2 \text{ and } \sigma_y^2 = \frac{1}{n} \sum_{i=1}^{i=n} y_i^2 - \bar{y}^2$$

where n is the number of data values in each set.

Similar to these definitions, the *covariance* is a measure of association between the variables and is defined by:

$$\sigma_{xy} = \frac{1}{n} \sum_{i=1}^{i=n} x_i y_i - \bar{x}\bar{y}$$

From these three definitions, the correlation coefficient, r, is expressed as follows:

$$r = \frac{\sigma_{xy}}{\sigma_x \sigma_y} \tag{4.7}$$

Table 4.14

Year	Primary	Secondary	Retail Price Index
	Expenditure per pupil indexes		
$y-5$	100	100	100
$y-4$	111	110	116
$y-3$	117	112	126
$y-2$	132	126	142
$y-1$	150	137	168
y	197	181	188

Table 4.15 Coefficient evaluation: primary and RPI data

Primary index x	RPI y	xy	x^2	y^2
100	100	10,000	10,000	10,000
111	116	12,876	12,321	13,456
117	126	14,742	13,689	15,876
132	142	18,744	17,424	20,164
150	168	25,200	22,500	28,224
197	188	37,036	38,809	35,344
Totals: 807	840	118,598	114,743	123,064

Calculation of coefficient:

$$\sigma_x = \sqrt{(114,743)/6 - (807/6)^2} = 32.15$$
$$\sigma_y = \sqrt{(123,064)/6 - (840/6)^2} = 30.18$$
$$\sigma_{xy} = (118,598)/6 - (807/6)(840/6) = 936.33$$

giving

$$r_1 = \frac{936.33}{(32.15)(30.18)} = 0.965$$

We can now calculate the correlation coefficient for first the primary and RPI figures, and secondly for the secondary and RPI figures. The calculations necessary for the two coefficient evaluations are set out in Tables 4.15 and 4.16.

Table 4.16 Coefficient evaluation: secondary and RPI data

Secondary index x	RPI y	xy	x^2	y^2
100	100	10,000	10,000	10,000
110	116	12,760	12,100	13,456
112	126	14,112	12,544	15,876
126	142	17,892	15,876	20,164
137	168	23,016	18,769	28,224
181	188	34,028	32,761	35,344
Totals: 766	840	111,808	102,050	123,064

Calculation of coefficient:

$$\sigma_x = \sqrt{(102,050)/6 - (766/6)^2} = 26.64$$
$$\sigma_y = \sqrt{(123,064)/6 - (840/6)^2} = 30.18$$
$$\sigma_{xy} = (111,808)/6 - (766/6)(840/6) = 961.33$$

giving

$$r_2 = \frac{761.334}{(26.64)(30.18)} = 0.947$$

The outcome from the calculation of a correlation coefficient, r, between data sets always gives a result for r lying in the range -1 to $+1$. The nearer the value of r is to $+1$ then the closer the relationship is in a 'positive' sense, that is with the values from both data sets increasing or decreasing together. The other extreme, with r near to -1, shows a close 'negative' relationship, that is with values from one data set increasing uniformly as the other values decrease. Correlation coefficient values around zero indicate a lack of correlation and that the two variables are essentially independent of each other. Therefore, the correlation coefficient result measures the 'degree' of correlation between the variables which is essentially the closeness of their relationship.

The above results, $r_1 = 0.965$ and $r_2 = 0.947$, show a positive and strong relationship in both cases. These results deserve a final comment to add to the earlier points of the political debate. What they show is that in both the primary and secondary sectors the expenditure per pupil has kept up reasonably well with inflation over the previous six-year period. Taking this on face value, while the 'secondary index' v. RPI correlation coefficient r_2 is the lower value of the two, it could not be considered low enough to add support to the case for a much improved secondary school provision and a cash injection of £2.5 million.

However, this is the outcome of one single information analysis and always the interrelated effects have to be considered, particularly in this case where the 11–15 population age group is projected to fall, and also presumably since a cash increase in one area of the county council's budget means at least a relative decrease in others.

4.5.4 Regression analysis

A strong positive correlation indicates a good linear relationship between the two variables. In such cases it is sometimes appropriate to determine the line of 'best' fit relating the variables. The technique for this is called *regression analysis*, and the line of best fit is the *regression line*. One use of regression analysis is to use the equation of the regression line to predict y-values from x-values.

To illustrate the approach let us consider the 'secondary index' (x-values) v. RPI (y-values) data and first of all plot the (x,y) values as points on a graph. Imagine that the line of best fit is drawn on the graph as well. The criterion that determines the equation of this line is that 'the sum of the squares of the vertical deviations of the points from the line is minimised'.

In representing the equation of the regression line by $y = a + bx$ we do not include here the mathematical analysis for the calculation of a and b which determines the relationship between the x and y variables. Simple formulae for their calculation will suffice, given in terms of values already calculated from the correlation analysis.

$$\text{First: } b = \frac{\text{Covariance of } x \text{ and } y}{\text{Variance of } x} = \frac{\sigma_{xy}}{\sigma_x^2}$$

Secondly, a characteristic of the regression line is that it passes through the point representing the arithmetic mean of the data sets, namely $(\bar{x}, \bar{y})$. Thus $\bar{y} = a + b\bar{x}$ which allows a to be calculated having previously found b from above.

For the data in question, and referring back to the results determined earlier in this section, a and b are found as:

$$b = \frac{\sigma_{xy}}{\sigma_x^2} = \frac{761.33}{(26.64)^2} = 1.0728$$

and

$$a = \bar{y} - b\bar{x} = (840/6) - 1.0728(766/6) = 3.039$$

The reader can confirm for himself that this is indeed the line drawn on the graph in Figure 4.15. The line and its equation could then be used to see if predictions for the following year(s) were in fact realised or not.

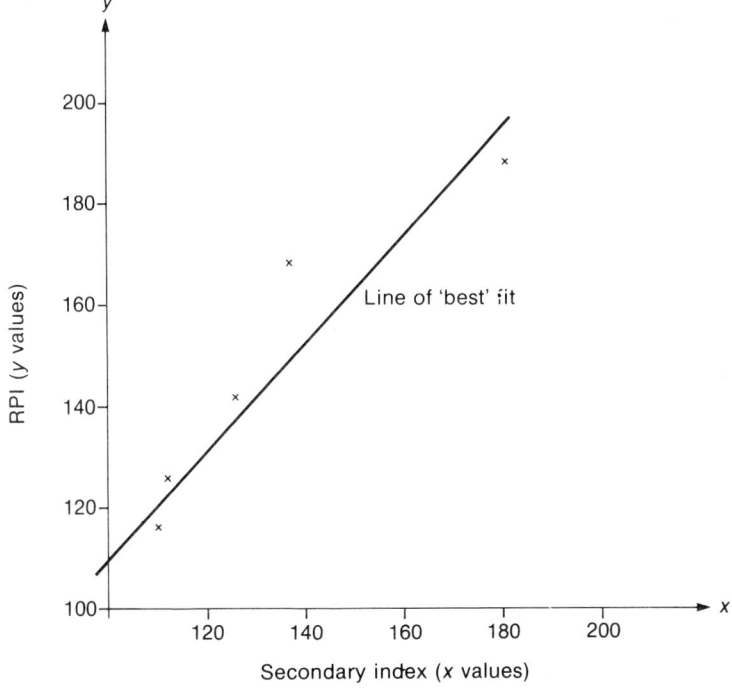

Figure 4.15 Line of best fit

4.6 Avoiding misrepresentation

It is not the intention in this section to concentrate attention on the misrepresentation of information. This, in fact, would be particularly unwise because as well as picking out isolated instances, in all probability either related information would be omitted from the discussion or perhaps the data and information would not be seen in its true context. Instead we shall concentrate on some fundamental points of good practice which should be observed in the presentation and analysis of information so that undue misrepresentation is avoided, and, where appropriate, reference will be made to items from the preceding sections.

4.6.1 Some guidelines to follow

Having collected or acquired data we saw the need in section 4.2 first to organise the data by forming a frequency distribution table. The road traffic accident casualty data analysed was such that convenient groupings were apparent. Initially, the data was presented in summarised form according to the category of casualty and the only matter to be decided was the form of visual presentation to be used, pie chart or histogram, according to the specified requirement.

However, the follow-up analysis necessitated a breakdown and classification of the data into age ranges. The selection of a ten-year age band was both convenient and sensible with this data. This, though, is not always the case and a more arbitrary classification has to take place. As a general rule you should not use less than five or more than, say, fifteen classes, otherwise the grouped data tends to become unrepresentative. A major factor in the decision of 'how many classes' there should be is the readability of the class ranges, for example classes 0–9, 10–19... are easier to assimilate than 0–7, 8–15... Clearly, also the class limits should be specified so that a data value can only be placed in one class. This means that classes should not be written 0–10, 10–20, and so on.

One last but important point with regard to data classification is the correct determination of the midpoint values as this is required for the evaluation of arithmetic means and standard deviations of grouped data. The correct determination depends on whether the data under analysis is 'continuous' or 'discrete'. To illustrate the difference, consider again the nature of the accident casualty data when classified into the various age ranges. The age bands 0–9, 10–19 actually meant 0 and under 10, 10 and under 20, respectively, so the class midpoints were 5, 15, etc., as age is a 'continuous' variable. If, however, the same class ranges 0–9, 10–19, etc., related to, say, the number of students studying on the various courses in a school or college then the data 'can' have only set values and the data is termed 'discrete'. The class midpoints are then $(0 + 9)/2 = 4.5$ and $(10 + 19)/2 = 14.5$ and so on.

Other guidelines that you should follow relate to information diagrams as well as to frequency distribution tables. Every diagram or table should be named and appropriately referenced if it is part of a report. Any units of measurement and keys should be clear. A table should not be too large. It is better to have more than one simple table rather than one single complicated one.

With histograms it is best not to picture too many bars as a cluster within a group. On this point if you refer back to Figures 4.6 and 4.7 you will see that although they are shown primarily as alternative ways of data presentation they are too crowded as diagrams and have too little clarity to be of much use. Six is too many components to group together in this way. Four is a suggested maximum, but the overriding factor should always be the ease with which the eye can take in the information presented.

4.6.2 Is the measure representative?

The arithmetic mean, median and mode were discussed as the three main measures of average. There is no 'best' measure of the three, the reason being that it is the value of the data itself as seen earlier which is the indicator to the information analyst which measure is the 'most' representative of average. It may be that the arithmetic mean is the most common and popular measure of average used. However, with large extreme values contained in the data the mean becomes much less representative of the data as a whole.

Also, if an end class is 'open-ended', and such cases are not rare, then an assumption has to be made with regard to the midpoint value of this end class. For example, with the accident casualty data grouped into age ranges, the last class (70 +) is open-ended and the midpoint value taken is an assumed one.

The only real guideline to be adopted is that whichever measure is quoted as representative of average it should not be quoted without justification and a tabular and/or pictorial representation of the data should always be provided.

4.6.3 Several points to note

The various points made above apply equally well to time series data. However, when trends are analysed and projections result, then the pictorial representation of the outcome is often via the use of a line graph. In the production of line graphs, distortion of the facts must be avoided. A line on a graph that is flat could be understating a growth trend. Similarly, one that rises sharply is likely to give the impression of rapid growth. Either or both may be a misrepresentation due to inappropriate scaling for the data placed on the vertical axis. A general rule to avoid any distortion is to make the graph a little wider than high, even with a small number of time periods on the horizontal axis.

Index numbers are often used in conjunction with line graphs and time series to represent comparisons of different data sets. Clearly, where comparisons are being made the same base period must be used for each index, and in general, the base period should be fairly recent. An overriding factor, however, is that the base period is 'normal' and so should not be set at an extreme value within a cyclic fluctuation.

To some extent the choice of the data in the trend analysis of Anyshire's recent live births and resulting line graph representation (see Figure 4.13) could be considered misleading as it was also stated that the birth rate had been erratic. A truer representation would have been achieved if more past data had been included in the analysis to reflect the fluctuations found in Anyshire and nationwide.

It was suggested in the previous section that one use of the equation of the regression line between two data variables might be to make predictions. It may be that regression analysis data is stable either by its very nature or that stability is achieved and controlled by external influences. With such data it is then possible to use the regression line to make reasonable predictions. However, especially with time series data, it is highly dangerous to predict too far ahead as relationships can often change very quickly. Generally, then, prediction using this approach is not a practice to be encouraged.

4.7 Summary

The main subject of this chapter has been the coverage of some basic statistical techniques linked to three broad but very common business requirements associated with the analysis of quantitative data. Seen through the eyes of the information analyst these were:

(1) to describe the characteristics of data;
(2) to analyse trends in data;
(3) to assess relationships between data variables.

All sections within organisations now use statistical methods in their operations, and many of their general requirements fit into one or more of these three categories.

It may be that the information analyst at times requires a deeper 'statistical' knowledge than it has been desirable or possible to develop here. However, the fundamental concepts have been introduced and a sound foundation of the techniques established. Clearly, should the reader wish, or find it necessary, to investigate any aspects further he/she should consult a statistics book with a good coverage of the particular area of study.

Whichever data analysis technique is used, it should be recognised that not only is it often desirable and necessary first to organise data appropriately but also it is important to consider fully the way(s) in which data and/or information are to be presented.

The diagram that is 'best' is the one matching the needs of the information analysis. Any diagrams, however, used to present the required features of the data must do so clearly without misleading the reader (for instance, omitting scales from graphs). All references to data sources should be included so that the decision-maker is fully aware of the origins of the data as well as its analysis.

CHAPTER 5

A case study of social services

5.1 Introduction □ 5.2 Background to social services □
5.3 Current organisation of Anyshire SSD □ 5.4 Defining the
problem □ 5.5 Summary

5.1 Introduction

The next two chapters are going to look in some detail at the approach
which the analyst might adopt to determine the information requirements of
an organisation. In order to emphasise the practical nature of such work we
are going to return to the case study introduced in Chapter 1 and concentrate on a single service area.

This chapter will provide the background to social services and a definition of the problem which existed in Anyshire Social Services Department. In
so doing it will provide the framework from which the analyst can build a
model to assist investigations into the information needs of an organisation.

Chapter 6 will extend the model and relate this to the information
analysis cycle developed in Chapter 3. Actual study findings will be examined and a proposal presented which could be used as a basis for future
information systems developments.

5.2 Background to social services

5.2.1 History

Social Service Departments (SSDs) were formed in 1971 as a result of the
enactment of the Local Authority Social Services Act 1970 which implemented most of the major proposals of the Seebohm Report (1968). Prior

to this, each main local authority (county boroughs and county councils) had a children's committee and children's department which were responsible for child case work; a mental health department dealing mainly with the provision of local authority services for the mentally disordered, usually as part of a large health department; and a welfare department dealing mainly with the elderly and handicapped. All these agencies were merged in the Seebohm re-organisation, and to their existing responsibilities were added some drawn from the health department, such as the provision of home help services and day care for children under five years of age.

The Seebohm Report had a bearing on the purposes as well as the functions of such departments:

'We recommend a new Local Authority department providing a community-based and family-oriented service, which will be available to all. The new department will reach far beyond the discovery and rescue of social casualties; it will enable the greatest possible number of individual to act reciprocally, giving and receiving services for the well-being of the whole community.'

This re-organisation was therefore a major upheaval in the provision of personal social services, and it was followed by a further disturbance when local government re-organisation took place in 1974, so that county councils and metropolitan district councils assumed responsibility for SSDs. The

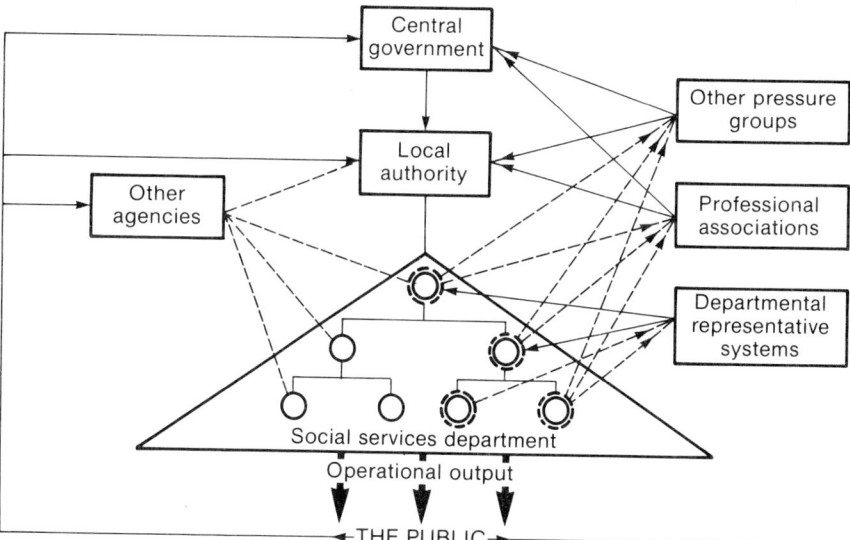

Figure 5.1 Overview of social services departments — a complex of interacting social systems

reduction of 173 authorities in England and Wales to 115 meant an increase in the size of SSDs, already large enough after Seebohm for most social workers' comfort, but other additions to SSD responsibilities were also made.

In general, however, these changes were viewed with approval by those involved. It was believed that greater power would derive in large measure from the concentration of responsibility in one place where the enormity of the problems to be faced could be more clearly seen, and from the greater professional authority social workers would derive from being independently responsible for a major government service with important duties.

The global structure which resulted is summarised in Figure 5.1. This, in fact, shows that no department within the system is a closed system in its own right. That is to say, they all interact with other departments and other environmental forces outside the SSD organisational structure. Consequently, various loops are built into the structure providing feedback from service receivers — the public and agencies — into the social service structure either directly or from a higher government level.

5.2.2 Structures

The organisation of the SSD itself will vary from one authority to another but an appreciation of the rule of social work suggests that there are certain organisational requirements which will have direct implications on structure. These are:

- Flexibility of structure
- Effective communiction and collaboration
- Good co-ordination, motivation and management in its widest sense

Certain structures may have paticular advantages in given situations but obviously these must be assessed within the terms of the communities they serve. What is likely is that no SSD operates in a simplistic mode; most combine a variety of structures using different role definitions within an apparently simple structure to create multiple lines of responsibility. A most noticeable trend has been the consistency of change — most SSDs appear to have a structure life of around 5–8 years — and while this obviously reflects the need to adapt to the changing environment and needs of social work, it may well inhibit the growth of formal planning and development of corporate and strategic policies.

Several writers have suggested structures along the lines of the 'individualistic' model discussed in Chapter 2 as the most suitable form for SSDs with the basic organisational element as the monitored and co-ordinated group. Attempts to achieve such fully fledged professional organisations, however, often fail due to the individual's misunderstandings of the information flows that are essential to the well-being of such an elite organisational form. This results in a sheer waste of talent, energy and enthusiasm which affects all facets of the SSD's operations. A large number of SSDs have moved towards a project-oriented model applying a matrix organisation as a co-ordination overlay on a basically hierarchical structure.

5.2.3 Functions

The general function of the SSD may be defined as 'the prevention or relief of social distress in individuals, families and communities in liaison with other statutory and voluntary agencies'. This can normally be split into a number of more specific functions as follows:

- Research and evaluation
- Strategic planning
- Operational work at the community level
- Operational work with individuals and families
  — basic social work
  — basic services
  — supplementary services
- Public relations
- Staffing and training
- Managerial and co-ordinative work
- Resourcing
- Finance
- Secretarial

5.3 Current organisation of Anyshire SSD

Anyshire SSD comprises four geographic divisions, each the responsibility of an assistant director.

The areas account for over half a million people, who naturally require a wide range of services to suit their needs. Most particularly, however, the areas themselves reflect different populations, such that within a division the needs may be varied. One division comprises Eastshire with a very large population of elderly (2 per cent above the national average), and Eastborough with a large ethnic influx and services developed for nineteen different ethnic groups.

The previous autonomy of the areas and their differing needs have also led to unique organisation structures within each area.

There is, therefore, no common reference framework of functional responsibilities across the divisions, or even within them. The area is largely rural, but with a large conurbation in Anytown itself (approximately one third of the county population) with the particular problems of any urban area.

The department employs around 2,800 staff of whom 42 can be classed as senior or middle managers. The total figure drops to around 460 when home-helps are excluded from the employee role. The management structure is shown on the organisation chart in Figure 5.2.

Each area has an area director and shares a divisional administrative officer. (The organisation for Southshire is shown in Figure 5.3.) Principal officers, however, reflect the particular divisional requirements, or in some cases may be based in one division although they perform their services for the whole county. Resources are historic, rather than reflective of area needs. Hence 75 per cent of residential and day care units for children are in Anytown, Eastborough and Eastshire having none. The headquarters and home of senior managers is situated in Anytown House, which also houses the Area 5 team. Central office support staff, who form a separate division, are also situated there. This particular group were subject to redundancies over the last three years with staff reduced from 52.5 to 29.5

			Paul Kemp Director		
			John Brown Deputy Director		
Asst. Director	Dave Marsh	Jane Cauldwell	Harry Mitchell	Peter Lawrence	Asst. Director
Division Policy	Westborough/ shire	Eastborough/ shire	Anytown	Southtown/shire	Central
Admin. Team: Peter Lawrence	DAO	DAO Area Director	DAO PO	DAO Area Director	Snr. Admin. Personnel
Children: Dave Marsh	DAO PRSW	AD PO	PRSW	PO PRSW AD	DO
Elderly: Jane Cauldwell	PO	DAO	AD PRSW	SSW PO	DO DO
Handicapped: Harry Mitchell	PO AD	PO	PRSW PO DAO		DO R&D

Key:
DAO = Divisional Administrative Officer
PO = Principal Officer
DO = Divisional Officer
AD = Area Director

PRSW = Principal Social Worker
SSW = Senior Social Worker
R&D = Research & Development

Figure 5.2 Anyshire SSD management structure

Administrative District Southshire

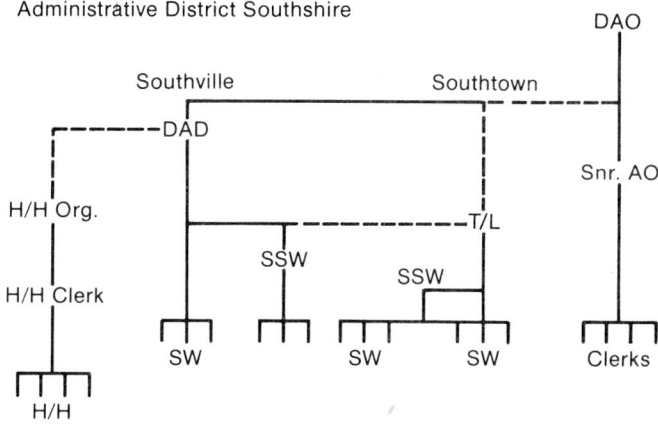

Key:

DAD = Deputy Area Directors

SSW = Senior Social Workers

T/L = A manager and supervisor of social work

SW = Social Worker grades 1, 2 and 3

H/H = Home help

Note: There have also recently been four new appointments of Senior Specialist Social Workers.

A further designation is Development Officers (DO), who represent the research grade and are all resident in headquarters.

Figure 5.3 Organisation chart for Southshire

and to a large extent their roles have changed as the impetus has moved from central administration towards divisional administration.

The matrix overlay on the divisional structure is the policy groupings. There are four policy groups PPDS — policy, planning, development and standards — with responsibilities for:

- Elderly
- Children
- Handicapped
- Administration

Policy groups meet at regular intervals and produce yearly reports delineating what has been achieved and what they should do next year. The current organisation, however, has existed for only two years and so many of the aims and objectives of the PPDS are only recently defined.

5.4 Defining the problem

As you will have perceived from the preceding section Anyshire SSD has undergone a complete re-organisation over the last few years, resulting in a rationalisation of services and structure.

The period of change has been accompanied by an almost complete change of senior management personnel and a fairly severe cut-back on central administrative support staff. Some computer-based information systems have been implemented during this time, but in a somewhat ad hoc manner both with respect to policy group and divisional involvement. There is currently no obvious strategy for future developments.

These changes have occurred at a time when severe constraints are being imposed on local government and forcing all services to become accountable. This has highlighted the urgent need within the SSD for some form of meaningful budgetary control. To some extent therefore the major emphasis over the last 18 months has been:

● The survival of change
● Establishing service priorities and policy objectives
● Establishing a pattern of delegation and responsibility
● Developing some form of budgetary control

This has resulted in a perceived need for information on which the new senior management team may base decisions as to the future development of the services. Dissatisfaction with the 'information' currently provided and considerable scepticism as to the viability of producing meaningful information has delayed any real systems development.

What exactly does 'information' relate to in the context of this problem? The answer to this question would normally be derived as part of the analyst's study but in order to allow the reader to understand the process described in Chapter 6 more clearly we need to define a basic system model at this stage. First, let us examine the problem in greater detail.

Prospective clients for social services will be introduced to an area office either of their own accord, through referral by another agency such as hospitals, police, school, etc., or by a second party contact — friend, relation, neighbour. The client may or may not need the help of social services, but in those cases where further action is to be taken the client becomes a 'referral'. The referred case will then be considered against the services which can be provided such as home help, residential care, day care, grants and a social service worker allocated to the case as appropriate. The basic data in the system will therefore concern the referral and information will be derived from records maintained on referred clients. At a basic level these will relate to geographic area, client category and service offered over certain time periods. Such statistics are already required to be maintained

Table 5.1 Example of monthly return

Number of clients registered blind and partially
sighted at end of year

Area	Blind	Partially sighted
Anytown	381	145
Westborough	43	39
Westshire	134	38
Eastshire	136	83
Eastborough	121	68
Southshire	111	52
Southtown	95	57
Totals:	1,021	482

by the Department of Health and Social Security and returns are made weekly and monthly. Typical examples are shown in Tables 5.1 and 5.2.

In any organisation information is used to improve organisational performance related to the quality of the service and the costs. In Anyshire the measurement of quality can only be related to movements and trends within the system and this can then be tied up to the costs involved. Both factors would be assessed in the context of the divisions and policy groupings within Anyshire but also comparatively with other SSDs across the country.

The examples given highlight the lack of value in available statistics and we should now be able to develop some ideas concerning the meaning of information in the context of this problem. We, then, need to relate this to a model of the system which can identify the information flow in the system. This will require the analyst to explore the full dimensions of the system in the terms expressed in Table 5.3.

Initially a very simple model can be developed. Figure 5.4 represents the global need to which the system responds with the client posing the problem and social services providing the solution — or at least attempting to!

This model obviously requires further development if it is to be of much use to the information analyst, and several models can be developed emphasising different features of the system. Figure 5.5 shows the processes which take place in the system by the person or people who perform them, whereas Figure 5.6 emphasises what is done.

Whilst both of these may form part of the model development, Figure 5.6 is infinitely more durable than Figure 5.5 since personnel and structures may change far more often than the processes to be performed. A model of the activities, therefore, can be linked to a model of the data which is stored (Figure 5.7) and these two together can form the basis for a logical model of the system that is a model which will describe the required behaviour of a system.

Table 5.2 Example of weekly return
Anyshire County Council — Social Services — Children in care statistics
General support section — Numbers of children in care for Anytown

	Male								Female								Grand total
	Age groups								Age groups								
Responsibility:	0–4	5–7	8–10	11–12	13–15	16–17	17+	Total	0–4	5–7	8–10	11–12	13–15	16–17	17+	Total	
Lodgings resid. employment	0	0	0	0	0	2	7	9	0	0	0	0	0	1	4	5	14
O & A centres	0	0	0	0	1	6	0	7	0	0	0	0	2	3	0	5	12
CHE's	0	0	0	1	5	8	3	17	0	0	0	0	0	3	0	3	20
A CC resid. accommodation	0	1	3	4	10	9	3	30	0	0	1	1	6	12	4	24	54
Voluntary homes/hostels	0	3	4	3	2	3	1	16	0	0	0	1	2	4	0	7	23
Boarding school	0	0	0	0	3	3	0	6	0	0	0	0	2	2	0	4	10
Homes/hostels for handicapped	0	0	1	0	0	0	0	1	0	0	0	0	1	2	1	4	5
At home	4	2	4	1	10	10	8	39	5	5	2	3	2	9	6	32	71
Penal estabs.	0	0	0	0	0	3	6	9	0	0	0	0	1	1	0	2	11
Foster home (Anyshire)	19	7	14	7	18	7	3	75	17	13	16	11	4	12	0	73	148
Foster home (elsewhere)	0	0	3	0	1	0	0	4	0	1	1	2	0	0	0	4	8
Other	1	0	1	0	1	0	2	5	0	1	0	0	0	0	1	2	7
Totals:	24	13	30	16	51	51	33	218	22	20	20	18	20	49	16	165	383

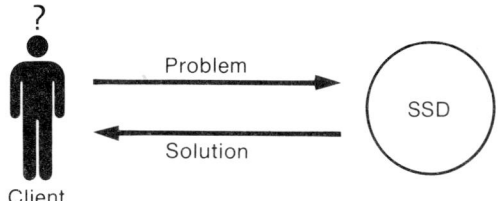

Figure 5.4 A simple model

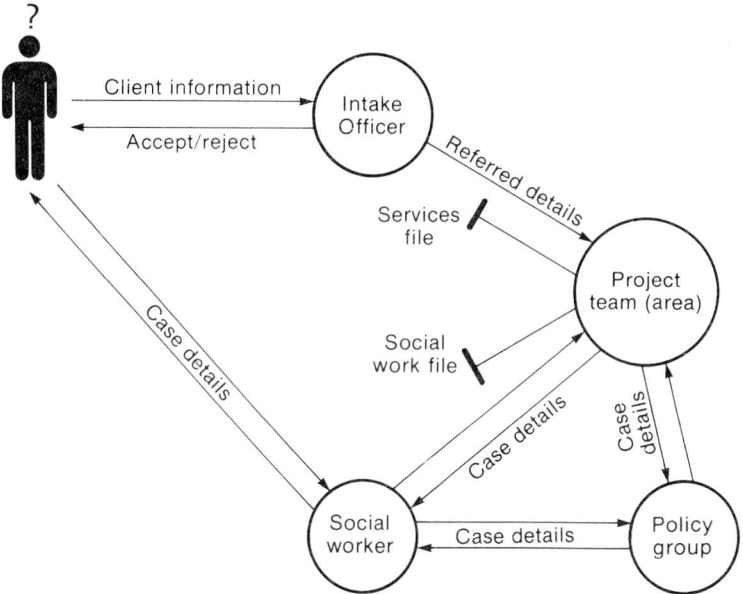

Figure 5.5 Model development 1 — activity flows by person

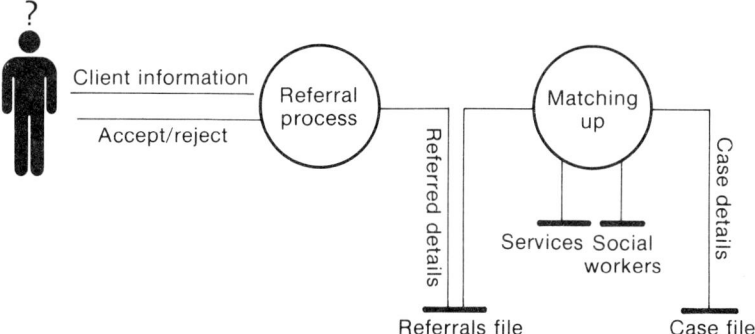

Figure 5.6 Model development 2 — process model

Table 5.3 Dimensions of a system

I. What the system is:	Needs to which the system responds: — names of responses — details of responses — names of people, departments, information systems which respond
II. How the system communicates:	Who from/to: — names of people, organisations, information systems, etc. What data and how: — names of data — details of data — media used
III. What data requirements exist:	Data stores: — names of data — details of data — media Data connections: — between responses and types of data — between various categories of data — between media, people, systems and data

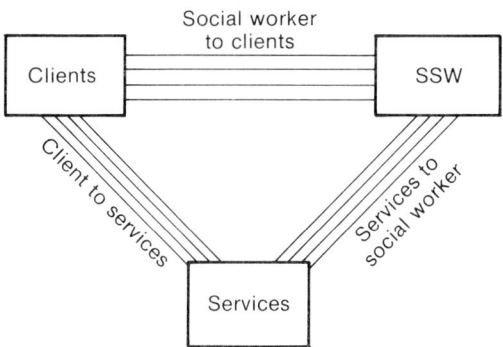

Figure 5.7 Data correction model

5.5 Summary

This chapter has introduced a problem within Anyshire Social Services perceived by senior management as: 'When you come to make a decision, on what information do you base it?' To some extent it has also provided a framework which allows the analyst to develop a clearer understanding of how to define a problem. This model would normally form part of the requirements analysis which we examine in Chapter 6.

At this stage, however, all we have developed to assist the reader is a model of the current system — this would not necessarily be the same as that required for an improved information system. The chapter which follows, therefore, will look in depth at the activities which the analyst would perform and show the impact on the analysis from the results of specific data collection exercises.

CHAPTER 6

A feasibility approach

6.1 Introduction

In Chapter 2 we developed a recommended approach to systems design which began with the diagnosis of needs and the setting of goals. This is essentially the job of the information analyst and is the subject of discussion for the rest of this chapter with particular reference to Anyshire Social Services Department. As part of this diagnosis the analyst will have to consider organisational factors, human requirements and appropriate technology, and as such will have to apply a variety of fact-finding techniques. These will have to be structured within a well-planned data gathering exercise and relate to the specific objectives of the study. This whole area of activity is often referred to as the requirements analysis stage of systems development and the output will be presented as a requirements analysis report, providing clear definitions of users' information needs and an outline strategy for meeting those requirements.

6.2 The scope of the study

The first step in any such study is to define the scope. The analyst and the user must agree as to the objectives which should be met and the boundaries which should be observed. This will include a statement of:

● Outline objectives
● Duration of study and deadlines
● Cost of study
● Approach and methods to be used within the study
● Required accessibility to personnel and resources

As an initial proposal for the study at Anyshire, outline documentation might be produced in the shape of a report as in Table 6.1. This implies a fairly formal and structured approach to the development of computer-based systems within the local authority as a whole since, in effect, this proposal would form an initial contract between the user, in this case Social Services, and the Computer Services. It can also act as a basis for direct costing of computer services personnel to be shared by all the users who benefit from their time. This can be very important when questions of accountability arise within the organisation or resource justification is required, but it may also act as a stimulus to user involvement. The stated commitment of time and personnel to the investigation, and hence the real or implied cost which will accrue generally, motivates the user department towards obtaining the maximum possible benefits from the exercise.

6.3 The study approach

The outline supplied in Report I identifies the particular method to be used as business systems planning or BSP. This is a formal systems planning approach which combines a top–down approach to the study of the organisation and motivation of personnel with a bottom–up approach to implementation of a developed system. It uses a framework based on three distinct but concurrent planning and control levels in the organisation (as identified in Chapter 2):

● Strategic planning
● Management control
● Operational control

and allows for the information system to address any one of these three levels as might be convenient.

The major concepts of BSP are as follows:

● An information system must support the goals and objectives of the business

Table 6.1 Anyshire SSD — Report I: Proposals for a study of management information requirements in Anyshire Social Services

---

1.0 Objectives
To provide:
— An evaluation of the effectiveness of current information systems
— An assessment of future information systems needs based on Anyshire SSD related impacts and priorities
— A defined logical approach to assist in solving senior management information control problems
— Outline proposals for systems to provide such detailed information

2.0 Boundaries
This study will be directed towards the needs of the senior management team but will inevitably take into account existing information systems throughout the organisation.

2.1 Time
The proposed study will occupy a period of three months from October—January and involve one analyst full-time or the equivalent thereof.

2.2 Access
It will be necessary to meet with the senior management team initially and establish the extent and purpose of the study. Thereafter it will require interviews with all senior managers, access to support staff and documentation and possible interaction with several other layers of responsibilities, in particular:
— central services support officers
— one or more social service area groups
— research and development officer
— divisional administration officers
The scope should be extended to provide a comparative study of at least one other SSD.

3.0 Action plan

3.1 Method
In order to impose some structure on the study it is proposed to follow a *Business Systems Planning* approach (BSP). This implies a top—down approach with a structured development cycle — outline details are provided for management as an appendix along with sample documents to be used as development aids.

3.2 Outline timetable
October—November
Initial meetings with senior management, background research and data collection, further meetings with senior management, primary model of needs defined.
November—December
— Interviews at support levels
— Intensive study of area groups
— Refinement of model

Table 6.1 (continued)

December–January
— Comparative study of another SSD
— Review of information systems at Anyshire
— Follow-up interviews with senior management
January
— Development of information system proposals
— Completion of requirements analysis report
— Presentation of report

4.0 Costs

- An information system strategy should address the needs of all levels of management within the business
- An information system should provide consistency of information throughout the organisation
- An information system should be able to live through organisational and management change
- The information system strategy should be implemented by subsystems within a total information architecture

The concepts applied to the study at Social Services preclude the possibility of the system being developed in isolation. Whilst the primary concern is obviously related to the information needs of senior management this must be extended to encompass the needs of all management levels and will require the analyst to identify consistent feedback and control information throughout the organisation.

Figure 6.1 provides a structural framework for this BSP approach and, as highlighted by the diagram, essential features are those of management commitment and user involvement. It is only in this way that the primary objective of BSP can be realised, that is to provide an information systems plan that supports the organisation's short- and long-term information needs and is integral with the overall objectives of the organisation. The approach therefore relies on detailed pre-planning and a controlled and well structured analysis cycle.

The major emphasis, however, is on data definition, that is the collection, organisation and analysis of data intrinsically related to the specific scope of the study within the organisation. The analyst must not only come to grips with the purpose, structure, functions and information flows of the organisation as identified in Chapter 2, but also select particular methods of data collection, as introduced in Chapter 3, appropriate to this environment.

As part of the study documentation several charts may be developed and will most certainly include models of the activities performed and the data

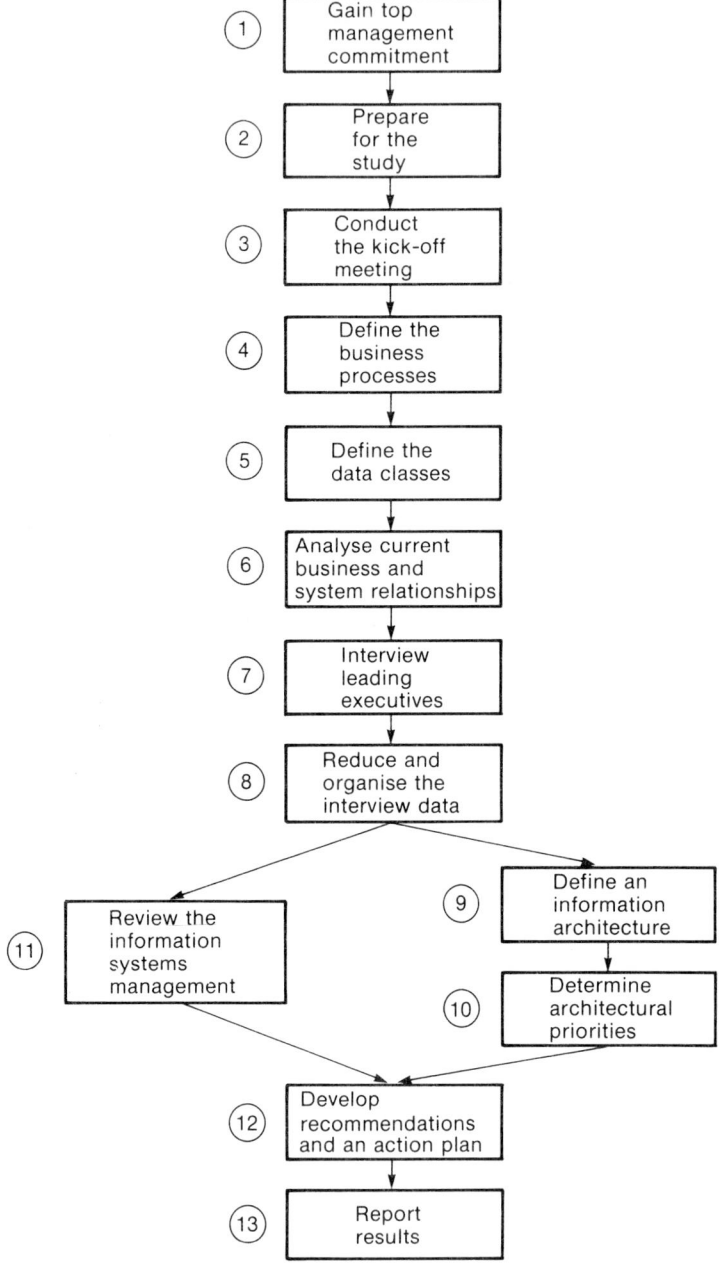

Figure 6.1 BSP framework

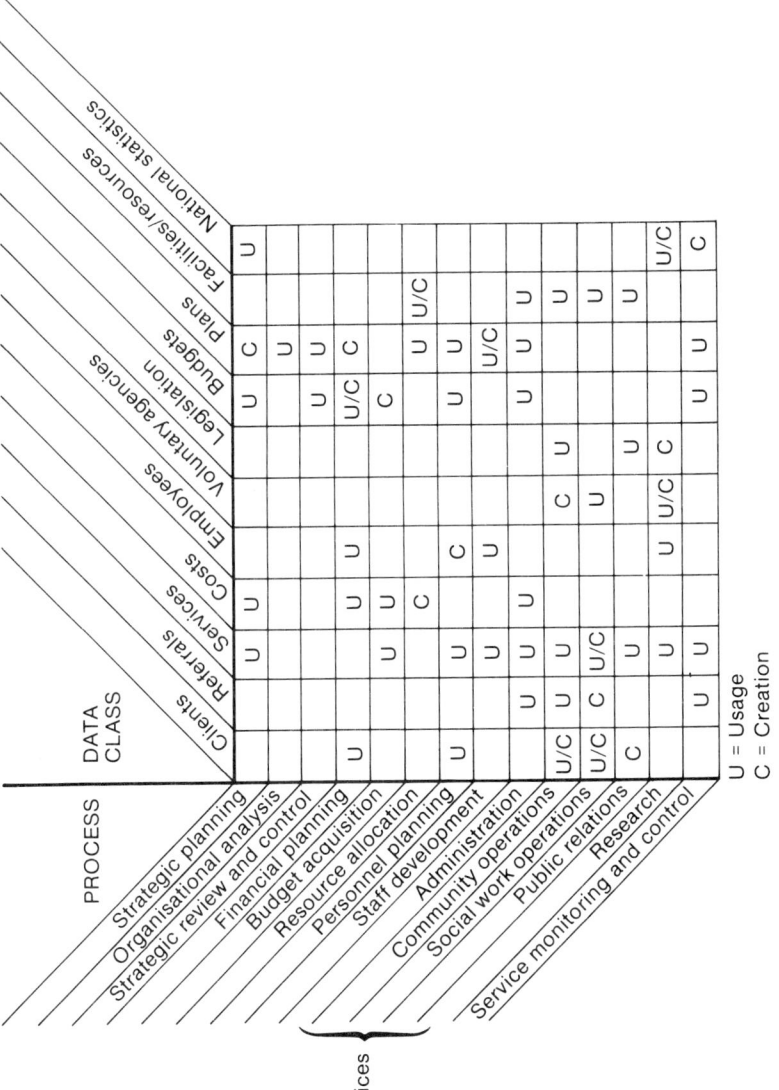

Figure 6.2 Data class by process showing data creation and usage: the processes are arranged in the life-cycle sequence of the key resource — SSD services

stored as introduced in the previous chapter. Several other aids, particularly
relevant to the BSP approach, can be developed including grid charts which
identify functional responsibilities, processes and data classes and their
relationships. A simple example of such a matrix showing data class by
process is provided in Figure 6.2. Such documents form part of the analyst's
work file but are only useful when used in combination with other information such as interview reports to provide a global overview of current
systems interactions

6.4 The detailed plan

Figure 6.1 identified thirteen possible stages in the study, two of which
precede the formal start date. The extent to which the analyst spends time
on these first two stages will relate to the way in which the study project was
initiated, but basically these relate to a definition of project scope agreed
by the project sponsors as outlined in section 6.2 of this chapter. This may
have involved the analyst in considerable prior research, most particularly
concerning the general organisation and the information systems.

This will form the background for the presentation of the study plan at
the first meeting with the senior executives and the analyst will be assisted
in this if a letter for the chief executive, in this case the SSD Director, has
acted as an introduction to the scope of the study and organisational
commitment.

The major activity in the study will probably revolve around Stage 4 of
the BSP framework (see Figure 6.1), and Figure 6.3 identifies three main
sources for the identification of processes:

- Planning and control
- Services
- Supporting resources

The planning and control processes effectively act as a secondary check
as all the processes relate directly to either services or resources and as such
are not stand-alone processes with their own life-cycle. It is possible,
however, to develop a life-cycle to both the services and resources process
as follows:

(1) Requirements planning — services and resources
(2) Acquisition — development of services and resources and referral of
    clients
(3) Operational maintenance — maintenance of services, control of
    resources and monitoring of clients
(4) Termination — end of services, use of resources, and of clients

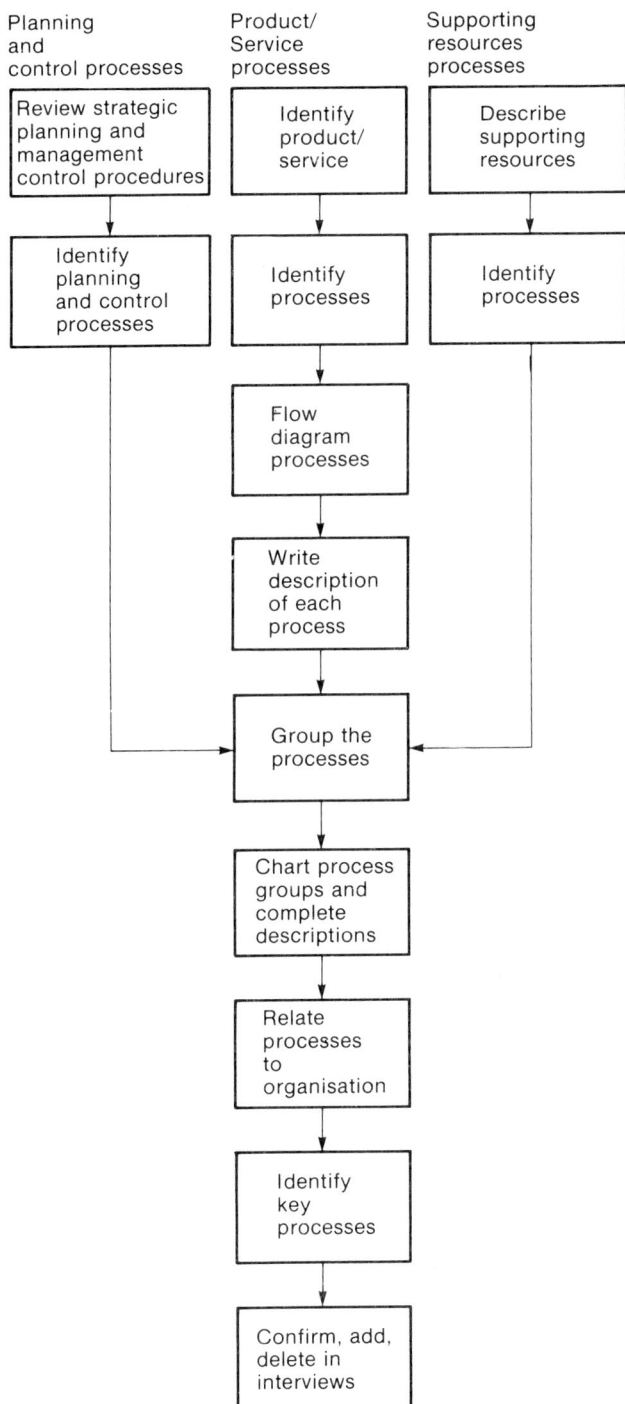

Figure 6.3 Definition of processes

It is at this stage that models of processes and flow of information such as that produced in Figure 5.6 are developed and prove particularly useful as discussion diagrams with the system users in order to further analyse and consolidate process relationships.

Once the processes are agreed upon and described they can be related to the organisational structure to help the analyst identify any additional personnel to be interviewed and to clarify further understanding of the organisational processes. In the case of Anyshire this will involve divorcing the structure from the processes so that processes such as provision of services, which will already have been identified in three out of the four policy groups, are shown only once but related in a matrix diagram as in Figure 6.4 to the actual organisation within the SSD.

The organisation/process matrix is one of several which can be developed as part of the BSP approach. Other forms of representation, however, may be more appropriate depending on the standards to be used throughout the study. A particularly useful function of any grid such as this is to identify the major recipients of information from the major decision-makers.

As we discussed at the end of Chapter 5 the next logical move is to identify the data required by each process. Within the BSP approach this will require the analyst to define data created and/or used by each process. The term data is used in this specific case to encompass information flows since at this stage we cannot *define* the information requirements, merely identify

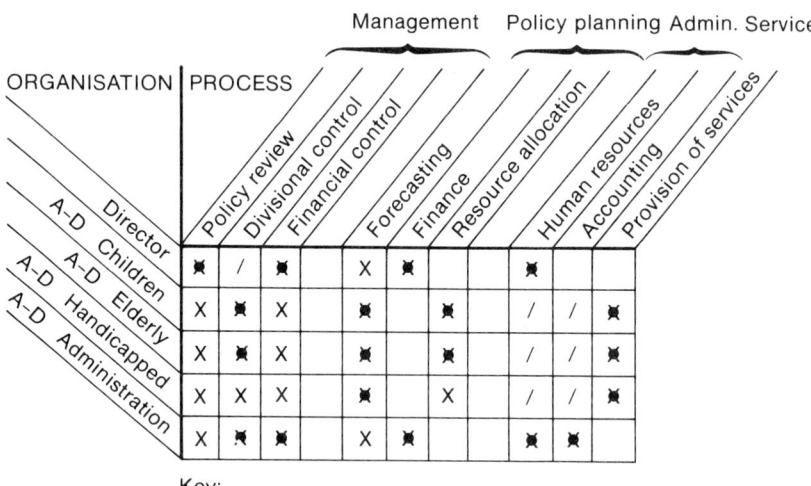

Figure 6.4   Organisation/process matrix

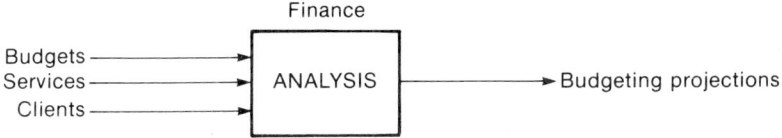

Figure 6.5 Input–process–output diagram

the flows. An example of the type of input–process–output diagrams to be developed is shown in Figure 6.5.

As each diagram relating to each process is developed it can be transcribed onto a data class by a process grid like that seen in Figure 6.2. This really forms the analysis of the current business environment and the analyst would then proceed to exercise the support currently provided within the organisation from information systems and the usage of current data. Effectively this review involves very similar processes as those already described, but against each process will be mapped the current systems and against each system the utilisation of data will be shown. In the case of Anyshire a number of systems have been partly implemented:

FAMIS —   the financial part of client costing
COLIS —   general purpose storage and retrieval system used for client register
CHILD —   a child-care tailor-made system to provide returns for DHSS and the children policy group
CLIENT —   a full client register and operational maintenance system developed by one divisional area — Southtown

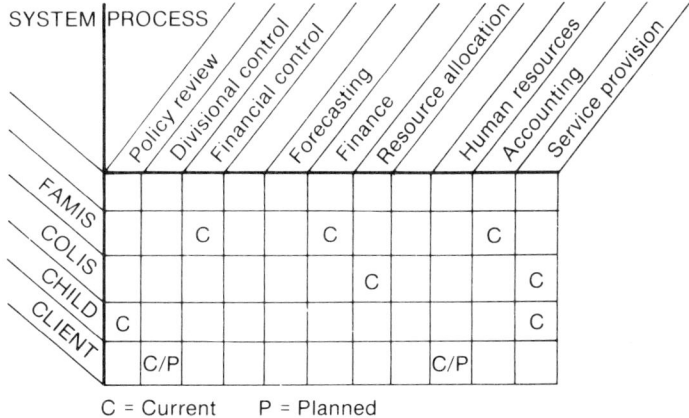

C = Current   P = Planned

Figure 6.6 Systems/processes matrix

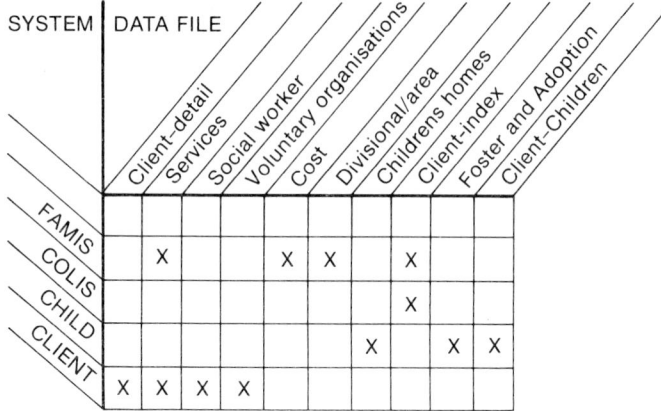

Figure 6.7 System/data matrix

Figure 6.6 shows the relationship of these systems to the processes defined at senior management level. Figure 6.7 shows a sample system/data file matrix which serves particularly to illustrate how much data is shared by various systems. This, in turn, helps point out the need for a database approach to provide consistency of data. The addition of planned systems such as a management information system would show a need for ever more sharing and consolidation of data files.

6.5 Data analysis

Interviews are the primary source of information for determining the business problem and management's need for support in solving their problems and supporting new opportunities. The interviews are not directed towards collecting data, but more specifically aim:

- To validate the data gathered, analysed and documented in the diagrams and grid charts
- To determine the information needed by individual executives as well as their problems and priorities
- To gain executive commitment and involvement
- To determine management values and quantify benefits to be derived by modifying or adding applications

The tasks that have to be accomplished in order to conduct the interviews are:

- Confirm the list of interviewees (this may have been added to during the study to date)

- Review the interview schedule to be certain it is practical and confirm it with the interviewees
- Review the questions that apply to all interviewees and develop individualised questions as appropriate
- Review the role of the interviewer(s) for each interview and the characteristics of individual interviewees
- Conduct the interview
- Prepare a summary of each interview to be approved by the interviewee

In order to direct the questions to specific issues the interviewer should have reviewed:

- Background of the interviewee
- Responsibilities of the interviewee
- Process in which the interviewee is involved
- Current information system support, if any

The interviewer should also have taken into account any specific questions to ask the interviewee based on prior interviews.

Within Anyshire interviews will be scheduled with the members of the senior management team. There will be a need, however, to collect information from other sources and this will include further interviews with:

Central administration
Divisional administration offices
Divisional members selected from one area (in this case Southtown where an information system is in the process of implementation)
Research and development officer

Interviews are extremely time-consuming and not always the best way to elicit information from a distributed base, so two further techniques will be employed:

- On-site observation and recording
- Questionnaire and document collection

The sites selected for detailed observation will be central administration where, in fact, the analyst will secure a base as the workroom for the BSP study. This means that charts can be displayed and commented on for accuracy by the operational staff. It also helps the analyst to gain acceptance as a member (albeit itinerant) of the user groups. A further site base will be maintained within a divisional area, in this case Southtown, and at least one week full-time will be spent on the observation.

In the particular situation at Anyshire with seven disparate areas it is important to include reference to all of their managerial styles and to gather information concerning their particular administrative systems. Simple questionnaires will be developed and issued to the divisional administration offices accompanied by requests for current data collection and processing forms. This will be reinforced by follow-up interviews with these officers as a group. Finally, all area directors will be circulated with a brief statement of the study scope and objectives and comments invited as to the intent and indications of further willingness to contribute to the study in greater detail.

Since Anyshire is in fact one of 39 such organisations in a non-competitive sphere, this particular study would be enlarged to evaluate systems within other comparable SSDs and include at least one in-depth study of an SSD with a more advanced information system.

As stated in Chapter 3, in any organisation there is an enormous amount of data available in primary and secondary form. The risk in information

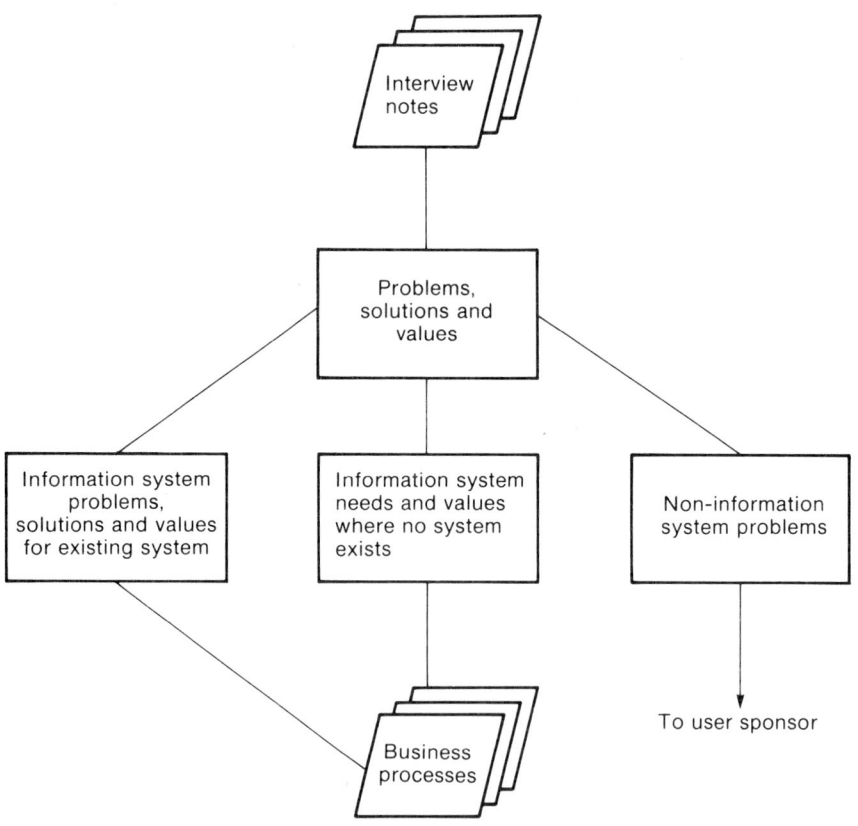

Figure 6.8 Interview structure

analysis is that the emphasis will be centred on the collection of this data rather than the analysis. The reduction and use of data obtained in the BSP exercise is therefore extremely important, and Figure 6.8 presents a structured procedure to organise interview data to provide a useful format for later use in determining the outline information architecture and priorities.

Basically this implies a review of all the 'perceived' problems and an objective assessment of cause and effect. The 'value' of a solution can then be quantified in terms such as 'improve client services', 'reduce costs'. Data can then be classified as to whether it is in the category of information systems solutions or outside, and finally related to the particular processes where it will have an impact both by creation and use.

6.6 Data management

The activities so far described provide the basis for developing an understanding of the processes within the organisation and the data required to support them. The next logical step is obviously to determine how to manage this data such that information systems can be developed as vehicles to insert data into and extract data from databases and formulate useful management information to support the organisational processes.

Figure 6.9 presents the global systems architecture diagram, but in order to identify the specific information systems and subsystems to be developed a detailed information architecture diagram must be produced outlining for each systems area:

- The data created, controlled and used
- The relationship of system to data
- Systems that support a given process

This will take into account the data requirements of later subsystems at the time of developing earlier subsystems in order to maximise storing of data.

Within the BSP approach a highly formalised method has evolved to develop the architecture through several iterations of a process/data class matrix (see Figure 6.2). But whilst this can prove an excellent aid it does

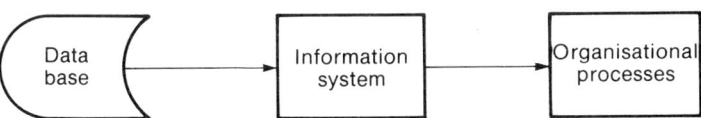

Figure 6.9 Global systems architecture diagram

nevertheless rely finally on the judgement of the analyst involved when it comes to a determination of the grouping of processes and data into major systems areas.

An alternative method is to use the grids as checklists and go directly to the development of an information flow diagram which represents the new logical model of the system. Both methods should result in the same outline of information architecture which will act as an excellent foundation for the determination of database requirements and an analysis of effective system processing modes. These two areas are somewhat outside the scope of this text but a review of the steps in the development of information architecture should show the reader where obvious links are formed.

From Figure 6.2 all the data classes along the horizontal axis should be placed in the order of creation by the processes. In other words, strategic planning creates plans and so plans will become the first data class. Figure 6.10 shows the resulting grid with all the 'creates' grouped diagonally from the matrix origin to the opposite corner. At this stage the object is now to group the processes and data into major systems areas which have respon-

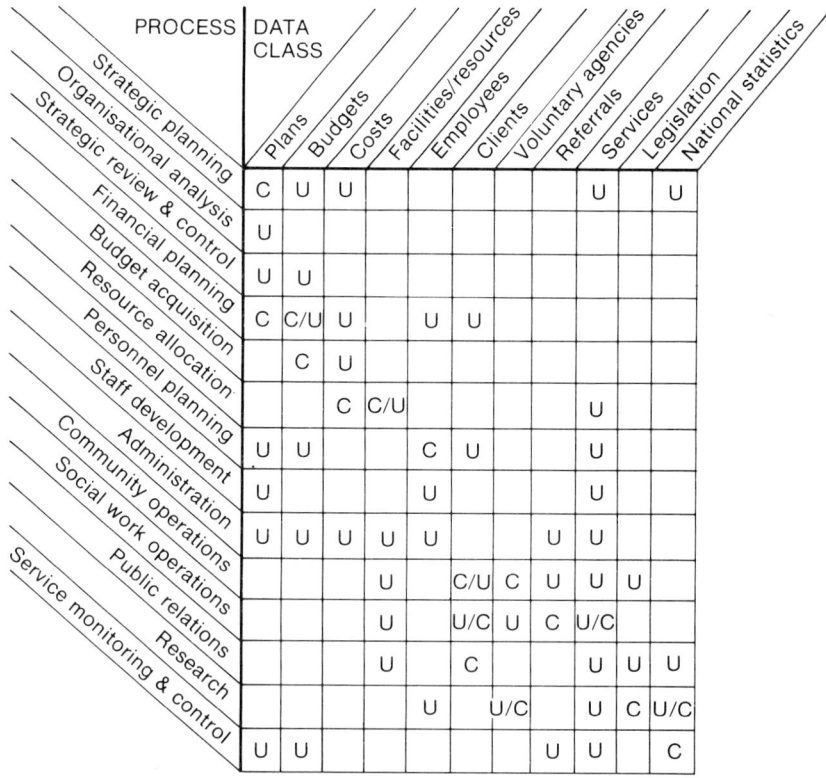

PROCESS \ DATA CLASS	Plans	Budgets	Costs	Facilities/resources	Employees	Clients	Voluntary agencies	Referrals	Services	Legislation	National statistics
Strategic planning	C	U	U						U		U
Organisational analysis	U										
Strategic review & control	U	U									
Financial planning	C	C/U	U		U	U					
Budget acquisition			C	U							
Resource allocation				C	C/U				U		
Personnel planning	U	U			C	U			U		
Staff development	U				U				U		
Administration	U	U	U	U	U			U	U		
Community operations					U	C/U	C	U	U	U	
Social work operations					U	U/C	U	C	U/C		
Public relations					U	C			U	U	U
Research					U	U/C			U	C	U/C
Service monitoring & control	U	U						U	U		C

Figure 6.10   Revised process/data class matrix

sibilities for creating and maintaining specific related classes of data. This can be accomplished by looking at the data created by processes and grouping these together in related boxes as shown in Figure 6.11. Where data usage falls outside the main boxes these should be examined and the flow identified from the process which creates the data to the process which requires it. Here a flow would come from system 4 — the service subsystem — into the strategic planning system 1, the resource allocation system 2, the personnel system 3, and the research system 5.

What we have arrived at, therefore, is a basic systems architecture which could now be divided into subsystems, all information flows could be identified between subsystems and priorities could be assigned to the system development schedules. A different way of approaching the same problem would have been to develop data flow diagrams for the logical model of the system as the information on processes and data classes was collected producing a global outline as shown in Figure 6.12. The basic architecture we should see is the same but the approach is more one of step-by-step development of the system from the major activating information flow, that

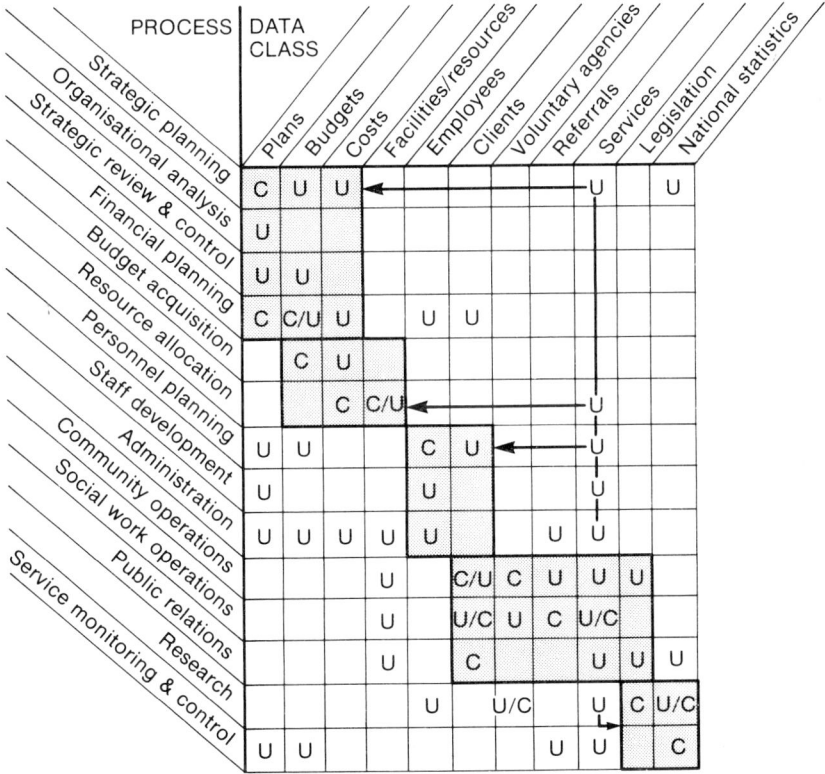

Figure 6.11 Process/data class matrix — final version

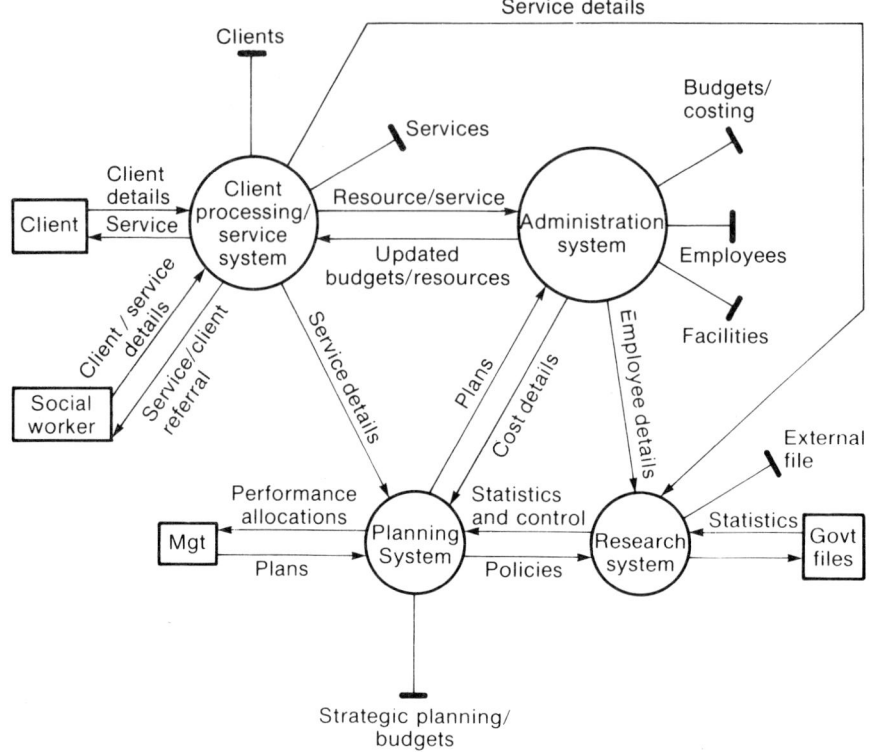

Figure 6.12 Global data flow diagram

is client request/or service rather than the top—down approach which was used in the BSP life-cycle approach. Hence the development of this flow diagram would begin with the impact of a service request from a client which would be matched against services available and if accepted would produce outputs as follows:

● Details to the social worker of client and service
● Details to administration of resources required
● Details to management for control and maintaining of commitment to client
● Details to research for statistical analysis and national returns.

In order to produce and maintain these flows of information this one process would require access to permanent files containing details of clients; the referral progress, that is case history; service provisions. Subsequent development of the flow diagram would take each output information flow in turn and examine the required processing within the organisation to develop an effective model of the system.

6.7 Outline strategies

Before looking at a possible solution we should clearly identify reasons which justify the implementation of a computer-based system in this case.

6.7.1 Data

There is a high volume of data to be maintained and, furthermore, to be cross-related in a variety of ways within the existing system. The data is distributed but required both locally and centrally causing duplication problems.

6.7.2 Information

Different and often discrete levels of information are required within the SSD but can all be provided for from the same base data. Reports are required at different time periods. Correlation between data sets is required to produce meaningful information for senior management.

6.7.3 Processing manually

The processing to produce the information from this data would require a large number of clerical staff with a variety of skilled techniques in information analysis. It represents a very large volume of often duplicated paperwork and imposes a standard clerical system throughout the organisation. It will require controlled data collection and information distribution procedures.

6.7.4 Processing by computer

In this particular situation a prime reason for this choice is the availability of computer resources from the local authority centralised services. Nevertheless, the justification for a computer-based system can be considered purely on:

- The ease of data collection from distributed sources
- Lack of skilled clerical staff
- Need for local on-line query facilities
- Need for centralised co-ordination of data
- Elimination of extra paperwork for professional social workers
- Provision of timely, up-to-date, relevant information to all levels of staff
- Speed of processing for large volumes of data

Carol Pattison, our information analyst, is therefore going to approach the design of a solution with some idea of the preferred implementation strategy. In this case, a distribution system with some local processing allowing down-loading from and up-loading to a centralised database would be the ideal. It is within this global context that she would propose the outline system architecture, although this design — while favouring the implementation we have just described — can still be assessed independent of the physical requirements.

6.8 The proposed systems architecture

When this project was commissioned by Social Services the problem was stated very simply: 'When you come to make a decision, on what information do you base it?'

Our information analyst, Carol Pattison, has obviously had to enlarge the problem definition and place this in the context of the overall objectives of social services in Anyshire. Preliminary discussions with the directorate identified the major group objectives as:

(1) The development of a much more integrated Social Service with the emphasis on co-ordination of resources and activities.
(2) The identification of ways in which better use could be made of resources both to identify the quality of service for outside bodies and to evaluate future resource needs.
(3) The provision of some form of cost centre management with regular monitoring reports.

These objectives really relate to the particular management information system required by senior managers but must be related to the definition of the organisation and its 'mission' statement. This was defined by Paul Kent, the Director, as follows:

'Our aim is to build on the strengths of the individual to enable him or her to lead a more independent life using the resources of the community, the family, and the skills and resources within this department, often together with those of other organisations, both statutory and voluntary.'

The basic building block of the system, therefore, must be formed around the life-cycle of the client within the social service system. Such information which is produced must match the organisation with reference to structure and services. Given the established pattern of delegation and responsibility within Anyshire SSD the service unit will form the crucial unit of analysis with several units forming a system within the division.

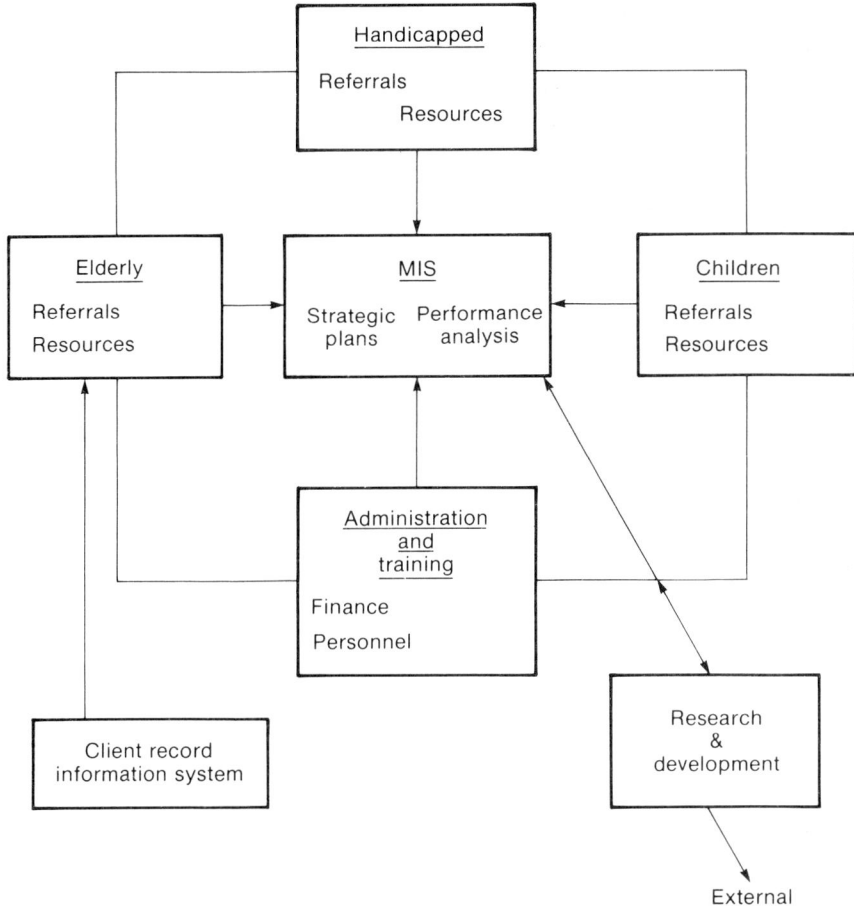

Figure 6.13 Proposed information architecture for Anyshire SSD

Using the techniques discussed previously a basic systems architecture, therefore, can be developed as shown in Figure 6.13. This shows the building block system as a client information system (CIS) which, in turn, feeds into the service unit systems — elderly, handicapped and children PPDS. All of these interface with the administration system but may also need to interface with each other since a client may not be exclusive to one service unit. These in turn will provide input to the management information system (MIS) used to develop strategic plans based on performance analysis and also input to the research and development subsystem.

This latter system is very much dependent on the quality of external information systems since it interfaces directly with national government sources, but given the state of national developments it will obviously not be a driving factor in the development of the other systems. All Carol will have to ensure is that interfaces exist which would allow for the full development of the R&D subsystem, when and if national developments make this a feasible and desirable proposition.

6.9 Defined information needs

The client information system forms the basis of the proposed management information system and needs to be examined within this context to identify the information flow requirements. Different information will be required at operational, tactical and strategic levels over different time periods, but broadly speaking will correspond to the outputs from the three layers of system identified:

- Client information system (CIS)
- Policy, planning and development group system (PPDS)
- Management information system (MIS)

Within each, however, the outputs will relate to the service and resource process life-cycle developed earlier in this chapter.

In order to provide for requirements planning, we must have information concerning services and resources, and to develop or acquire these we need details of client demand and usage. To operate efficiently we need regular monitoring of all three — clients, resources and services — and termination of any one will automatically affect the others.

6.9.1 Operational needs

The resource process life-cycle at this level basically revolves around the life of a client in the system and may be very short-term. It is also likely, however, to require urgent action rather than long-term decision-making and will relate initially to the level of seriousness of the client problem.

Table 6.2 At-risk register (AR)

Three digits are available to code up to three at-risk conditions. The options have been kept to a minimum so as to avoid unnecessary sophistication. The likely number of names on the register will allow easy perusal of the whole list if necessary.

C   Child at risk
H   Hypothermia risk
U   At risk if public utilities are disrupted
E   Vulnerable in emergencies/disasters
W   Wanted or missing person

Note: Where only one or two conditions exist, the vacant digit(s) will be left blank.

Table 6.3 Priority categories (PP)

This constitutes two digits. It is included to accommodate the department's established policy on the subject

A	Situations which are resulting in serious damage which will continue unless the department takes action.
B	Situations which it is highly probable will develop into category A unless the department takes action.
C1, C2, & C3	Situations in which individuals or groups are likely to deteriorate to the extent of falling into categories A and B unless the department intervenes,

And it is predictable that action that the department is actually able to take will change the situation with one of the following results:

● C1 improvement will occur, or
● C2 Deterioration will be avoided, or
● C3 Deterioration will be significantly slowed down.

D1 & D2	Situations in which:
	D1 Even though deterioration may be likely it is doubtful whether action by the department could significantly affect the situation; *or*
	D2 Individuals or groups that might benefit from action by the department but are unlikely to deteriorate significantly if the department does not act.

Table 6.4 Logical record description

Field	Name	Description
1.	Location — code	Area code
2.	Name of client	
3.	Address and telephone number	Own home, foster home, special home
4.	Date of birth	
5.	Sex	
6.	Date of entering the system	
7.	Name of senior officer	
8.	Name of worker	
9.	Review date	
10.	Client classification	
11.	Problem on referral	
12.	Resources requested/implied	
13.	Action taken on referral	
14.	Referral source	From other classification tables
15.	At risk register	
16.	Priority situation	
17.	Closure code/date	
18.	Other information	

Most newspaper readers are aware of the difficulties encountered within social services in properly identifying cases in need of urgent action, and hence to provide an effective level of operational maintenance this must form part of the information flow. Tables 6.2 and 6.3 define priority categories in accordance with current policy within Anyshire SSD and provide a coding structure which can be incorporated into data input to this system. These classifications have obviously to be linked to other items of data such as details on client, social workers and services, problems and actions to produce activating or monitoring reports, and a number of such classification tables would therefore be developed. Table 6.4 provides an example of the logical record requirements based on these. You will note that there is no reason why the physical system should preclude local areas from maintaining further information as appropriate to their needs.

While the client information system is basically designed to satisfy operational needs, it nevertheless provides information at area and divisional level for tactical and strategic planning concerning the allocation of local resources and their future acquisition. Such information will concern the workload of social workers and case officers, demand for local resources, and effectiveness of service provided.

6.9.2 Tactical/planning needs

At the PPDS system level the resource process life-cycle relates to the yearly budget allocations and hence concerns planning for specific service requirements based on a pattern of previous demand and any known activators for change such as government legislation; acquiring budget allocations and developing such resources to meet the service requirements on a priority basis; and monitoring the use of these and evaluating the effectiveness of the service on closure. The information output for the client information system will, therefore, be integrated with details of services and resources and matched against costs.

At this level the recipients of information will be both battling for a share of scarce resources out of the overall SSD allocations and besieged by areas and divisions for increases to their local share. It is therefore imperative that they should have a means of comparing the use of resources against the resource demand for that particular category of service over the whole SSD.

Again this system is not solely concerned with one level of management information. Operational information such as the level of residency in child-care hostels, etc., will be required in order to allocate this type of resource fairly across the county. For strategic planning an analysis of shifts in demand over five-year periods would prove useful with major trends highlighted for particular consideration.

6.10 Strategic planning and control

The management information system is the central axis of this hierarchically distributed system and so will require operational monitoring of both levels of subsystem in order to produce a performance analysis. Basically, all of the sub-groups are competing within the SSD for the resources to be allocated by senior management and as such the allocation will be governed by:

(1) evidence of demand for that service/resource; and
(2) analysis of the effectiveness of usage by that sub-group.

In other words, if Southtown request more resources for counselling because of increased demand this would then be compared to:

(1) The level of demand in the other areas — is it higher?
(2) The effectiveness of current counselling practices in Southtown — are clients recorded as satisfactory closures after a counselling referral?
(3) Are clients in counselling for an average time duration?

At a more strategic level, senior management have to forecast demand for the future and this may require a 20 or 30 year view if they are considering, say, investments in building residential accommodation for specific purposes. To provide effective information at this level considerable input will be required from external sources. Figure 6.14 shows the current split in

Note: Administration costs are subsumed within the service PPDS units.

Figure 6.14 Net expenditure on social services

available expenditure between the PPDS allocations, but this needs to be related to other information such as:

- Numbers of National Health Service patients entering and leaving Anyshire
- Anyshire projected population figures

in order to project estimates for the next five years allocated. At the same time, this has to be related to competing resources within the local authority itself as the scenario in Chapter 1 clearly identified.

6.11 Systems development

In the preceding section the analyst has explored the dimensions of the system. The considerations are as follows:

- What the system is
- How the system communicates
- What data requirements exist

This leads to a model resembling that in Figure 6.15, from which it is clear that a much more detailed interpretation of needs exists at the bottom level of implementation than at the top. The reader will recall that the BSP approach advocated in this text suggests top–down design but bottom–up implementation, which implies that we will build systems within the global strategic needs. At the same time, however, we will, in fact, be clarifying the specific user needs as we progress through each level of the system.

Modern day approaches to systems development often use a prototyping approach which in many ways reflects this style. A basic model is developed and then refined through several interactions with the user until an acceptable systems model is produced. Within the context of this whole MIS system, therefore, the CIS system will not be developed by itself but within the character of the total systems architecture. In other words it must support the organisation's processes and must:

(1) fit properly into and interface with the other (future) systems of the overall architecture, and
(2) provide for proper implementation of the appropriate database(s).

In this way refinement of the first system models will more clearly identify the specifications for other systems.

Systems development is a complex process. It requires technical expertise, effective communications and skilful handling of conflicting objectives of

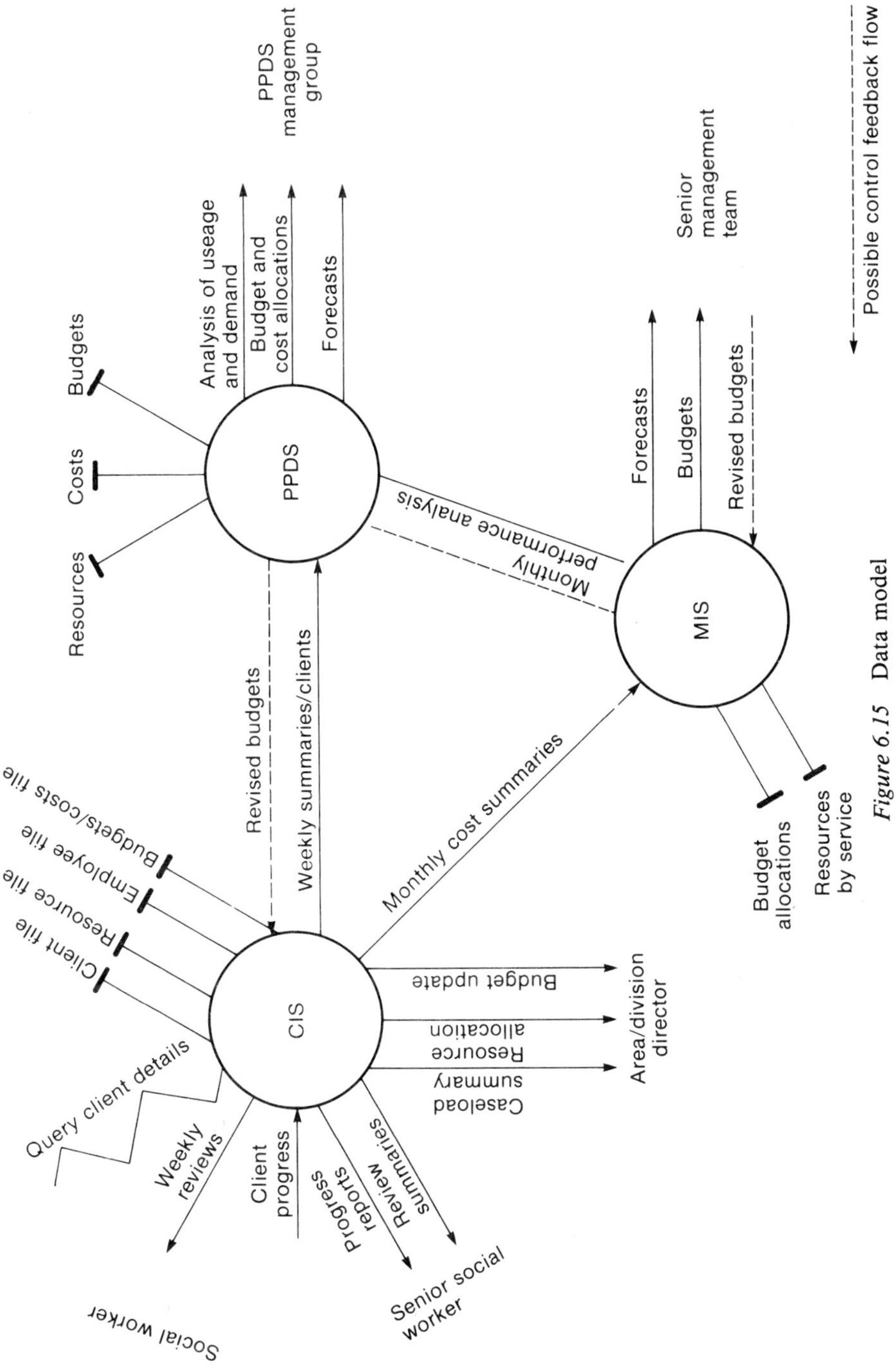

Figure 6.15 Data model

users, management and data processing. Underlying this, however, the system is only as good as the information which it produces and hence a thorough analysis of information needs cannot be over-emphasised as a prerequisite to the development stage.

6.12 Summary

This chapter has provided the basis for a solution to the information system needs at Anyshire SSD. It has not specifically identified the content and format of output reports as this is an exercise suitable for the reader to practise the concepts so far outlined. The reader is therefore asked to complete the relevant selected exercises which are to be found in the Appendix to this text.

CHAPTER 7

Introduction to accounting techniques

7.1 Introduction

It has already been stressed that to operate efficiently and effectively it is essential for an organisation to have a clear understanding, through all levels of management, of its objectives. Whatever the objectives, because there are generally financial aspects associated with any organisational activity, it is important for anyone concerned with information analysis to be aware of some accounting techniques.

The purpose of this chapter is to present a number of concepts, principles and conventions which are basic to all accounting processes. The intention is to give an insight into accounting procedures for those students who have little or no previous grounding in finance or accounting.

The financial section or department is often regarded as the hub of an organisation since everything seems to revolve around it. Its work and reporting procedures are central to the way in which an organisation is able to meet, or not meet, its objectives.

Decisions made by managers at all levels are incorporated into an organisation's master plan by way of the estimating and budgeting process. The management accountant and the finance department is at the centre of this planning which consolidates individual departmental budgets into the organisation's total budget for a financial year. Then, as the financial year unfolds, the various managers are periodically kept informed of actual costs etc. Any variations from the plan are monitored. This control and feedback gives managers up-to-date information concerning the operations under their responsibility, so ensuring that appropriate adjustments to plans can be made as necessary.

Even from what has been said above the obvious implication is that all managers need to have a grasp of accounting procedures in order not only to make effective use of the resources under their control but also to liaise from time to time with the central finance section of the organisation. In particular, the finances of Anyshire County Council, as a local authority, are closely controlled across the various departments. A stringent economy makes this necessary as does accountability to the ratepayer and voter. In much the same way an organisation in the private sector is accountable to its shareholders. So, regardless of the nature or type of organisation, for all managers who have a responsibility for the planning, development and control of resources there is a need for a good appreciation of standard accounting techniques.

The first two sections in the main body of the chapter cover the background of accounting and the general procedures observed by organisations. The two sections following then concentrate more on specific accounting techniques dealing with those matters which any business manager would require knowledge of when incorporating financial aspects into an information analysis requirement.

7.2 The accounting framework

The coverage of basic accounting techniques in this chapter is far from exhaustive for any student. The intention is to consider the modes of management accounting adopted by organisations with regard to the needs in this area of other management personnel who deal with the costs and figures relating to the activities and operations within their own departments.

In the light of this it would be useful, perhaps, at the outset to list some of those areas of accounting and finance outside the scope of this text. These are:

- Monetary policy
- The capital market
- Banking
- Insurance companies
- Pension funds
- Investment trusts
- The Stock Exchange
- Trade credit

In order that the stated intention can be fulfilled it is necessary first to discuss the accounting framework within which organisations operate.

Any accounting system maintains separate accounts to record all the financial details of the various operations of an organisation. In the context of Anyshire County Council separate accounts are maintained to record:

- Salaries and wages paid
- Income from rates
- Equipment bought by schools and colleges
- Grants to various bodies, e.g. voluntary organisations
- Borrowed and loan finance
- Income from car parks, leisure centres, etc.
- Purchase/sale of land and buildings

The list is not quite never-ending, but it seems it!

All these separate accounts are brought together to create the central system, forming a vast amount of accounting data useful to the organisation. The way in which data is useful to an organisation splits, by and large, into two categories: information for either external or internal purposes. Externally, accounting information is required by and/or has to be passed on to government departments, banks, the inland revenue, etc., as well as shareholders (in private sector companies) or the public at large (in local authorities and other public sector organisations). Internally, the provision of accounting information is vital to the on-going effectiveness of managers and the operations and resources for which they are responsible.

Broadly, these two categories form the difference between financial and management accounting. The financial accountant is concerned with global accounting principles and the preparation of the organisation's accounts. The basis of these accounts, usually produced yearly, are the 'balance sheet' and the 'profit and loss account'. They are statements of how an organisation *has* used the resources at its disposal. In essence they are concerned with historical financial data, forming a total picture of the financial affairs of an organisation.

Primarily, the management accountant's responsibility is the provision of management information which is of a financial nature. This specifically will vary according to the nature and workings of the organisation. Typically, however, it covers all the formal generation and preparation of the financial aspects of costing and forecasting data. The associated examination and interpretation of this data enables the management accountant to act very much as an information manager to the organisation so that management generally is in a position to make more effective decisions.

There will, of course, be interaction between the two aspects of accounting as they will both provide and use items stored on the same database.

7.3　Basic accounting

7.3.1　Debit and credit entries to accounts

Accounting practices have existed for and evolved over many centuries. They have developed from the simple systems devised by the early traders to the complex integrated systems of today. However, while practices are forever developing to meet the demands of the day, one of the basic principles of accounting has been with us since the fifteenth century. This is the principle of *double-entry* whereby every transaction has a two-fold outcome. Simply, for every debit there is a corresponding credit and vice-versa.

The reader does not need to master fully the many and varied ways in which entries to accounts are made. He or she should, however, acquire an understanding of the principles involved in order that the information analyst is in a position to interpret financial data extracted from an accounting system.

The standard rule of 'debit and credit' is that the account 'receiving value' is 'debited' and the account 'giving value' is 'credited'. Thus:

Increase in assets
Decrease in liabilities　　are all debit entries
Decrease in capital

Decrease in assets
Increase in liabilities　　are all credit entries
Increase in capital

As a simple example to illustrate the workings of debit and credit across various accounts, consider the following dated transactions made by Anyshire County Council's Social Services Department:

8.9.89　Purchased a microcomputer for £750 cash
8.9.89　Sold an old minibus for £500 cash
9.9.89　Purchased a new minibus for £8,500 on credit from Motorbus Co.
9.9.89　Paid wages of £50 cash

The entries to the various accounts would be as seen in Figure 7.1. Extended application of this principle ensures a systematic treatment of an organisation's transactions, whatever their type, into the appropriate account. When consolidated, the records in these accounts form a comprehensive accounting system showing the *performance* and *financial* position of the organisation.

ANYSHIRE COUNTY COUNCIL
SOCIAL SERVICES DEPARTMENT

Dr (Debit)	Cash Account		Cr (Credit)
	£		£
8.9.89	500	8.9.89 Microcomputer	750
		9.9.89 Wages	50

Dr	Purchases Account		Cr
	£		£
8.9.89 Cash	750		
9.9.89 Motorbus Co	8,500		

Dr	Sales Account		Cr
	£		£
		8.9.89 Cash	500

Dr	Motorbus Account		Cr
	£		£
		9.9.89 Purchases	8,500

Dr	Wages Account		Cr
	£		£
9.9.89 Cash	50		

Figure 7.1   Organisation of debit and credit entries

7.3.2 Summarising accounts

At the end of a trading period the transactions that have taken place during that period are summarised by way of:

(1) A profit and loss account
(2) A balance sheet

These two are often confused by non-accountants and thought to be the same. They are related but their purposes are different.

(1) Profit and loss account

This account summarises the transactions over a trading period in order to illustrate the *performance* of the organisation, that is how successful the organisation has been in making profits and/or using its resources. In addition it will indicate the factors that have influenced changes from the previous trading period. The trading period may be a month, a quarter, a half-year or a year.

Profit and Loss Account for the year ended........

Income	*Expenditure*
Sales, cash and credit	Purchases, cash and credit
Other income and cash	Services used and paid for
Cash inflows	Other expenses and cash outflows (including depreciation if charged)
Loss	*Profit*
Excess of expenditure over income	Excess of income over expenditure

Figure 7.2 Structure of a profit and loss account

The profit and loss account shows items of income and expenditure relating to that period only. The basic structure of the account is shown in Figure 7.2. Organisations often consider it appropriate, for comparison purposes, to show on the profit and loss account the figures from the previous trading period as well.

Fund Balance Sheet as at 31 March 19..

	£	£		£	£
Long-term liabilities			Fixed assets		
Loans fund			Capital outlay		
Stock			Other long-term outlay	___	
Bonds/mortgages			Current assets		
Superannuation fund loans			Work in progress		
Other internal loans	___		Stocks in hand		
Current liabilities			Investments		
Temporary borrowing			Debtors — deferred		
Creditors			— others	___	
Internal advances			Other balances		
Cash overdrawn	___		Deferred charges		
Provisions			Suspense accounts		
Renewal and repairs fund			(if any)		
Other (to be specified)	___		Revenue account		
Other balances			deficiency	___	___
Capital discharged				£	
Capital fund					
Capital receipts unapplied					
Suspense accounts (if any)					
Revenue account surplus					
Stock sinking funds	___	___			
		£			

Figure 7.3 Structure of a fund balance sheet

(2) The balance sheet

First of all, the balance sheet is a statement rather than an account. It is a statement of the organisation's financial position at a particular point in time, this being at the end of a trading cycle — usually the last day of that organisation's financial year. It records all the assets and liabilities in order to give a financial view of the organisation on the set date.

For Anyshire County Council, in common with all local authorities, profit and loss accounts and balance sheets are drawn up for each of the constituent departments. Each service department's balance sheet,

BIG BROTHER DEVELOPMENT PLC
Group Profit and Loss Account for the year to 31 December 1984

	£m	£m	£m	£m
			Year to 31 December 1983	
Turnover		292.9		277.7
Operating profit		27.1		25.0
Share of profits of associates		3.6		2.5
Profit before taxation, minority interests and extraordinary items		30.7		27.5
Taxation		(6.8)		(5.2)
		23.9		22.3
Minority interests		(0.8)		(1.7)
Profit before extraordinary items		23.1		20.6
Extraordinary items		3.9		1.0
Profit attributable to Big Brother Development PLC shareholders (of which £18.2m (£8.8m) is dealt with in the accounts of the company)		27.0		21.6
Appropriations Dividends Preference—£4,000 (£4,000) Ordinary				
Interim 1.00p (1.00p)	2.8		2.4	
Proposed final 2.35p (2.10p)	6.5	(9.3)	5.1	(7.5)
		17.7		14.1
Retained profit brought forward		99.4		85.3
Retained profit carried forward		117.1		99.4
Earnings per ordinary share		8.3p		8.0p

Figure 7.4 A large organisation's profit and loss account

BIG BROTHER DEVELOPMENT PLC
Group Balance Sheet at 31 December 1984

	£m	£m	31 December 1983 £m	£m
Assets employed				
Fixed assets		170.9		169.9
Associates		65.3		30.5
Investments		7.2		8.2
Goodwill		0.2		0.2
Net assets of the Little Brother Group		37.1		33.1
Current assets				
Stock and work in progress	110.3		75.3	
Debtors	62.2		57.7	
Short-term deposits	2.0		17.2	
Bank balances and cash	9.2		8.8	
	183.7		159.0	
Current liabilities				
Creditors	94.5		66.2	
Short-term loans and overdrafts	35.0		15.5	
Taxation	6.8		3.6	
Dividends	9.3		7.5	
	145.6		92.8	
Net current assets		38.1		66.2
		318.8		308.1
Financed by				
Share capital		69.6		69.6
Reserves		155.1		137.5
		224.7		207.1
Investment grants		2.4		2.0
Long-term liabilities		75.4		82.1
Minority interests in subsidiary companies		15.8		16.0
Deferred taxation		0.5		0.9
		318.8		308.1

J. Burn (signature) ⎫
                     ⎬ *Directors*
M. O'Neil (signature) ⎭

These accounts were approved by the board of directors on 15 May 1985

Figure 7.5   A large organisation's balance sheet

commonly called a fund balance sheet, can then be aggregated to form a consolidated balance sheet for the local authority. The basic structure of a fund balance sheet is shown in Figure 7.3.

In commercial accounting, individual company accounts and balance sheets can be consolidated in the same manner to give the picture for a group of companies. An example of this, for a large organisation, is shown in Figures 7.4 and 7.5 so that the reader can appraise their form and content.

At the other end of the scale, the profit and loss account and balance sheet for a small organisation, in this case a residential home run by Anyshire County Council, are shown in Figures 7.6 and 7.7. The reader should note here:

(1) the level of detail that can easily be recorded in the profit and loss account, and
(2) the lack of complexity in the balance sheet.

ANYTOWN HOUSE RESIDENTIAL HOME
Income and Expenditure Account for the year ended 31 March 1985

Income	£	Expenditure	£	Total £
Anyshire County Council	32,000.00	Employees		
Contributions from residents	31,851.25	Salaries	24,505.50	
Staff board and lodgings	490.80	Sleeping-in allowance	2,311.06	
Sick pay recovered	263.25	National Insurance	3,210.39	
		Superannuation	2,390.50	
		Wages	11,285.70	43,703.15
		Premises		
		Repairs & cleaning	62.20	
		Heat and light	4,361.24	
		Furniture & fittings	345.83	
		Water rates	306.48	
		Rent	3,120.00	
		Insurance	254.43	8,450.18
		Equipment & materials		
		Bedding, linen, etc.	186.63	
		Other equipment	175.34	
		Provisions	7,597.75	7,959.72
		General expenses		
		Adverts & telephone	536.90	
		Travel & subsistence	338.03	
		Miscellaneous	710.08	
		Bank charges	21.76	1,606.77
				61,719.82
		Excess of income over		
		expenditure		2,885.48
	64,605.30			64,605.30

Figure 7.6 A small organisation's profit and loss account

ANYTOWN HOUSE RESIDENTIAL HOME
Balance Sheet as at 31 March 1985

	£			£
Creditor (PAYE)	950.50	Cash floats		180.00
Trustees of S Ward	204.39	Bank		495.43
(resident)		Income & expenditure account		
		Balance 1.4.85	£3,364.94	
		Excess income over		
		expenditure for year	£2,885.48	479.46
	1,154.89			1,154.89

Figure 7.7   A small organisation's balance sheet

Anyshire County Council, as are all local authorities, are publicly accountable so they must comply with the legal requirements in force and produce their accounts according to recognised accountancy principles. They must be drawn up on 31 March each year and be independently audited.

While these accounts, as they stand, clearly will convey the correct information to those with a financial training or background, they are not necessarily that communicative to non-financial managers and the public at large to which they are accountable. Accordingly, present practice is such to communicate the information in an alternative manner in addition. The council's finances are set out, service by service, in a form showing relevant information, sometimes together with useful associated statistics (for example percentage changes in expenditure from last year). Service departments even go as far as producing handbooks to give a yearly progress and information report including summaries of expenditure and use of resources, etc.

Anyshire County Council as a whole has found a useful and welcome format to summarise their consolidated accounts as was shown in Chapter 1, Tables 1.7 and 1.8.

This section puts into perspective the role of financial management and the basic accounting principles. The next sections discuss some aspects of management accounting which will be useful to all business managers.

7.4 Budgeting and control

The reader will have seen from Table 1.8 that one way Anyshire County Council chooses to present its financial information is in the form of estimated expenditure and actual expenditure, 'estimates' and 'actuals'.

'Estimates' are always based on historic costs. Nowadays, however, it is essential to allow for inflation. From the last entry shown in Table 1.8 Anyshire County Council chooses to show this as a global figure labelled 'Provision for contingency sum for pay and price increases'. Last year and this year the calculated figures approximate to 7.5 per cent and 6.3 per cent respectively.

Allowance for inflation is important when preparing budgets on 'estimates' in the subsequent controlling of 'actuals'. The Retail Price Index (RPI) has already been mentioned as an index used to identify and measure the level of inflation. Its use, associated with inflation, is in the preparation of supplementary balance sheets with their values adjusted in order that realistic comparisons can be made with the effects of an unstable monetary unit removed.

7.4.1 Planning and controlling

Planning and *controlling* are the two activities central to effective management. Much of the information associated with these operations relates to cost and so comes under the realm of the management accountant. The quantitative information they collate and provide for other managers is at the centre of the financial administration of an organisation and affects all levels of management.

The financial processes covering these two activities are summarised by way of the two following definitions, partly due to the ICMA (Institute of Cost and Management Accounting):

'*Budgets* are financial and/or quantitative statements, prepared and approved prior to a defined period of time, of the policy to be pursued during that period for the purpose of attaining a given objective.

Budgetary control is the continuous comparison of actual with budgeted results either to secure by individual action the objective of the policy or to provide a basis for its revision.'

7.4.2 Budgetary control

These definitions quite rightly pre-suppose the existence of a policy prior to the preparation of the budget. The policy will be guided by the aims and objectives of the organisation and how it sees them being fulfilled. For private sector organisations this is invariably seen in terms of a profit target. The various budgets are then prepared covering all income, expenditure, assets and liabilities to ensure that the profit target is reached. For public sector organisations, and Anyshire County Council in particular, once the objectives are settled and the public's needs identified, the organisation has

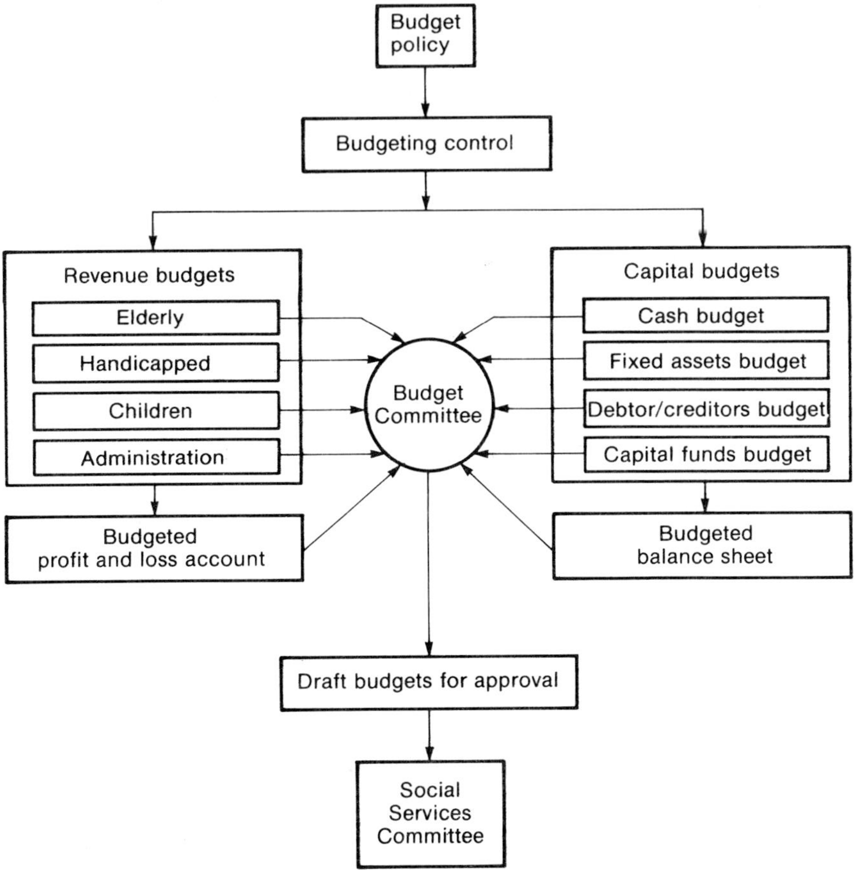

Figure 7.8 Framework for budgetary control

to decide on the directions that the departmental services are to be altered or developed.

Figure 7.8 describes a framework for budgetary control. It is attributable to the Social Services Department of Anyshire County Council, but in essence its form is applicable to any organisation.

The 'Budget Committee' consists of the Director of Social Services, his Assistant Directors and the Department's Chief Financial Officer. Its task is to administer the budgetary control system. Its functions are threefold, namely:

(1) to prepare draft budgets
(2) to keep under review their control procedures
(3) to monitor the on-going operation of the system.

A Budget Committee will enlist the help of other specialists, as appropriate, as the budget is being prepared. Standard procedures for monitoring the system will be set out in detail and include, for uniformity, the manner in which accounts are to be presented, the frequency that periodical reviews are to be carried out and reports produced comparing actual results with budgeted figures. Generally, the Social Services Budget Committee will need to liaise throughout with personnel in the Treasurer's Department as their budget will later be consolidated with the budgets from the other committees. Much groundwork will also be covered by way of regular meetings between the Director of Social Services, as an officer of the Council, and the Chairman of the Social Services Committee, as an elected member.

Whatever the nature of the business it is vital that budgets are prepared in accordance with the structure of the organisation. With Anyshire County Council Social Services Department, while the Assistant Directors have a clear responsibility for their own divisional operations, the department's overall structure is by client-group classification. Accordingly, it is this overall structure which directs the form of the budget as the objectives in each of the client-group areas are identified, with local needs, on a divisional basis, implicitly taken into account.

Anyshire County Council would be unworkable as an organisation without an annual budget. The principles adopted, however, are not universally applicable and each local authority has its own interpretation. As such there is no 'model' practice. Here, by identifying the main requirements for Anyshire County Council, the discussion will convey general practices adopted within local authorities. They are, however, also equally applicable to other organisations of any size.

All departments and many officers contribute towards the annual budget. Its preparation is a method of 'objectively' classifying expenditure (set against the rate and any other income). It reveals the cost of the whole and any specific service, and allows the comparative cost-of-service studies, already referred to, to be made amongst local authorities. Legally the adoption of the annual budget fixes the rate demand. However, from an internal and managerial viewpoint the budget itself encompasses both decision-making and control in that all must abide by its contents.

7.4.3 Approach to budgeting

The traditional budgeting approach adopted by local authorities was based wholly on the various claims put forward by the authority's departments. This allowed departments much freedom and as a result they over-emphasised their claims and what they wanted to do. This was done in the full knowledge that the council could not permit it and would reduce their draft estimates so that an acceptable rate could be fixed.

While such traditional budgeting techniques served local authorities well until fairly recently, economic stringencies led to chief financial officers rigorously scrutinising budgets to the extent that departments struggled to substantiate their requests, ad-hoc costs occurred and much in-fighting ensued.

More popular now, and adopted by Anyshire along with other more realistic and forward-looking authorities, is the 'predetermined rate' approach. This approach starts from the precept of setting pro-rata allocations to departments, much of this due to the comparative information available through CIPFA. It allows the authority to look initially at the total expenditure permissible at various rate levels. Then once the rate level is chosen, resources are allocated to departments according to the agreed council policy objectives as developed through both their short- and long-term plans. This system not only gives departments more actual control of their own affairs and responsibilities but it is seen to be more in keeping with current practices of corporate planning and integrated management.

Further, with the development and refinement of planning and costing techniques, the adoption of the predetermined rate approach is now considered an improvement on previous practice. In fact, present views are that this approach to budgeting is indeterminately linked to what is a corporate management system.

7.4.4 Forward planning

What has been said about budgeting so far has been mainly concerned with revenue budgets. Clearly, organisations need to plan in the longer term as well. How far ahead an organisation will realistically be able to plan depends on its size and nature. However, a common length of time for forward planning is five years. Accordingly, organisations produce five-year rolling programmes. These incorporate the fairly conventional five-year capital programme with a five-year action plan of desirable projects. Those projects included in an action plan, especially the major ones, have to be presented in sufficient detail for the full implications and alternatives to be considered. This aspect is particularly important in local authorities because much of their development work is by way of capital schemes. Thus, the consequent loan charges and revenue expenditure has to be included in the planning and budgeting process.

The annual budget, then, is part of a comprehensive planning exercise. To avoid unsatisfactory results, sufficient time has to be allowed and a timetable drawn up for its consideration through the various levels of administration. This is important because of the varying nature of the matters under consideration. For Anyshire County Council these include changes in government policies, particularly with regard to public sector growth rates (teachers' pay etc.), together with the different departmental and service needs.

Budgets should be as free as possible from hurried projections that can easily be made on unclear assumptions and inaccurate calculations. Budgets should also differentiate between what is recurring expenditure and expenditure over which there is no control mechanism.

A detailed budget should be in terms of measurable quantities to facilitate some form of later assessment. For consolidation purposes across an organisation budgets should be uniformly compiled. This means that there must be guidelines laid down centrally. Then, not only are the financial arrangements integrated, but also such practices lead to better inter-departmental liaison resulting in good lines of communication and an information provision helpful to all.

7.5 Accounting measures

There are demands in all organisations for business managers to appraise the results from the activities under their responsibility. Appraisal in this sense is quantitative measurement and is seen not only as a means of control but also as an aid to future planning. Fortunately business performance can often be measured simply in terms of percentages or unit costs.

Although many of the activities within local authorities and other public sector organisations are similar to those in the private sector, there are some aspects which are quite different. These we will examine first in a discussion of useful accounting ratios.

7.5.1 Profitability ratios

Profitability is the key indicator of performance in private sector organisations. Seen from both external and internal viewpoints profitability, as a percentage, may be judged as follows:

(1) By shareholders interested in the profits generated by their funds expressed as:

$$\text{Return on investment} = \frac{\text{Net profit after tax}}{\text{Shareholders' capital}} \times 100 \qquad (7.1)$$

(2) By business managers interested in the profits generated by the capital input expressed as:

$$\text{Return on capital employed} = \frac{\text{Net profit before tax}}{\text{Total capital employed}} \times 100 \qquad (7.2)$$

The second profitability ratio given by equation (7.2) gives a measure of the efficient use of funds and, as such, is a commonly used ratio for evaluating investment in any enterprise or venture.

Clearly, to improve profitability then either 'net profit' has to be increased or 'total capital employed' reduced. The latter, while possible, is generally the more difficult to effect. The former, however, can be increased in three ways:

(1) Increase in selling price
(2) Increase in sales volume
(3) Reduction in costs

If prices increase customers may buy from a competitor. If sales increase then more customers may still not buy; also there may be associated problems in organising any significant increase in sales volume. These two ways tend to lead to less controllable situations whereas a reduction in costs can be effected directly under management control.

The ratio given by equation (7.2) is often expressed as a combination of two ratios. We have, by rearrangement:

$$\frac{\text{Net profit}}{\text{Total capital}} \times 100 = \frac{\text{Net profit}}{\text{Total sales}} \times 100 \times \frac{\text{Total sales}}{\text{Total capital}} \qquad (7.3\text{a})$$

or

$$\begin{pmatrix} \% \text{ return on} \\ \text{capital employed} \end{pmatrix} = \begin{pmatrix} \% \text{ net profit on} \\ \text{sales} \end{pmatrix} \times \begin{pmatrix} \text{Turnover on} \\ \text{capital employed} \end{pmatrix} \qquad (7.3\text{b})$$

Both parts of the right-hand side of equations (7.3a) and (7.3b) are contributory to the result, but they contribute in different ways depending on the type of the organisation. In industries where profit margins are low, compensation is achieved with a high sales turnover. Supermarkets, chainstores and others involved in retailing are typical to this situation. However, in heavy engineering type organisations where there is a low turnover then a good return on capital is obtained from much higher profit margins. So, depending on the type of industry, business managers consider and seek to improve profitability in different ways.

These and other similar accounting ratios can be gleaned directly from the organisation's balance sheet and profit and loss account(s).

7.5.2 Unit costing

The sorts of activities that are similar in both public and private sector organisations are cleaning, printing, computer services, maintenance of vehicles, equipment and buildings and building work itself. With all these activities the accounting information required by business managers is that concerned with operational control. This means that data pertaining to the activity to be controlled must be kept and made readily available. For example, a data processing manager in charge of computer services needs to have access to the running and maintenance costs of all computing equipment in his charge so that comparative costings can be made for different departments and different periods, and also idle and down time statistics can be produced. Having such information available in appropriate detail will enable him to see in what ways actual costs over a period of time have varied from estimates thus enabling him to review his short- and long-term strategies.

To achieve this much use these days is made of the 'unit costing' technique, that is expressing costs in relation to an appropriate unit. It may be that a 'unit cost' is the only measure available, but invariably it does serve the purpose and acts as a focal point on an aspect of a service. In this way unit costs can be very useful measures, not only in the processes of budgeting and on-going operational control but also in the general appraisal of services.

We have seen examples of unit costs in our 'comparative statistics' table between a number of local authorities (see the case study at the end of Chapter 1).

Some of the unit costs used as measures are:

Education	— Gross cost per pupil
Social services	— Gross cost per child of children in care
	— Gross cost of supported elderly residents per week
	— Home help contact hours per 1,000 aged 65 +
Highways	— Maintenance cost per kilometre of road
Police	— Population per police officer
All services	— Net cost per 1,000 population.

Unit costs are seen to be useful measures of local authority services as they often have more significance than global or other totalled figures. Accordingly, they allow for a better and more proper assessment of trends and clearly give meaningful comparisons on services for use by government and the local authorities themselves.

One last point, however, that must always be remembered is that such statistical information only forms a basis from which judgements and decisions can be made, and often other subjective points have also to be taken into account.

7.6 Summary

The purpose of this chapter has been twofold: first, to explain the differing roles of financial and management accountants, specifying the nature of their work and how each role complements the other; secondly, to identify a number of areas of overlap where the management accountant needs to communicate and liaise with other managerial staff within an organisation.

As discussed in the opening chapters, organisations are structured such that, through their structure, delegated responsibility is encouraged as a good management principle to be followed. This perhaps is one hidden but prime advantage that results from an informative budgetary control system. A budget itself serves as a means of communication. It encourages staff participation, reduces 'them and us' attitudes, and also makes managers at all levels more appreciative of others' responsibilities as well as problems.

Budget control is a form of 'management by exception' in that it is the significant differences of 'actual' from 'budgeted' figures that should lead to investigation and possible action. Interaction between managers on budgetary matters is vital also as sometimes some managers have to be persuaded that budgeting is not necessarily a means just of limiting expenditure but it is, in fact, an important management technique designed so that efficient use can be made of the resources at an organisation's disposal.

CHAPTER 8

Business models and their development

8.1 Introduction

It is important for any information analyst to have a good understanding of the range of data analysis techniques employed within organisations. It is also highly desirable for many other people working in today's business environment to have a fundamental understanding of such techniques. In Chapter 4 some of the common statistical techniques, as they apply to data analysis, were examined. In this chapter the emphasis is geared towards the understanding of the basic mathematical techniques that underpin many business applications.

A business manager, whatever his area of responsibility, will often need to evaluate data quantitatively prior to making a recommendation or a decision. For a financial manager the decision could concern company profit. A sales manager could be forecasting supply targets based on an analysis of product demand. A production manager makes decisions with regard to control of stock levels and production costs. Although these examples are simplifications of decision-making in general, data items such as profit, cost and sales are all measurable quantities. Accordingly, it is the examination of related quantities and factors, together with the resultant analysis, that inevitably has a bearing on any decision made and its consequences.

The objectives of Anyshire County Council as a local authority are different in essence from an organisation in the private sector which has to sell its product or service at a profit to stay in business. However, many of its operational procedures are similar. The costs of local authority activities are continually under review department by department. Further, ways of improving cost effectiveness are investigated by the same methods that ways to improve profit margins are investigated elsewhere.

Many of these methods are nowadays based on modelling techniques. Some techniques are very complex and their use needs expert knowledge well beyond the scope of this book. Other simpler techniques only require some basic mathematical knowledge and understanding. Accordingly, it is the aim of this chapter to introduce the student to some relevant mathematical topics in the context of selected applications important across general management.

While the mathematical content of this chapter is not very deep, parts of it do rely on an understanding of simple calculus and associated techniques. Accordingly, the reader lacking in this background knowledge is advised to study this aspect separately before continuing.

8.2 Modelling in business

8.2.1 Quantitative methods and subjective decision-making

Few will argue against the statement 'business decision-making is mainly a human process'. The very environment of business administration supports this and the reader will surely have realised this from the discussion in Chapter 2. Of the contributory factors affecting a decision, many are human ones and accordingly are based on the decision-maker's experience and intuition, or perhaps just plain common sense. It is only the human mind that can judge whether or not there are missing, conflicting or ambiguous details in a report tabled before a board or committee.

While not pretending that the human 'thought and decision' process can be replaced, quantitative methods are increasingly being used to advantage in business practice. It must be said, however, that such methods should be used only to *supplement* and *complement* the basis on which decisions are made.

Recent years have seen a rapid advance in the development of quantitative methods to support decision-making. Linked to the advent of computers with their power, speed and accuracy of calculation, such techniques are now central to many information analysis requirements. Some of these techniques that are widely applicable in modern business organisations, whatever the industry or type of organisation, will be discussed in Chapter 9. In this chapter, however, we will confine ourselves to laying the quantitative foundations that are fundamental to many of the techniques employed in the 'science of management'.

In today's society, all types of business organisation have to be adaptive to change. This change could be for development purposes or it could be necessary due to circumstances within an organisation that have changed. For example, a company could suddenly be experiencing cash-flow problems. Have sales been worse than the seasonally adjusted expectations? Is the inventory system working properly, or indeed are stock-levels being kept too high?

Anyshire County Council is facing a reduction in its rate support grant from the government and will naturally have to have a re-think on the provision of its services to see whether cuts can be averted or minimised in certain areas. In both these cases data values will change. The result(s) of these changes will need to be calculated, first in a quantitative sense. The outcome of this will then determine what changes in policy, if any, are necessary.

Clearly, in some situations, a change in policy comes first. Often, however, as in the above descriptions, the data varies and the implications need to be ascertained and appraised. It is thus important to match the human side of any decision with the quantitative side. The basic facts and data have to be combined with the subjective judgement of the decision to establish a logical framework which describes the situation.

8.2.2 The modelling approach

A *model* is a representation of a real-life object as in Figure 8.1. The concept of a model is familiar to us as it is a term we are all used to — we have all seen models from our earliest days.

A *mathematical model* can be considered similarly. It is basically a representation using numbers and symbols of the relationships among data items which occur in a real-life situation.

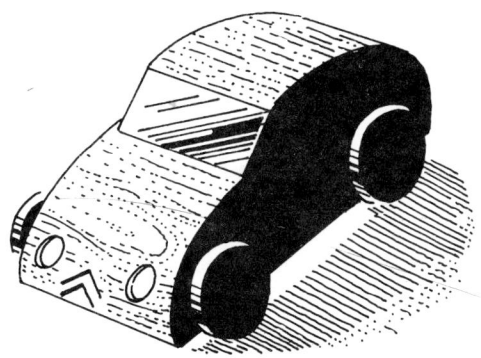

Figure 8.1 A toy model

Figure 8.2 Model of a house in three stages of development

Sometimes a simplified model is considered initially and other relationships are introduced at later stages. Each stage of the development then makes the model a closer representation of its real counterpart. Thus, mathematical models can be developed or 'built' in a manner similar to some children's toys (see Figure 8.2). The reason for using a mathematical model is that it provides the logical framework already mentioned within which a manager, as an information analyst, can sensibly work.

To create the model, the important factors, together with any assumptions, have to be explicitly stated, and the relationships between data items have to be described. The means for this is the language of mathematics. It eliminates ambiguities. Thus, results are not misleading in the same way that human assertions can be. Further, the unambiguous nature of computer languages and processes indicates that the computer is a very powerful 'tool' when applied to mathematical models.

Instances of the use of a computer modelling a real-life situation are actually more apparent to us than the nature of the mathematical model itself. Airline pilots train from mock-up flight decks with computers simulating the behaviour of the aeroplane when landing or in other situations. In an analogous manner, the computer simulation of the mathematical model allows realistic training to take place at reduced cost and, in this case, without putting lives in danger.

At another level, games on home computers are interpretations of the behaviour of modelling situations. Some common ones that spring to mind are chess, decathlon, even snooker, as well as all the different types of adventure and attack games.

In a strictly business sense, mathematical models can be investigated and explored to identify the strategies and features that are most appropriate to the existing situation. Also, if the relationships specified in a model are such that its behaviour is unrealistic or fails to match anticipated results then the very mathematical nature of the model will usually help to detect errors in its formulation or indicate which characteristics need to be adjusted.

Models can be complex both mathematically and in structure, typically the 'pilot trainer' model. Similarly, government economic models contain numerous different parameters and interrelationships between the data items.

Many models, however, are simple in formulation in that their representation in mathematical terms is fairly straightforward, relying only on a basic understanding. Often, this directly results from the purpose of creating the model — to bring simplicity and clarity to a complicated and unclear situation. Accordingly, simple mathematical models are to be found employed in a wide range of business activities and across all functional areas of an organisation, incorporating operational, tactical and strategic situations.

Generally, the justification of using mathematical modelling techniques is increasing. All levels of management, not just students, are becoming more aware of the basic methods and the underlying concepts. As a result, with present-day students becoming tomorrow's management, an expanded use of modelling techniques is envisaged.

More and more small businesses are now using computers in their everyday work. Payroll, inventory, financial planning, and other packages are readily available for immediate use. Mathematical models are likely to be embedded in such software. Clearly, some awareness and understanding is desirable in order to be in a position to judge whether a particular mathematical model is suitable or not.

There is one other useful advantage that can be gained by adopting the modelling approach to quantifying a business situation. A model developed in an organisation to represent one situation may well be conceptually similar and use the same techniques as another in a completely different area or field of work. Thus, the models introduced in the next section should not be viewed solely in the given context, but the quantitative methods employed should be considered for wider application in any number of situations.

8.3 Some simple business models

In this section, three different aspects of mathematical modelling are examined (see Figure 8.3). Each aspect is essentially stand-alone but a central theme is adopted in order that the reader can perceive some connections and relationships that might apply between them.

The chosen theme is 'catering' within Anyshire's education service. Perhaps an unusual choice, but most organisations of reasonable size will operate a catering service of some kind. Elsewhere within Anyshire, for instance, there is the town hall restaurant, the police canteen, the leisure-centre cafeteria and the museum coffee-room.

This choice of theme can in many ways be considered organisation independent in that it is both product and service oriented and so reflects characteristics common across a wide spectrum of organisations.

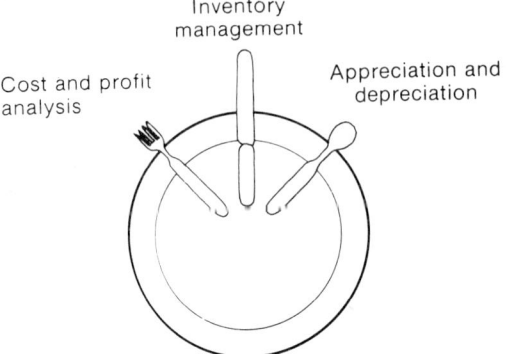

Figure 8.3 The three business models

8.3.1 Cost and profit analysis

Anyshire's primary school meals system operates like most others in the country: there are set charges for a lunch-time meal. Costings are currently based on the overall operation and there is a central administration system. However, with the introduction of more stringent economic targets (previously 'school meals' was heavily subsidised) the viability of each school's operation is to be periodically reviewed. To aid this review, it has been decided to develop a mathematical model based on a typical primary school.

Features of the model

First, there are a number of general factors to be identified in connection with any 'cost and profit analysis' model. The key factor is that there are two types of cost involved:

- Fixed costs
- Variable costs

Fixed costs are those that do not respond to changes in sales, that is the volume of meals. These are rent and rates, salaries and wages, other administration costs and depreciation of equipment. They are readily identifiable from available figures. Other costs such as gas, electricity, telephone, breakages and reviewals we will include as fixed costs although they are not wholly fixed in the true sense of the word. *Variable costs* are those that vary in proportion to the volume of sales/meals. They relate to the food and beverage costs, that is the raw materials.

Other factors include the *break-even point*, which is reached when sales revenue is equal to total cost, that is no net profit, and *profit* itself, as income minus expenditure, defined simply as total revenue minus total cost.

Before formulating a mathematical model incorporating these factors it is necessary to denote them in symbolic form. Let:

- F = Total fixed cost
- V = Variable cost per school meal
- q = Number of school meals
- r = Price of a school meal
- P = Amount of profit (or loss)

In general business terms, the 'school meal' is referred to as the 'unit'. Accordingly, V = unit variable cost, q = volume of units and r = unit revenue.

The relation between the variables is thus:

$$\text{Profit} = \text{Total revenue} - \text{Total costs}$$
$$P = rq - (F + Vq) \tag{8.1}$$

Example

Anytown Central Primary School has 400 pupils. In any one week there are between 1,450 and 1,525 school meals taken. The weekly fixed costs have been calculated at £450. The variable costs are 35p per school meal. The price of a school meal is 65p.

Putting these values into the model given by equation (8.1), we have:

r = £0.65
F = £450
V = £0.35.

and so:

$$P = 0.65q - (450 + 0.35q) \tag{8.2}$$

P is a function of q, where q varies from 1,450 to 1,525, where P is called the dependent variable and q the independent variable.

This model, given in equation (8.2), is a linear equation in one unknown in that the profit P varies with respect to the number of school meals q in a linear or straight line manner. This is shown in Figure 8.4, by drawing the graph of P (profit) against q (number of school meals).

The break-even point is reached when the number of school meals is 1,500 per week. Above this number a net profit is achieved, below it a loss is recorded.

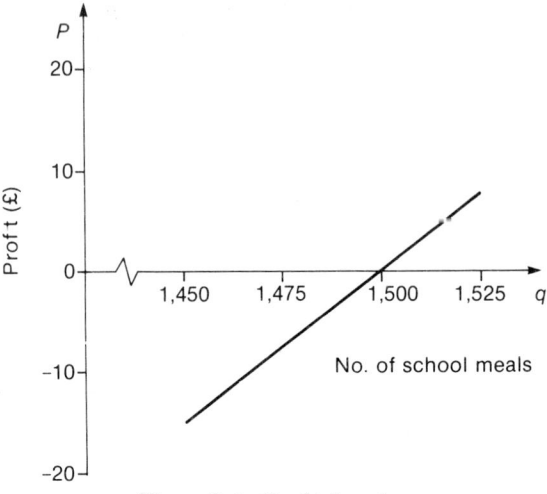

Figure 8.4   Profit function

Model development

The above simple model can now be developed in a particular way to take account of the fact that the percentage of primary school children taking school meals is falling. To suit this changing situation it has been decided to incorporate the following modifications:

(1) Reduce the fixed costs to a level based on a new break-even point of 1,450 meals per week.
(2) Vary variable costs such that they are 35p per meal at 1,450 meals per week rising to $36\frac{1}{2}$p per meal at 1,525 meals per week, these increased costs being due to varying overtime payments to staff.

The effect of (1) on the model given by equation (8.2) is straightforward. It becomes:

$$P = 0.65q - (435 + 0.35q) \qquad (8.3)$$

The figure of 435 being the amount of fixed costs necessitating a break-even point of 1,450.

The effect of the second modification is less straightforward and needs to be analysed before the new variable costs can be properly specified. The assumption made in (2) is that the new variable costs increase uniformly from 35p at 1,450 meals to $36\frac{1}{2}$p at 1,525 meals. This means that a linear relationship exists between the two variables, V, variable cost per school meal, and q, the number of school meals.

The form of the relationship is thus:

$$V = aq + b \qquad (8.4)$$

where a and b are values to be determined from the data provided. Substituting the appropriate values into equation (8.2) we have:

and
$$\left.\begin{array}{l} 0.35 = 1{,}450a + b \\ 0.365 = 1{,}525a + b \end{array}\right\} \qquad (8.5)$$

The two equations in (8.5) are *simultaneous linear equations*, and in order to determine how V varies with q they are solved to give values for a and b. Subtracting one of the equations in (8.5) from the other gives:

$$0.015 = 75a, \text{ therefore } a = 0.0002$$

With the value of a known, the value of b can be found by substituting the value of a into either of the equations in (8.5), and b is found to be 0.06. Thus:

$$V = 0.0002q + 0.06 \qquad (8.6)$$

and is the revised form from which variable costs are calculated.

Note: The reader should be familiar with the 'elimination' and 'substitution' ways of solving any pair of simultaneous equations. These methods can be applied to the solution of systems of more than two linear equations. However, it is more usual in such cases to employ particular matrix or numerical methods and other, more mathematically oriented books should be consulted.

Incorporating the expression for V (equation (8.6)) into the model given by equation (8.3) leads to a new profit function, namely:

$$P = 0.65q - [435 + (0.0002q + 0.06)q] \qquad (8.7)$$

Combining the terms together we have:

$$P = -0.0002q^2 + 0.59q - 435 \qquad (8.8)$$

P is now a quadratic function of q. A table of calculated values is given below and the corresponding graph is shown in Figure 8.5.

q	1,450	1,475	1,500	1,525
P	0	0.125	0	-0.375

A quadratic function like this in which the coefficient of q^2 (q, the independent variable) is negative gives the graph shape shown, and a maximum value for the dependent variable, here P, can be found. On the other hand, if the coefficient of q^2 had been positive, the graph shape would have been 'cupped' with a minimum value being possible.

From the graph, it can be seen that a maximum profit, albeit only £0.125, is achieved when $q = 1{,}475$. Above this level, profit is reducing and actual losses are incurred above $q = 1{,}500$ as the costs considerably outweigh the revenue. This aspect is further investigated as the model is developed.

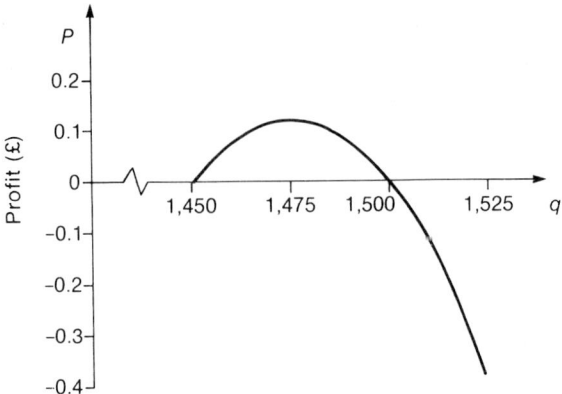

Figure 8.5   Modified profit function

It is often well worth while to draw a graph in order to show the overall effect of the mathematical model formulation. To determine maximum profit, however, it is best to employ also the techniques of *differential calculus*.

From Figure 8.5, it can be readily seen that at the point of maximum profit the tangent to the curve is horizontal, and the gradient or slope of the curve is therefore zero. In calculus terms, this means that the first derivative with respect to the independent variable is also zero.

Differentiating equation (8.8) with respect to q gives:

$$\frac{\mathrm{d}P}{\mathrm{d}q} = -0.0004q + 0.59 \qquad (8.9)$$

For a maximum or minimum:

$$\frac{\mathrm{d}P}{\mathrm{d}q} = 0$$

This condition occurs when:

$$q = \frac{0.59}{0.0004} = 1,475$$

which is in agreement with the graphically determined value.

Substituting this result, $q = 1,475$, back into equation (8.8), the maximum profit is again found to be £0.125.

Generally, a maximum or minimum occurs where $\mathrm{d}P/\mathrm{d}q = 0$.

Also, for a maximum: $\dfrac{\mathrm{d}^2P}{\mathrm{d}q^2} < 0$

for a minimum: $\dfrac{\mathrm{d}^2P}{\mathrm{d}q^2} > 0$

at the maximum/minimum point.

Before finishing with this model we can look at one further modification. For the next financial year it is anticipated that variable costs can be kept to the same level. However, inflation will lead to an increase in the level of the fixed costs to £460 or even £465. The model can now be used to work out a new price for a school meal in order to balance out these increases in fixed costs.

The model becomes:

$$P = -0.0002q^2 + (r - 0.06)q - F \qquad (8.10)$$

where r is the price of a school meal and F is the total fixed costs.

F is independent of q and so does not affect the value of the first derivative which is:

$$\frac{dP}{dq} = -0.0004q + (r - 0.06)$$

Adopting the established approach to determine the number of meals to give maximum profit, we find:

For $r = 0.66$, $\frac{dP}{dq} = 0$ where $q = 1,500$, giving $P = 450 - F$

For $r = 0.67$, $\frac{dP}{dq} = 0$ where $q = 1,525$, giving $P = 465.125 - F$

For $r = 0.68$, $\frac{dP}{dq} = 0$ where $q = 1,550$, giving $P = 480.5 - F$

These results give one viewpoint of this model. However, it is just as significant to identify the break-even points in each case, these occurring when $P = 0$. Thus, there will be break-even points when:

$$-0.0002q^2 + (r - 0.06)q - F = 0 \qquad (8.11)$$

The solution of this quadratic equation is best found by applying the well-known formula, which for the general equation:

$$ax^2 + bx + c = 0$$

is:

$$x = \frac{-b \pm \sqrt{(b^2 - 4ac)}}{2a}$$

With $r = 0.66$, there are no real solutions of the quadratic equation if $F < 450$. Other results found are given in Table 8.1, where q_1 and q_2 are the two solutions of the quadratic equation. The graphs, with these combinations of r and F, are shown in Figure 8.6.

These results show clearly that should the fixed costs work out to be £465 rather than £460 per week then a rise in the price of a school meal to 68p is desirable to ensure a reasonably safe profit margin.

Table 8.1

r	F = 460	F = 465
0.67	$q_1 = 1,365$ $q_2 = 1,685$	$q_1 = 1,500$ $q_2 = 1,550$
0.68	$q_1 = 1,230$ $q_2 = 1,870$	$q_1 = 1,272$ $q_2 = 1,828$

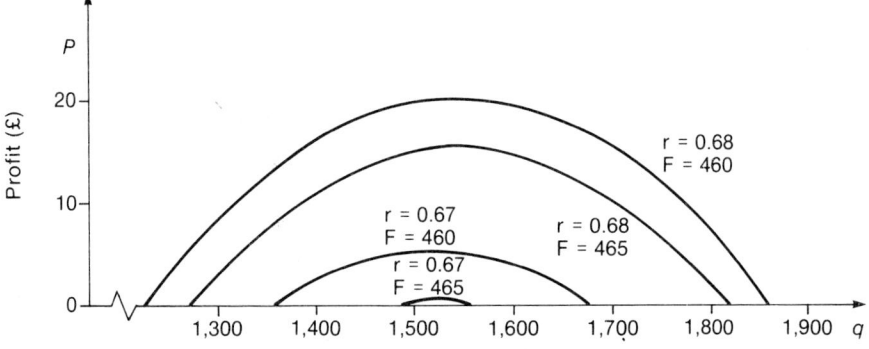

Figure 8.6 A range of profit functions

8.3.2 Inventory management

One of the activities of many business organisations is inventory management. It is usual to think of an item or commodity to be stored, used and replenished as a raw material in a production or manufacturing environment. However, the formulation and use of an inventory model is just as pertinent if the commodity, for example, is available beds in a hospital or reams of paper in Anyshire's schools.

Any items or commodities that are stored or reserved in order that future demands are met are called *inventories*. The main aim of an inventory policy is to minimise the total cost of maintaining the inventory, while maintaining an adequate supply of the commodity. In order to be able to make decisions regarding optimal levels of inventories, inventory models are formulated and analysed.

In a catering operation, fresh food items and other perishables are generally ordered on a daily or weekly basis. Such items may not form part of a long-term inventory model. However, frozen, tinned and other stored foods as well as non-consumable items would be typically included in an inventory control scheme.

Factors to consider

In a simplified inventory model, a realistic assumption to start with is that the demand for an item is known. To match a known demand, it is the function of the inventory model to identify the best supply policy that minimises the costs appertaining to the inventory. A supply policy is based on the answers to the following questions:

● How often should an item be ordered?
● How much should be ordered?

More and more inventory systems are being computerised. Accordingly, the control aspects are being programmed whereas previously inventory control relied very much on a manager's intuition. It is thus important that the underlying concepts and methods of quantitative analysis are understood.

Before actually developing an inventory model, the different types of costs that can occur need to be identified:

(1) *Holding costs:* These costs result directly from the storage of the inventory items. They are expressed in units of money per item stored for a specified time period. They include costs incurred from maintaining the storage facilities, insuring the inventory as well as interest lost due to capital tied up in the inventory.
(2) *Reorder costs:* These costs occur each time the inventory is replenished. They are expressed in units of money per order. They relate to the cost of preparing a purchase order but they do not depend on the size of the order.
(3) *Stockout costs:* These costs occur when the available supply is non-existent. They are expressed in units of money per item short. They relate particularly to situations where a customer does not buy an item because the stock is depleted.

Let:
● C = Cost of order
● H = Holding costs
● R = Reorder costs
● S = Stockout costs
● T = Total costs

The general form of an inventory model is therefore:

$$T = C + H + R + S \qquad (8.12)$$

Making the assumption that there is a known demand for an item over a specified period leads to what is called a *deterministic inventory model*.

With this assumption the answers to the two questions posed earlier are related in that if we know how much to order every time then we must also know how often to order. In this situation, the optimal order quantity, known as the *economic order quantity* (EOQ), is easily determined from the model equation.

This basic model is important as it adequately describes the large class of inventory problems in which the item stored is subject to a stable demand. Further, deterministic inventory models in general describe the procedures adopted for the control of stocks of many regularly used low-value items — the classic institutional catering situation.

Example

The Catering Division of Anyshire's Polycollege is large and has an expected use of sugar in the forthcoming year of 3,000 kg. The demand rate will be reasonably constant throughout the year because even in the student vacations Polycollege is an attractive and well-used conference centre.

Sugar is bought in 10 kg catering packs. A supplier is willing to provide the Catering Division with the required amount, if ordered in sufficient quantities, for £3.52 per pack which includes transport costs. The storage and insurance costs of holding one pack of sugar in inventory are estimated to be 80p per year. The clerical costs associated with placing an order are estimated to be £1.20. A mathematical model is to be developed to enable the Catering Division to determine what order quantity will minimise their total annual sugar costs.

Using the EOQ model approach the necessary assumptions are:

(1) Replacement stock arrives as existing stock runs out.
(2) Stockouts are not permitted (not tolerated in catering!).
(3) Inventory items are used at a constant rate.
(4) For each reorder the same number of units are ordered.

Graphically, this basic EOQ model can be represented as in Figure 8.7.

The mathematical model is first to be formulated in symbolic form. To allow this, let:

- c = cost of one unit, i.e. one pack of sugar
- q = order quantity, i.e. number of packs per order
- h = holding cost per unit, i.e. holding cost per pack of sugar
- r = reorder cost
- d = demand rate, i.e. number of packs used per year.

There are no stockout costs so that the general model given by equation

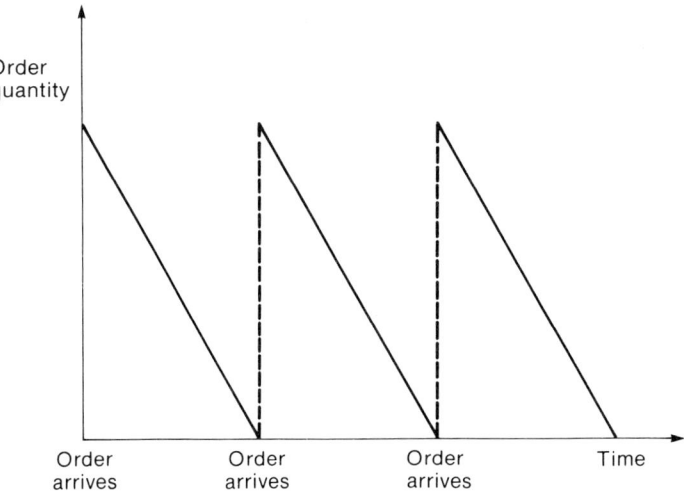

Figure 8.7 Basic EOQ model

(8.12) reduces to:

$$T = C + H + R$$

where C = cost of order, H = holding costs and R = reorder costs. For the sugar inventory system we have:

$$c = 3.52 \qquad h = 0.80$$
$$d = 300 \qquad r = 1.20$$

The following relationships are now established:

C = (cost of one unit) × (demand)
$\quad = cd = (3.52)\,(300) = 1{,}056.00$
H = (cost of holding one unit for one year) × (average number in inventory)

$$= (h)\,\frac{(q + 0)}{2} = hq/2 = 0.80q/2 = 0.4q$$

R = (cost of each reorder) × (number of reorders per year)
$\quad = (r)(d/q) = rd/q = 1.20(300/q) = 360/q$

Thus

$$T = C + H + R$$
$$= cd + hq/2 + rd/q$$
$$= 1{,}056 + 0.4q + 360/q \qquad (8.13)$$

These costs, for varied q values, are shown in Table 8.2.

The variable costs in the equation are the holding costs H and the reorder

Table 8.2

Order quantity q	Cost of order $C = 1,056$	Holding costs $H = 0.4q$	Reorder costs $R = 360/q$	Total costs T
10	1,056	4	36	1,096
20	1,056	8	18	1,082
30	1,056	12	12	1,080
50	1,056	20	7.2	1,083.2
60	1,056	24	6	1,086

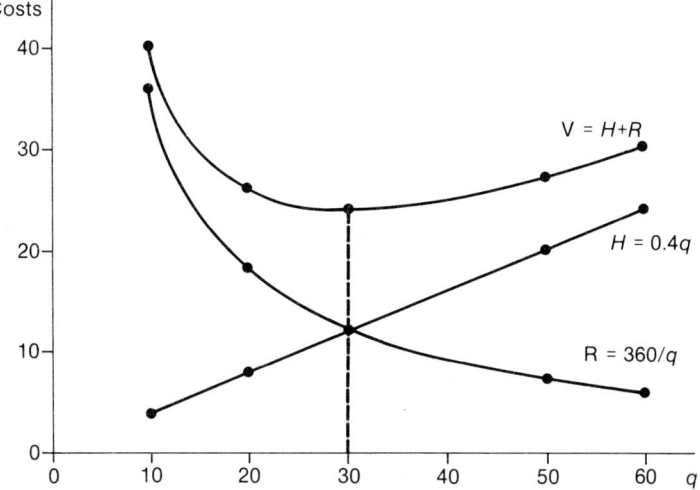

Figure 8.8 Variable cost functions

costs R. These values, together with the total variable costs, $V = H + R$, are graphed in Figure 8.8.

It can be seen that the total variable costs V, thus the total costs C, are minimised when the order quantity is such that the holding costs equal the reorder costs. Mathematically:

$$V = 0.4q + 360/q$$

are the total variable costs. These are minimised when $dV/dq = 0$. Applying the rules of differentiation, we find:

$$\frac{dV}{dq} = 0.4 - \frac{360}{q^2}$$

Therefore, setting $dV/dq = 0$ to determine a maximum/minimum value, we find:

$$0.4 = \frac{360}{q^2}$$

$$q^2 = \frac{360}{0.4} = 900$$

giving $q = 30$ as the economic order quantity.

Likewise, if holding costs are equated to reorder costs:

$$0.4 = \frac{360}{q}$$

giving the same result, albeit in a different way. Thus, generally, in the basic EOQ model the economic order quantity occurs when

$$\text{Holding costs} = \text{Reorder costs}$$

or, from above, when:

$$\frac{hq}{2} = \frac{rd}{q}$$

that is when:

$$q = \sqrt{\left(\frac{2rd}{h}\right)} \qquad (8.14)$$

Equation (8.14) is known as the EOQ formula.

Model development

The outcome of this model analysis resulted in the stockroom supervisor advising the Catering Division manager to order sugar in quantities of 30 packs, this being the economic order quantity. The stockroom supervisor has also contacted the supplier informing him of the proposed ordering policy. The supplier has indicated his agreement.

Prior to the placement of the first order, however, the Catering Division manager looks at the basis on which the model was formulated and now asks the stockroom supervisor to include in the model the effect of capital costs. The modification to the model is as follows.

The present cost of money is 10 per cent per year. Therefore, the capital cost of one pack of sugar held in inventory is $0.10 \times £3.52 = £0.352$. Thus, the holding cost per pack of sugar per year will now be this capital cost plus the storage and insurance cost:

$$£0.352 + £0.80 = £1.152$$

With $h = 1.152$ the total variable costs become:

$$V = H + R$$
$$= hq/2 + rd/q$$
$$= 1.152q/2 + 1.2(300)/q$$
$$= 0.576q + 360/q$$

Equating holding costs, H, to reorder costs, R, in order to determine the new economic order quantity, we find:

$$q^2 = 360/0.576 = 625$$

giving $q = 25$.

The stockroom supervisor advises the Catering Division manager of the new EOQ. He also contacts the supplier to inform him that the sugar contract is now likely to be 12 deliveries per year, 25 packs at a time, rather than 10 deliveries per year, 30 packs at a time.

With $q = 25$, the total cost for the year's sugar supply is:

$$T = C + H + R$$
$$= 1,056 + 0.576(25) + 360/25$$
$$= 1,056 + 14.4 + 14.4$$
$$= £1,084.80$$

The supplier is not keen on the proposed change and prefers to make 10 rather than 12 deliveries over the year. Accordingly, even though profit margins are tight on sugar, the supplier offers the Polycollege a discount of 2p per pack for orders of 30 packs or more, and 4p per pack for orders of 50 packs or more (only 6 deliveries in the year).

To assess the overall value of the alternative offers the stockroom supervisor re-analyses his model for each. He knows, however, that in each case it would be wise only to order the minimum number of packs each time, either 30 or 50, as the greater the number of packs in inventory the greater the holding costs, and these costs now contribute much more to the total cost than the reorder costs as the number of packs under consideration are well above the EOQ value.

Case 1: 2p per pack discount on order of 30 packs
Cost per pack: £3.52 − £0.02 = £3.50
Capital cost per pack: 10% of £3.50 = £0.35
Total holding cost per pack: £0.80 + £0.35 = £1.15
Total costs are given by:

$$T = C + H + R$$
$$= cd + hq/2 + rd/q$$

With $q = 30$:

$$T = (3.50)(300) + (1.15)(30)/2 + (1.20)(300)/30$$
$$= 1,050 + 17.25 + 12$$
$$= £1,079.25$$

Case 2: 4p per pack discount on order of 50 packs
Cost per pack: £3.52 − £0.04 = £3.48
Capital cost per pack: 10% of £3.48 = £0.348
Total holding cost per pack: £0.80 + £0.348 = £1.148
Total costs are given by:

$$T = cd + hq/2 + rd/q$$

With $q = 50$:

$$T = (3.48)(300) + (1.148)(50)/2 + (1.20)(300)/50$$
$$= 1{,}044 + 28.70 + 7.20$$
$$= £1{,}079.90$$

Thus, although the 4p per pack discount offer looks tempting, the most favourable option (that is the option minimising overall costs) is for Polycollege to order 30 packs of sugar at a time, each pack at the discounted price of £3.50.

8.3.3 Appreciation and depreciation

The previous two modelling types were both of a financial nature. Although their basis was different, both models were investigated by the same criterion, namely the minimisation of costs. Costs of items are likely to be included in the development of many business models. Further, costs or the price of money will change with time due to inflation and other factors. This influence of time on all costs is a fundamental factor in financial modelling situations. This section examines this influence, the appreciation or depreciation of monetary items with time.

Example

Part of the forward planning of Anyshire's Education Service is to refurbish the equipment in the kitchens of the county's schools every fifteen years. The current cost on average is £5,780 per school. Questions to ask are:

(1) What is the depreciation per year of this amount if in fifteen years time the equipment will have an unchanged scrap value of £80?
(2) What will be the cost of refurbishment in another fifteen years, and how could the meeting of this cost be planned for now?

A modelling approach is to be used to determine the answers to these questions. They are considered in turn.

In answer to Question (1)

Often in financial accounts deductions are made in balance sheets to allow for the decrease in value of equipment. This is depreciation and is due either to obsolescence or wear and tear.

Model 1a

Assuming depreciation is assessed as a fixed amount each year, let this amount be £x. So, if initially the equipment is assessed as being worth £5,780:

After one year it is worth $(5,780 - x)$ pounds

After two years it is worth $(5,780 - 2x)$ pounds

$$\vdots$$

After fifteen years it is worth $(5,780 - 15x)$ pounds

After fifteen years the equipment is to be scrapped for the sum of £80. Thus the mathematical model describing the situation is simply:

$$5,780 - 15x = 80$$

giving x = £380 as the yearly depreciation. This means that the 'book value' of the equipment starts at £5,780 and, as an accounting item, decreases each year by £380.

This mathematical model of the situation is formed from the quantities 5,780, $5,780 - x$, $5,780 - 2x, \ldots$, $5,780 - 15x$. These quantities form a series as there is an identifiable relationship — a common difference — between the successive terms or quantities. This type of series is known as an *arithmetic progression*.

In general, an arithmetic progression has the form a, $a + d$, $a + 2d, \ldots$, $a + (n - 1)d$ where:

- a is the first term
- d is the common difference
- n is the number of terms in the series

Note: In a situation of depreciation as above, the common difference is negative.

Denoting the sum of the general arithmetic progression by S_{AP}, we have:

$$S_{AP} = a + (a + d) + \cdots + [a + (n - 2)d] + [a + (n - 1)d]$$

which can be rewritten in reverse order as:

$$S_{AP} = [a + (n - 1)d] + [a + (n - 2)d] + \cdots + (a + d) + a$$

Now adding these two expressions for S_{AP} by summing corresponding terms in each expression, these sums being the same throughout, namely $[2a + (n - 1)d]$, we find:

$$2S_{AP} = n[2a + (n - 1)d]$$
$$\therefore \quad S_{AP} = n[a + \tfrac{1}{2}(n - 1)d] \tag{8.15}$$

which gives the sum of an arithmetic progression as a concise expression.

Model 1b

Taking a different accounting approach, depreciation can be calculated as a fixed percentage of the current book value at the end of each year. In this case the yearly depreciation is not fixed but varies according to the book value at that time. With depreciation considered in this manner a revised model is now formulated.

Let r denote the constant percentage to which the book value of the equipment reduces each year. Again, initially, the equipment is assessed as being worth £5,780. Then:

After one year it is worth £5,780r
After two years it is worth (£5,780r)r

and so on.

Again, the mathematical model is formed as a series of quantities. However, the pattern we observe this time is that each term in the series is obtained by multiplying the previous term by a common ratio, here by the constant rate r.

Generally, this type of series can be defined as:

$$a, ar, ar^2, \ldots, ar^{n-1}$$

where:

● a is the first term
● r is the common ratio
● n is the number of terms in the series

This type of series is called a *geometric progression*.

The kitchen equipment model becomes:

$$5,780r^{15} = 80$$

as its initial value is £5,780($= a$) and after 15 years its value is £80.

$$\therefore \quad r^{15} = \frac{80}{5,780}$$

The solution to this equation is found using logarithms. Taking logs of both sides:

$$15 \log r = \log 80 - \log 5,780$$

178 Business models and their development

Logarithms to any base can be employed to find the value of r that satisfies this equation. As the reader may find it a useful exercise to confirm for herself/himself the result, the intermediate calculations are given using logs to both base e and base 10.

To base e	*To base 10*
$15 \log_e r = \log_e 80 - \log_e 5{,}780$	$15 \log_{10} r = \log_{10} 80 - \log_{10} 5{,}780$
$= 4.3820 - 8.6622$	$= 1.9031 - 3.7619$
$= -4.2802$	$= -1.8588$
hence $\log_e r = -0.2853$	hence $\log_{10} r = -0.1239$
giving $r = 0.7518$	giving $r = 0.7518$

Both results are the same, as expected. Rounding to two decimal places the constant reducing factor becomes 0.75 which gives a percentage depreciation value per year of 25 per cent. On face value, this figure may seem large but actually it is, as we see, quite accurate, and it is in fact the sort of realistic figure that is commonly used to represent depreciation of equipment for accounting purposes.

In answer to Question (2)

In order to estimate the cost of refurbishment in another fifteen years an average annual inflation rate needs to be assumed. One way of covering the costs for the future replacement of equipment is to establish a sinking fund whereby a set amount is put into the fund each year and interest is earned year by year at the rate which is currently applicable. For the purposes of this exercise it is necessary to assume an annual average investment rate.

It should be noted that this approach is an alternative for those organisations who do not show the value of machinery or equipment directly in their accounts.

Model 2

We know that present cost of refurbishment is £5,780 and the scrap value is £80. Let us suppose average annual inflation and investment rates of 6 per cent and 8 per cent respectively.

With an inflation rate of 6 per cent the cost equivalent to £5,780 now will be:

In one year's time £5,780 × 1.06
In two years' time £(5,780 × 1.06) × 1.06 = £5,780 × 1.06^2 . . .
In fifteen years' time £5,780 × 1.06^{15}

that is:

$$£5{,}780 \times 2.39656 = £13{,}852.12 \tag{8.16}$$

The value of the sinking fund in fifteen years' time, with a set amount £a being invested each year at a rate of 8 per cent, is given by:

$$a \times 1.08^{15} + a \times 1.08^{14} + \cdots + a \times 1.08^2 + a \times 1.08 \qquad (8.17)$$

In general terms this is:

$$ar^n + ar^{n-1} + \cdots + ar^2 + ar \qquad (8.18)$$

with $r = 1.08$ and $n = 15$.

The expression (8.18) can be rewritten as:

$$r(a + ar + \cdots + ar^{n-2} + ar^{n-1})$$

The contents of the brackets is seen to be the sum of the terms in the standard geometric progression. Denoting this sum by S, i.e.:

$$S = a + ar + \cdots + ar^{n-2} + ar^{n-1}$$

multiplying by r gives:

$$Sr = ar + \cdots + ar^{n-2} + ar^{n-1} + ar^n$$

By subtracting these two equations like terms cancel each other out leaving:

$$Sr - S = ar^n - a$$

i.e.

$$S(r - 1) = a(r^n - 1)$$

Thus the sum of a geometric progression is expressed in concise form as:

$$S = \frac{a(r^n - 1)}{(r - 1)} \qquad (8.19)$$

From equation (8.16), the actual cost in fifteen years' time will be £13,852.12 minus the scrap value, still taken to be £80, which gives £13,772.12. This is to be matched by the value of the sinking fund which, from equation (8.17), will be:

$$1.08 \, (a + a \times 1.08 + \cdots + a \times 1.08^{14})$$

which using (8.19) is:

$$1.08 \, \frac{a(r^n - 1)}{r - 1}$$

where $r = 1.08$ and $n = 15$.

The mathematical model for the situation, as described, is thus:

$$1.08\left[\frac{a(1.08^{15} - 1)}{(1.08 - 1)}\right] = 13,772.12$$

$$\therefore \quad a = \frac{13,772.12(1.08 - 1)}{1.08(1.08^{15} - 1)}$$

$$= \frac{13,772.12(0.08)}{1.08(2.17217)} \text{ (using logarithms to determine } 1.08^{15})$$

$$= 469.65$$

Full accuracy is not possible due to the use of logarithms and rounding errors in the calculations, so the answer is best quoted as about £470. This then is the set amount each year which needs to be put aside and invested in order to cover estimated costs of refurbishment fifteen years ahead.

8.4 Summary

The three business situations and models considered in the previous section were all deliberately fairly simplistic both in nature and analysis. The approach should, without being too formal, allow the reader to assimilate the idea of modelling with the use of some fundamental mathematics in analysing various features of each model.

8.4.1 The cost and profit analysis model

This first model illustrated the way in which a cost, revenue and profit model is formulated. As a model it typified only a certain category of catering. 'School meals' is an environment which operates with low fixed costs and enjoys a relatively stable volume of business. Other environments in this category are notably hospitals and industrial canteens, whereas hotels, guest houses and restaurants suffer from higher fixed costs and a more unstable demand. Thus, different catering environments vary widely in their cost and demand structure.

The use of differential calculus is central to the analysis of all cost, revenue and profit models as they involve consideration of relative rates of change of variables which have a connecting and functional relationship. In particular, the reader may also come across such terms as marginal cost, marginal revenue and marginal profit.

To explain briefly their meaning let us consider again a profit function used in section 8.3.1, namely that given by equation (8.8):

$$P = -0.0002q^2 + 0.59q - 435$$

The derivative of P with respect to q given by equation (8.9):

$$\frac{\mathrm{d}P}{\mathrm{d}q} = -0.0004q + 0.59$$

is the relative rate of change of the profit P with respect to the quantity q, and is known as the marginal profit. Similar definitions apply for marginal cost and marginal revenue.

Other than cost, revenue and profit functions, managers more interested in market research would be modelling supply and demand functions. For instance, the use of calculus here allows these managers to ascertain whether or not small changes in prices leads to significant changes in quantity sold.

8.4.2 The inventory management model

The economic order quantity model of a deterministic inventory system as described in section 8.3.2 provides a sound basis from which other models can be developed. Some of the common variations on the EOQ model itself are briefly described below.

An 'order-level' inventory model is one where the time period between orders is fixed. No matter what the current stock level is, at the prescribed time a sufficient amount of stock is obtained for the inventory to be brought up to a set level. This fixed time period between stock replenishments might be as much as yearly for farm produce or seasonal goods in a retail outlet, or it could even be daily as in the case of bread and milk deliveries to a supermarket. The other assumptions made with the order-level model are similar to those of the EOQ model except that in the model formulation stockouts are allowed to occur, particularly if they help reduce total costs.

It might be noted here that inventory systems that do not allow stockouts do not necessarily lead to lower overall costs. The reason for this is a straightforward one — to prevent stockouts invariably large inventories must be held thus increasing holding costs, or stock needs to be frequently replenished thus increasing reorder costs.

Sometimes it is usual for retail organisations to increase occasionally their inventory holding, for example to be ready for the busy Christmas selling period. Another situation similar to this is when an organisation places a large order having announced a future price rise. The organisation would then anticipate increased sales for a short period followed probably by a drop afterwards. For this duration, the organisation's ordering and inventory profile will be as shown in Figure 8.9.

In inventory systems clearly orders do not arrive at the same instant that an order is placed as assumed in the EOQ model. Often the *lead time*, the time between placement and arrival of an order, is not precisely known. It is common practice, however, in building inventory models to assign to the lead time a constant value.

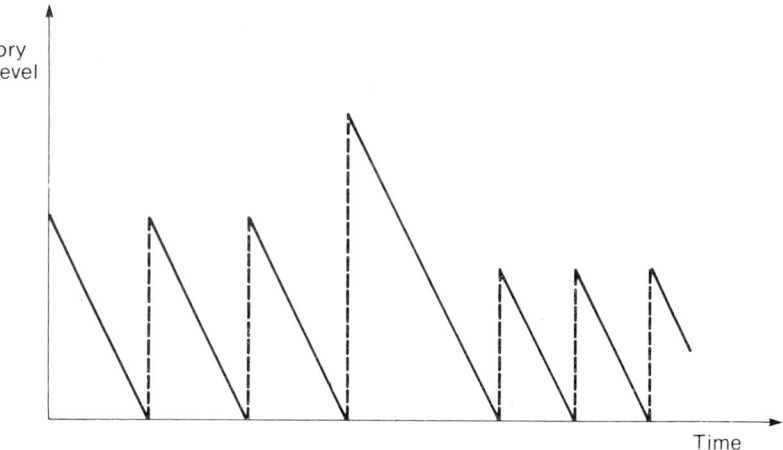

Figure 8.9 A different ordering and inventory profile

Another approach to inventory management, and so another modelling situation, occurs when an order is placed once the amount of stock in the inventory is reduced to some threshold value, the reorder quantity being the amount required to bring the inventory back up to a set level. Here the model is more complex as the demand rate is not constant, but its virtue is that the inventory level is continuously being monitored.

An understanding of deterministic inventory modelling is also necessary when considering other inventory systems where the demand and lead time are random variables.

8.4.3 Appreciation and depreciation model

The last of the three models considered the relationship of arithmetic and geometric progressions to appreciation and depreciation. This model basically extended the ideas of simple and compound interest to a modelling situation. With knowledge and understanding of the approach taken it becomes fairly straightforward to extend the techniques further to other applications. For instance, one other category of application relates in particular to annuities, loans and mortgages.

To illustrate their workings, consider the following two short examples.

Example 1

Determine the cost of an annuity of £100 for 10 years if compound interest is allowed at 8 per cent per annum.

Any payment of £a to be made in n years' time will have a 'present value' of £a/r^n where r is the common ratio or compound interest rate. An *annuity* is a payment at the end of each year for a certain number of years, so the cost or present value of the annuity is the sum of the present values of each of the yearly payments.

Letting the present value of the annuity be £P, we have:

$$P = \frac{a}{r^n} + \frac{a}{r^{n-1}} + \cdots + \frac{a}{r^2} + \frac{a}{r}$$

This is just a geometric progression in reverse order with the first term a/r, the common ratio $1/r$, and n terms in the series.

With these values appropriately substituted into equation (8.19) of section 8.3.3, then:

$$P = \frac{\left(\frac{a}{r}\right)\left[\left(\frac{1}{r}\right)^n - 1\right]}{\left[\left(\frac{1}{r}\right) - 1\right]}$$

which simplifies to:

$$P = \frac{a(r^n - 1)}{r^n(r - 1)} \tag{8.20}$$

For the example in question $a = 100$, $r = 1.08$ and $n = 10$. The cost of the annuity is thus:

$$P = \frac{100(1.08^{10} - 1)}{1.08^{10}(1.08 - 1)}$$

Using logarithms, P is found to be £671 approximately.

Example 2

A company borrows £20,000 over three years. Repayments are to be made at the end of each of the years. Determine the amount of each payment allowing for compound interest at $12\frac{1}{2}$ per cent.

This situation is the inverse of that above. Here, the amount of the loan is simply the present value of the annuity. Thus, re-arranging the formula given by equation (8.20):

$$a = \frac{Pr^n(r - 1)}{(r^n - 1)} \tag{8.21}$$

and a is the annual repayment on the loan.

Substituting P = 20,000, r = 1.125, n = 3 into equation (8.21) gives:

$$a = \frac{20,000 \times 1.125^3(1.125 - 1)}{(1.125^3 - 1)}$$

$$= 8,398.62$$

Check

		20,000
+ $12\frac{1}{2}$%		2,500
		22,500
1st repayment		8,398.62
		14,101.38
+ $12\frac{1}{2}$%		1,762.67
		15,864.05
2nd repayment		8,398.62
		7,465.43
+ $12\frac{1}{2}$%		933.18
		8,398.61
3rd repayment		8,398.62

1p over (due to rounding error)

A mortgage loan is considered in this way, except that normally the calculations are made on a monthly rather than a yearly basis.

The concept of 'future values' and 'present values' is an important one which we will see taken up in the final chapter.

CHAPTER 9

Operational research in business

9.1 Introduction

The quantitative methods discussed earlier in the book covered some basic statistical and mathematical techniques together with an introduction to 'modelling' as a problem-solving approach. These techniques were really quite straightforward. This was seen to be so as it became relatively easy to draw informed conclusions following their application, and they do have widespread use. However, in the present day, there are many business operations where more complex problems arise which cannot be solved by those simple and unsophisticated methods.

The emergence of such complex problems first became apparent during the Second World War (1939–1945) with the vast organisation necessary to plan and co-ordinate the many operations required at that time. Consequently, new techniques had to be developed in order to begin to analyse the complexity created by many interdependent activities and, out of it all, the term *operational research* was born.

Over the following decades, a host of such techniques have been developed to the extent that their application is playing an increasingly important role across all areas of organisations. To state what operational research is and does, is not easy, as OR, as it is commonly known, comprises several scientific disciplines. In fact, investigating more widely, the reader will find many written variations for the term. A suitable concise definition is:

> 'OR is the application of scientific methods to complex problems arising from the management of resources in organisations.'

One implication of this definition, or any other, is that Operational Research is playing an important role in the evolution of computerised systems for 'Decision Support'. The purpose of a decision support system is to provide decision support for management. To this end the approach widely taken is first to develop a scientific model describing the system, that is the complex problem under consideration. OR techniques are then used to determine the unknown characteristics of the system from which sound decisions can be made.

These days, such is the range of applications analysed using OR techniques that many large organisations have special departments containing trained personnel in this one area. Further, their widespread use is indicative of the need for any business manager, in a large or small organisation, to have a good insight into some of the techniques. This chapter will provide some of this insight.

9.2 Introduction to linear programming

In a business environment decision-making is often constrained in some way. The cash flow situation within an organisation can restrict the scope of a development programme. The nutritional and protein requirements of certain foodstuffs can dictate the allowable ways in which the raw materials can be mixed to obtain a desirable, and edible, end product.

These are vastly different situations but there is a common denominator between them: that they each must satisfy a number of constraints. On the one hand the first organisation will want to maximise its return from the development programme, whereas the second organisation will want to minimise its costs in the production of its foodstuffs. The process by which a business manager specifies decision variables to maximise or minimise something is called *optimisation*.

There is a vast range of business problems that match this type of application in which the *objective* is to seek an *optimal solution*. The problems that arise can vary enormously in their complexity with different problems requiring different solution approaches. The general term for the set of techniques used to solve this type of problem is *mathematical programming*. *Linear programming* is the simplest, and also the most widely used of these. The initial sections of this chapter introduce the reader to the basic concepts of linear programming.

First, a simple and straightforward problem is considered in order that the reader is able to follow and easily understand the approach taken to arrive at the desired optimal solution. The example identifies the basic concepts and illustrates a consistent technique for the solution of similar problems.

Example 1

Anyshire County Council Planning Department has been asked to determine how much the County Council should invest in two development projects. The recommendation is to be based on the following information.

The maximum outlay allowed for Project 1 is £110,000 and for Project 2 is £140,000. Expected yearly benefits to the County Council for each project as a percentage of capital outlay are estimated as 10 per cent for Project 1 and 5 per cent for Project 2. Total investment on both projects is restricted to £200,000, and there is the further proviso that at least 40 per cent of this total is invested in Project 2.

Model formulation
A more concise written statement of the problem is:

Maximise expected yearly benefit : $0.10 \times$ (amount invested in Project 1) $+ 0.05 \times$ (amount invested in Project 2), subject to:

(1) Amount invested in Project 1 $\leqslant$ £110,000
(2) Amount invested in Project 2 $\leqslant$ £140,000
(3) Total of amount invested in Project 1 plus amount invested in Project 2 $\leqslant$ £200,000
(4) Amount invested in Project 2 $\geqslant$ 0.4 (total amount invested).

Let us denote:

f = expected yearly benefit
x_1 = amount invested in Project 1
x_2 = amount invested in Project 2

These definitions are convenient as they allow us to translate the 'concise written statement' into a mathematical business model format, namely:

Maximise $f = 0.10x_1 + 0.05x_2$
subject to:
(1) $x_1 \leqslant 110,000$
(2) $x_2 \leqslant 140,000$
(3) $x_1 + x_2 \leqslant 200,000$
(4) $x_2 \geqslant 0.40 (x_1 + x_2)$

This mathematical model as it stands is a true representation of the problem. It is not, though, in 'standard' form. This is only achieved by having all the variables on the left-hand side of the constraint sign and a constant on the right-hand side. Constraint (4) thus needs amending. Algebraic manipulation converts this constraint to its required form:

$$-0.40x_1 + 0.60x_2 \geqslant 0$$

The above business model is now expressed as a 'consistent' linear programming model by:

Maximise $f = 0.10x_1 + 0.05x_2$
subject to:
(1) $x_1 \leqslant 110,000$
(2) $x_2 \leqslant 140,000$
(3) $x_1 + x_2 \leqslant 200,000$
(4) $-0.40x_1 + 0.60x_2 \geqslant 0$

where f is termed the *objective function* of the model, and x_1, x_2 are its *decision variables*.

'Consistency' is achieved in that linear programming models are formulated by a set sequence of activities. These are:

(1) Identify the objective function
(2) Identify the decision variables
(3) Write concise statements for the objective function and constraints
(4) Define notation
(5) Translate the concise written statement into a mathematical format
(6) Amend, if necessary, this mathematical model in order that it conforms with the standard linear programming format.

MODEL SOLUTION
Linear programming models with just two decision variables are conveniently solved using a graphical approach. First, each constraint is taken in turn and re-written ignoring their inequality signs. This gives:

(1) $x_1 = 110,000$
(2) $x_2 = 140,000$
(3) $x_1 + x_2 = 200,000$
(4) $-0.40x_1 + 0.60x_2 = 0$.

Lines are then drawn on the same graph representing each of these equations. These are shown in Figure 9.1.

The next stage is to determine the region on the graph which constitutes *feasible* solutions to the problem. It is readily seen that this region is the

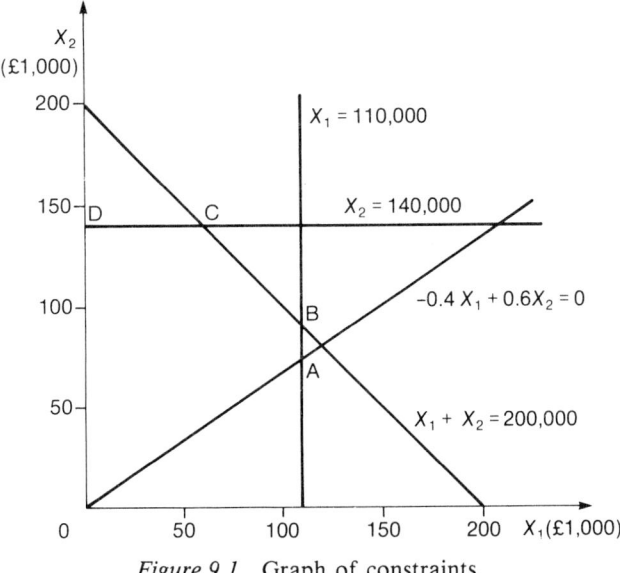

Figure 9.1 Graph of constraints

area whose boundary is defined by the points OABCD. Within this region, all the constraints apply. The reader can easily check this by choosing one point within this region, say $x_1 = 50$, $x_2 = 100$, and testing the actual constraints (including their inequality signs) one at a time.

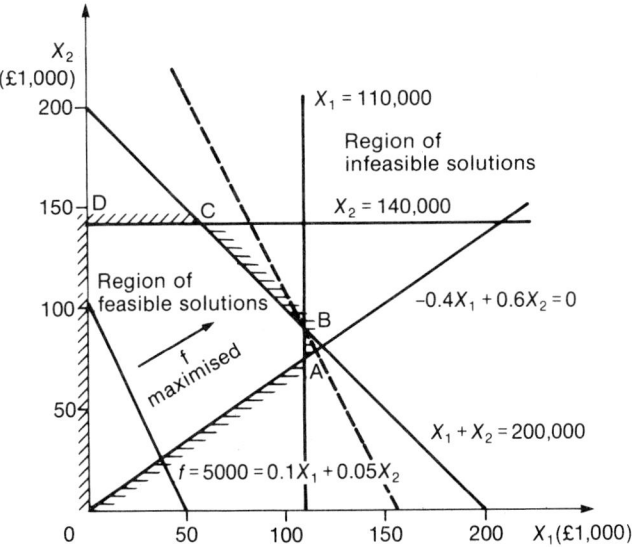

Figure 9.2 Identification of optimal solution

In order to obtain the *optimal* solution to the problem the objective function, f, is given some value, say 5,000, and the resulting equation:

$$5,000 = 0.10x_1 + 0.05x_2 \qquad (9.1)$$

is superimposed onto the 'constraints' graph.

The requirement is to maximise the objective function, f. As f takes different values, the equation of the line representing the objective function moves in parallel to that of equation (9.1). The position of this line, with f as large as possible within the region of feasible solutions, is shown in dotted form in Figure 9.2. The value of f in this case, $f = 15,500$, thus represents the optimal solution to the problem. The corresponding values of the decision variables are $x_1 = £110,000$ and $x_2 = £90,000$.

It is seen that an optimal solution will be located at an extreme point on a graph (here point B). The values of the decision variables giving the optimal solution are then determined from the equations of the lines intersecting at the extreme point.

9.3 The generalised linear programming model

The graphical method of solving a linear programming model is clearly only practicable in cases where there are only two decision variables. For cases where there are three or more a different technique is necessary. The technique, called the *simplex method*, is based on an extension of the graphical approach. However, because the calculations required are so complex, the optimal solution is invariably found by computerising the model using a software program for the method. This aspect is considered more closely later. First, let us consider the structure of the model in a generalised form.

9.3.1 Formulation of the model

The formulation is given in general terms as follows.

Maximise the objective function given by:

$$f = c_1x_1 + c_2x_2 + \cdots + c_nx_n$$

subject to the m constraints:

$$a_{11}x_1 + a_{12}x_2 + \cdots + a_{1n}x_n \leqslant b_1$$
$$a_{21}x_1 + a_{22}x_2 + \cdots + a_{2n}x_n \leqslant b_2$$
$$\vdots \qquad \qquad \vdots \qquad \vdots$$
$$a_{m1}x_1 + a_{m2}x_2 + \cdots + a_{mn}x_n \leqslant b_m$$

where the decision variables, $x_1, x_2 \cdots x_n$, are all greater than or equal to zero, that is:

$$x_1 \geqslant 0$$
$$x_2 \geqslant 0$$
$$\vdots \quad \vdots$$
$$x_n \geqslant 0$$

The values $a_{11} \ldots a_{mn}$, $b_1 \ldots b_m$ and $c_1 \ldots c_n$ are the sets of constants pertaining to the particular problem.

Any problem which can be set up in this manner formulates a linear programming model, which can be solved using the simplex method. This model formulation *must* be presented in a way that satisfies these three conditions:

(1) The objective function, f, is to be *maximised*
(2) Every constraint is of the same, less than or equal to ($\leqslant$) type
(3) The decision variables, $x_1 \ldots x_n$, are all *positive*

The reader will recall that in Example 1 of the previous section one of the constraints, constraint (4), was re-arranged in order to get the decision variables x_1 and x_2 onto the left-hand side of the inequality sign to become $-0.40x_1 + 0.60x_2 \geqslant 0$. This move was alright as far as it allowed us to draw the appropriate line on the 'constraints' graph. However, as it stands it fails to satisfy condition (2) above. In order for the model to become acceptable for solution by the simplex method this constraint must be further amended to change the $\geqslant$ sign to a $\leqslant$ sign. This is achieved by negating the left-hand side at the same time as changing the sign. The acceptable form for that constraint (4) is thus

$$+ 0.40x_1 - 0.60x_2 \leqslant 0.$$

Also, an objective function, f, which is to be minimised can be similarly converted to an objective function which is to be maximised. This is done by negating the terms in the original objective function f to obtain a new expression.

The above three conditions are restrictions implicit to the model for solution by the simplex method. Models that do not satisfy all the conditions in their original form must be converted into equivalent models by such manipulations as are necessary. Any solution for a converted model then becomes the solution for the original model.

9.3.2 Solution of the model by computer

The simplex method itself is well documented in most specialist books on operational research and is beyond the scope of this text. Indeed, most

```
PROBLEM DATA
MAX       0.1 X1 + 0.05 X2  (maximise the objective function)
SUBJECT TO
   2)      X1 <=   110000         (list of
   3)      X2 <=   140000          constraints)
   4)      X1 +  X2 <=   200000
   5)      0.4 X1 - 0.6 X2 <=    0


PROBLEM SOLUTION

         OBJECTIVE FUNCTION VALUE

   1)         15500.0000

VARIABLE            VALUE          REDUCED COST
   X1          110000.000000        0.000000
   X2           90000.000000        0.000000


ROW                 SLACK          DUAL PRICES
   2)              0.000000         0.050000
   3)          50000.000000         0.000000
   4)              0.000000         0.050000
   5)          10000.000000         0.000000
```

Figure 9.3   Typical problem data and solution formats

worthwhile computing installations will have at least one proven software linear programming package available to its users. It is then simply necessary to input the data to the computer in some predetermined order and form. The data will be those values found in the model formulation.

A good design philosophy for a linear programming package is that its documentation and use should be straightforward for the user with a simple problem as well as providing the capability of solving large real industrial problems. As an illustration, a typical package is used to solve the problem of Example 1 from the previous section. Figure 9.3 shows the problem data in the form required by the package together with the optimal solution.

As can be seen from Figure 9.3 the output from a linear programming package may also give other results relating to the problem formulation.

Reduced costs

It may be that a decision variable has a zero value in the optimal solution, that is it does not contribute towards maximising the objective function. A reduced cost is the decrease in the objective function value due to introducing one unit of that decision variable.

Slack variables

Slack variables represent unused quantities of the decision variables. The output from the above example indicates the amount of 'slack' there is in each of the constraints.

Dual prices

The right-hand side constants in each of the constraints are binding to a problem as presented. The dual price associated with a constraint is the increase in the objective function value due to a unit increase in the right-hand side constant, assuming the same implied cost for that unit. 'Dual prices' are often referred to as 'shadow prices' or 'shadow costs'.

Many linear programming packages also include a 'sensitivity analysis' facility. Such a facility will provide a fuller analysis of the implications of possible changes to model formulations.

9.4 Business applications of linear programming

Solving a linear programming problem by computer means that the results from quite complex problems can be found virtually as easily and quickly as they can from relatively simple problems. Thus, it is the model formulation that is really the crux of the solution to a linear programming model. A business manager faced with a particular problem may be able to call upon a specialist adviser from within the organisation to help with the model formulation. Whether this is so or not, the business manager should still be able to make certain assessments pertaining to the problem. First, it should be possible to recognise the type of problem that can be solved using linear programming techniques. It should also be possible to state the problem in a form from which the model can be formulated, even if a specialist is involved with any development work. Lastly, the manager should have sufficient skill to be able to assess whether or not the model so formulated is actually representative of the problem in question.

9.4.1 Resource allocation problems

The range of applications of linear programming and other mathematical programming techniques is now very large. Accordingly, it is impossible to list more than a handful. Many, however, while they may arise from totally different application areas, are similar in their nature. This broad group of problems is concerned with some kind of *resource allocation*. In fact, most of the problems which can be solved by linear programming techniques are concerned with determining the best allocation of available resources, whether these resources be money, equipment or manpower. Example 1 was typical of a resource allocation problem — what was required was the best allocation of available investment resources where the amount of the resources was limited, that is constrained. Generally, any real investment appraisal will be subject to decisions constrained in some way. This being the case, then linear programming will play a vital role in the appraisal. Other common financial applications of linear programming are in the budget planning and break-even analysis areas of accounting.

Machine-allocation problems are often solved using linear programming techniques, typically when different machines are used to manufacture a number of different products. The machines may have different running costs associated with them. Some machines may be faster than others requiring less time for the same process. Production of the different products will require different combinations of processes and hence machines. What is the best use of the machines available? How many units of each product should be manufactured in order to maximise profit? These answers are easily found by formulating the problem into the standard linear programming model.

Another group of resource allocation problems is concerned with the identification of the best mix or blend of items for different products. In product-mix problems the component items are mixed together to form the marketable products. Each product is constrained to meet certain specifications, say a maximum of one item and a minimum of another. These specifications along with other relevant information form the constraints. A product-mix plan maximising total revenue is then only acceptable if it doesn't violate any of the resource constraints. Hence it is a linear programming problem.

Many private sector organisations are applying linear programming techniques in order that they can decide on appropriate strategies for the marketing of their products. The interaction of packaging, promotion and price factors of a product is clearly one of business experience and market insight. There will, however, be restrictions set that are out of the control of the marketing manager responsible for recommending a strategy. For example, the ceiling defining the availability of funds or the need to more than match the prices of a competitor. Given such constraints the marketing manager has then to allocate the amount to be spent on each of packaging, promotion and price as well as on product development. With proper model formulation linear programming techniques have been found to provide valuable assistance in this respect.

Another aspect of marketing as it applies to public sector planning is shown in the following example.

Example 2

Anyshire County Council is planning a new industrial estate in a recently designated development zone. It is to contain large, medium and small sized standard work units measuring 25,000 sq. ft, 5,000 sq. ft and 1,000 sq. ft respectively. It is vital to attract purchasers to the large and medium sized units as in turn they will attract small business to the small sized units. So annual rates have been set at £100,000, £25,000 and £10,000 respectively. The total area of the development zone is two hundred thousand square feet. The guidelines for a suitable blend of different sized work units within the development zone are:

- At least two large units
- Between two and four medium units for every large unit
- The combined total area taken up by the small and medium units must be less than the total area taken up by the large units.

Model formulation
As before, we first express the problem as a concise written statement, namely:

Maximise total annual rent = £100,000 × (number of large units) + £25,000 × (number of medium units) + £10,000 × (number of small units), subject to:

(1) Total area of large units + total area of medium units + total area of small units ≤ 2,000,000
(2) Number of large units ≥ 2
(3) Number of medium units ≥ 2 × (number of large units)
(4) Number of medium units ≤ 4 × (number of large units)
(5) Total area of small units + total area of medium units ≤ total area of large units

Let us denote:

f = Total annual rent (objective function)
x_1 = Number of large units
x_2 = Number of medium units
x_3 = Number of small units

The model becomes:

Maximise $f = 100,000x_1 + 25,000x_2 + 10,000x_3$
subject to:
(1) $25,000x_1 + 5,000x_2 + 1,000x_3 < 200,000$
(2) $x_1 \geq 2$ or $-x_1 \leq -2$
(3) $x_2 \geq 2x_1$ or $2x_1 - x_2 \leq 0$
(4) $x_2 \leq 4x_1$ or $-4x_1 + x_2 \leq 0$
(5) $1,000x_3 + 5,000x_2 \leq 25,000x_1$
     or $-25,000x_1 + 5,000x_2 + 1,000x_3 \leq 0$

MODEL SOLUTION

Figure 9.4 shows the computer printout of the solution obtained using a linear programming software package.

Luckily, the results for x_1, x_2 and x_3 do turn out to be whole numbers which the problem expects. Clearly, in general linear programming problems the optimal solution is arrived at by assuming that the decision variable values are infinitely divisible. If this is not the case, as clearly it can't be here, then either the solution needs to be adjusted accordingly or more special *integer programming* techniques are required.

```
MAX          100000 X1 +  25000 X2 +  10000 X3
SUBJECT  TO
    2)        25000 X1 +   5000 X2 +   1000 X3  <=      200000
    3)    -   X1  <=  -  2
    4)       2 X1  -    X2  <=     0
    5)    -  4 X1  +    X2  <=     0
    6)    -  25000 X1 +   5000 X2 +   1000 X3  <=      0
END


        LP  OPTIMUM  FOUND   AT  STEP       4

            OBJECTIVE  FUNCTION  VALUE

    1)          1200000.00

    VARIABLE          VALUE           REDUCED  COST
      X1           4.000000            0.000000
      X2           8.000000            0.000000
      X3          60.000000            0.000000


    ROW               SLACK           DUAL  PRICES
      2)           0.000000            6.000000
      3)           2.000000            0.000000
      4)           0.000000        25000.000000
      5)           8.000000            0.000000
      6)           0.000000            4.000000

    NO.  ITERATIONS=      4
```

Figure 9.4 Solution to Example 1

9.4.2 Transportation and assignment problems

This double category of problems again is quite commonly encountered in business. Such problems can, of course, be formulated as linear programming models and solved appropriately by computer. However, there is a quicker computational method of solution available than the general simplex method. So, if a problem is recognised as falling into one of these categories it should be formulated as such.

However, as, these days, it is likely that the potential user will want to apply a software package to the problem, the categorisation into a transportation or assignment problem is only necessary if separate packages are available at the computer installation. Otherwise, the model can be formulated as normal and the computer can be left to do the work. Therefore, we will only briefly describe the nature of transportation problems.

The essence of a *transportation problem* is one of determining the best way to transport items from a number of despatch points, or sources, to a number of destinations. Transportation problems display the following characteristics:

(1) The objective is to minimise the total cost or total time required to transport items from sources to destinations
(2) Items can be sent from any source to any destination
(3) The total amount of items available at the sources equals the total amount of items required at the destinations

In some applications clearly there could be a larger total amount of items available at the sources than is required at the destinations. To take this situation into account it is then necessary to introduce a fictitious or dummy destination in order that the problem can still be formulated as a true transportation model. The dummy destination is created to receive the number of items which is the difference between the total amount available and the total amount required. To satisfy the data requirements of the model, the unit cost of transporting goods from any source to the dummy destination is designated as zero. On finding the optimal solution the items to be transported to a dummy destination are summarily ignored.

An *assignment problem* is a special form of transportation problem. Its characteristics are:

(1) The number of sources is equal to the number of destinations
(2) There is only one item available at each source
(3) There is only one item required at each destination.

Computationally, assignment problems are much easier to solve than the more generalised transportation problem, especially when there are only a few sources and destinations. That of 'job allocation' is an assignment problem common to many business activities. Example 3 is such a problem that serves to illustrate the approach to be taken with assignment problems.

Example 3

Anyshire County Council's Data Processing Department has four computer programmers who could be assigned to write four different but urgently required computer programs. On analysing the results from previous similar programs, the estimated number of errors that each programmer is

Table 9.1 Estimated number of program errors

	Program type			
	A	B	C	D
Programmer 1	9	13	8	4
Programmer 2	6	12	8	7
Programmer 3	11	21	12	9
Programmer 4	2	5	9	4

likely to make on each type of program is given in Table 9.1. How should the programmers be assigned to the different programs in order that the number of errors is minimised?

SOLUTION

Step 1
Subtract the smallest value in each row from every value in the same row. This reduces Table 9.1 to:

	A	B	C	D
1	5	9	4	0
2	0	6	2	1
3	2	12	3	0
4	0	3	7	2

Step 2
Subtract the smallest value in each column from every value in the same column. This further reduces the table to:

	A	B	C	D
1	5	6	2	0
2	0	3	0	1
3	2	9	1	0
4	0	0	5	2

Using this data we are able to reach the same conclusions concerning optimal solutions.

Step 3
Test whether it is possible to make an assignment using only zero values in the table. This is done by drawing on the table the minimal number of lines through each row and/or column to cover every zero value. The table becomes:

	A	B	C	D
1	5	6	2	0̸
2	0̶	3̶	0̶	1̶
3	2	9	1	0̸
4	0̶	0̶	5̶	2̶

If, in the resulting table, the number of these lines equals the number of assignments to be made then an optimal solution is possible. Only three lines are needed here to cover all the zeros, thus the optimal solution has not yet been reached.

Step 4
Take the value of the smallest uncovered element in the table and:

(1) Subtract it from all uncovered element values
(2) Add it to the element values at the intersection of two lines

leaving all the other element values unchanged. The table now reduces to:

	A	B	C	D
1	4	5	1	0
2	0	3	0	2
3	1	8	0	0
4	0	0	5	3

Steps 3 and 4 are re-applied until an optimal solution is possible. Applying Step 3, we re-draw the minimal number of times to cover all the zeros in the table. The table becomes:

	A	B	C	D
1	4	5	1	0
2	0	3	0	2
3	1	8	0	0
4	0	0	5	3

Whichever way the lines are drawn, the zeros in the table cannot be covered by less than four lines. Hence, we can ascertain an optimal solution as the number of lines now equals the number of assignments to be made. An optimal solution is determined by selecting one zero in each column (row) so that no two selected zeros are in the same row (column). The ringed zeros in the following table show this optimal solution:

	A	B	C	D
1	4	5	1	(0)
2	(0)	3	0	2
3	1	8	(0)	0
4	0	(0)	5	3

Thus the optimal assignments are:

Programmer 1 to program D
Programmer 2 to program A
Programmer 3 to program C
Programmer 4 to program B

In this particular example there is only one optimal solution. In other examples there may well be more than one optimal solution possible.

9.5 Project planning and network models

The examples seen so far in this chapter have been concerned with aspects of project planning, and were problems that could be formulated as linear programming models. The remainder of the chapter is more directly concerned with the methods by which complex project scheduling operations are monitored and controlled, that is methods used in the management of projects. The analysis of *network models* has been found to be a powerful tool in this respect.

As implied above, there is an area of overlap, as some linear programming problems can be expressed by a network structure. For example, transportation networks are familiar to us all. The solution to this type of problem is, in fact, often aided by initially analysing the problem as a network from which the linear programming model can be directly formulated. On the other hand, some linear programming can be solved more easily by network analysis techniques rather than having to resort to the generalised linear programming solution.

The form the approach to the solution should take will depend on the objective to be achieved. The nature of the objective will give rise to particular characteristics within the network structure associated with the problem. The network type can then be categorised and a decision made whether the problem is best solved using linear programming or network analysis.

The following sub-section on network models describes the basic terms that relate to the structure of a network, identifies categories for different types of problem, and considers how project activities are represented in a network model. Section 9.6 discusses a network analysis technique in common usage that is used to solve project planning problems, namely the critical path method.

9.5.1 Network models

A *network* is a graphical structure consisting of *nodes* and *arcs*. The arcs connect up the nodes. Each node can be connected with one or more of the other nodes. Figure 9.5 shows a simple network. The circles, with the numbers inside, represent the different nodes. The arcs are the lines connecting the circled numbers, that is the nodes.

Directed networks

In many networks, including, as we shall see, those resulting from an analysis of a project's operations, the sequencing of the nodes in a network is significant, that is there is a direction associated with each arc in the

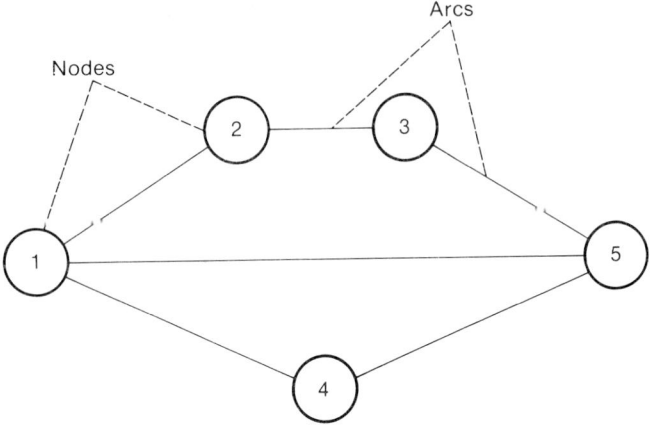

Figure 9.5 A network

network. As it stands, Figure 9.5 is unclear in this respect as the network does not indicate any direction between connected nodes. Is node 3 connected to node 2 because it follows on from it? If it does then the direction 2 to 3 is applied to the arc connecting these nodes. If this sequencing applies throughout then a directed network results. The directions in the sequencing are indicated by arrows as in Figure 9.6.

The node in a directed network which only has directed arcs emanating from it is termed a *source node* — node 1 in Figure 9.6. The node in a directed network which only has directed arcs coming into it is termed a *destination node* — node 5 in Figure 9.6.

A *path* of nodes through a directed network is a sequence of nodes passing along directed arcs from the source node through to the destination

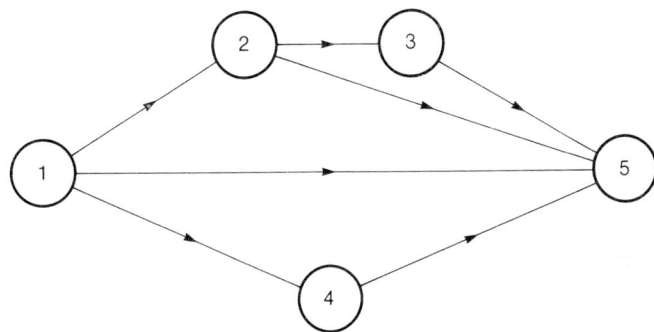

Figure 9.6 A directed network

node. In the directed network of Figure 9.6 such paths are:

- 1–2–3–5
- 1–2–5
- 1–5
- 1–4–5

This chapter is only concerned with problems that give rise to directed networks. Thus, hereafter, 'directed networks' will just be referred to as 'networks'. Also, because of the nature of the applications to be discussed, networks containing loops will be deemed invalid as loops appearing in project networks represent logical errors.

Types of network model

There are basically three categories of network model:

(1) Maximum flow models
(2) Shortest path models
(3) Activity models

(1) Maximum flow models
General maximum flow problems assume that a certain commodity flows into the network along directed arcs and out of the network at the destination node. A typical application is a network of pipelines carrying, say gas, water or oil. Each directed arc on the network represents a pipeline carrying the commodity in a set direction between two nodes. Each pipeline has a carrying capacity associated with it. The object would be to formulate a network model for maximising the total flow of the commodity from the source node through to the destination node.

Transportation and assignment problems also fit into this category. The structure of a transportation network is a series of sources, say production plants, linked directly to a series of destinations, say warehouses. Given information on the unit profit margins of items shipped from each production plant to each warehouse, taking into account the transportation costs, then the problem is how to maximise total profit.

(2) Shortest path models
Problems associated with these types of models are, as the term implies, concerned with finding the shortest path between two nodes in a network. Finding the shortest path between the source node and the destination node is just one special case of a shortest path problem. Other possibilities

include:

(*a*) the shortest path between any two nodes in the network
(*b*) the shortest path from one node to all the other nodes in the network.

A typical example of (*a*) is the need for a driver despatching goods to be informed of the shortest path between two towns in a road network. Optimising the location of a new plant is an example of (*b*). The network consists of roads, and associated distances, emanating from the new plant to, say, various distribution centres, the problem being to site the new plant in order to achieve the shortest path from one node, the plant, to all the other nodes in the network, the distribution centres.

(3) *Activity models*
A complex project consists of a number of interrelated activities. Some activities must be completed before others are embarked upon. Thus, overall, the project's activities must be performed in some specified sequence. This sequence must be carefully planned at the outset by the project manager in order to ensure that the work is completed within a pre-specified time or budget limit. The use of networks is important in the analysis of these activity type models.

An *activity* is defined as any part of a project that has a distinct beginning and a distinct end. An *event* is defined as the beginning or end of one or more activities. In a network the nodes depict the events and the arcs are the activities.

A *precedence relationship* indicates the activities that *must* be completed before a particular activity is begun. This is 'translated' to form a directed network whose structure simply represents the logical sequencing of the various project activities.

Suppose we have a precedence relationship for a project's activities set out as:

Activity	Immediate predecessor
A	None
B	None
C	A
D	A, B
E	C

The network representation of these precedence relationships is shown in Figure 9.7.

The precedence relationships are represented by arrows so producing a directed network. Activity C cannot start until A has been completed. Likewise activity E cannot start until C has been completed. Hence the

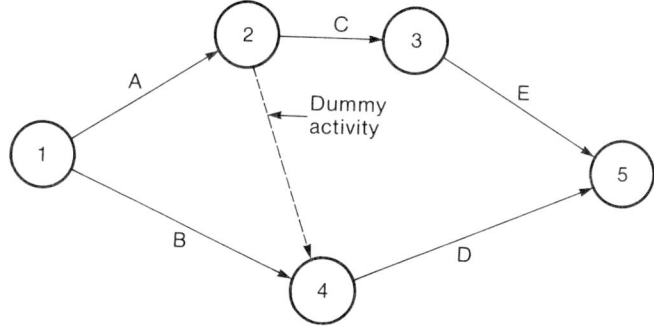

Figure 9.7   Example network

representation shown in the top part of Figure 9.7. Now, activity D cannot start until both activities A and B have been completed. In order to incorporate this precedence relationship in the network it is necessary to create a dummy activity so completing the network. As this network stands, there is no significance to the lengths of the arrows; activity D may not take up more time than activity E. Further, zero activity time is always associated with a dummy activity. The reader should also note that, as shown, activities are conventionally denoted by letters and events by numbers, the number for an event being greater than those of the events preceding it.

As we are primarily concerned with project planning we will henceforth concentrate on network analysis as applied to activity models only.

9.6 The critical path method

The critical path method (CPM) for network analysis is applicable to projects which display the following characteristics:

(1) The project can be sub-divided into a number of separately identifiable activities
(2) The time required for each activity can be given or estimated
(3) The precedence relationship for each activity is known

Generally, each activity is some combination of available manpower, equipment, raw materials and money. The combination of these resources for a particular activity results in a time estimate for that activity.

We have seen briefly already how the interrelated activities of a project can be represented graphically as a network. We now consider those aspects of network analysis which are important to an overall project schedule. This is done in the context of Example 4 that follows.

Example 4

Anyshire County Council, in conjunction with its own Data Processing Department, is planning to set up a new Microcomputer Business Information Unit. An in-town office block has been purchased and is to be converted into the Unit.

Preliminary project planning has identified a number of interrelated activities that necessarily need to be carried out before the Unit can become operational. These activities, their duration estimates and precedence relationships form a *project activity table* and are listed in Table 9.2.

Perform an appropriate network analysis on these activities.

Table 9.2 Project activity table

Activity	Description	Duration (in weeks)	Precedence relationships
A	Final negotiations	4	None
B	Order and await delivery of hardware/software/office equipment	10	A
C	Conversion work	12	A
D	Installation of equipment	3	B, C
E	Determine staff requirements	4	A
F	Recruit some existing DP staff	5	E
G	Send those existing staff on external courses for training	4	F
H	Recruit new staff	10	E
I	Train new staff on-site	4	H, G, D
J	Order and await delivery of office consumables	6	F
K	Prepare for opening of Unit	2	I, J

9.6.1 Network analysis

Networks can be analysed from one of three aspects, namely time, resources or cost. Clearly, the main planning objective of this example is to ascertain a date for the opening of the Unit. Accordingly, having set up the network model we will analyse it from the point of view of time. A time analysis provides information on:

(1) The minimum time in which the project can be completed
(2) The activities which must be completed on time if the project is to be completed in its minimum time — these are called *critical activities*
(3) The time amounts by which the non-critical activities can be delayed without affecting the minimum completion time

First of all, using the guidelines from the previous section, a network is

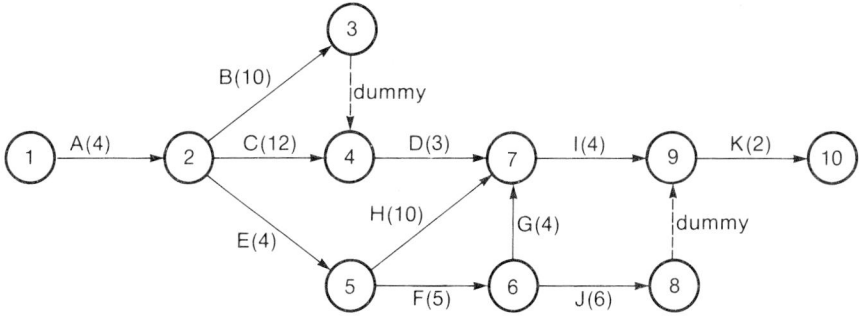

Figure 9.8   Activity network

drawn up from the project activity table (Table 9.2). Figure 9.8 shows the resulting network. The reader should verify the network against precedence relationships given in the project activity table. The notation used on the network should be self-explanatory, that is A(4) denotes that time duration of activity A is 4 weeks.

The network model is then analysed in stages.

Stage 1: Earliest event times

To be able to determine the minimum time in which the project can be completed we must examine every route through the network. Doing this enables us to find the earliest times for each event, or alternatively the earliest starting and finishing times for each activity. The rules to apply are:

(1) The earliest starting time of an activity is the earliest time by which all immediately preceding activities can be finished.
(2) The earliest finishing time of an activity is the earliest starting time for the activity plus the time needed to perform the activity.

On application of these rules, the earliest times for each event can be deduced.

First of all, it is assumed that activity A starts at zero time, that is week 0 is associated with event 1 as shown in the network. Activity A requires 4 weeks for completion thus the time associated with event 2 is week 4.

Activities B, C and E can start as soon as activity A is completed (event 2). Adding their times onto week 4 gives the earliest event times for events 3, 4 and 5 as weeks 14, 16 and 8 respectively. Note here, also, the dummy activity connecting events 3 and 4.

Activity F can start as soon as activity E is completed. Hence the earliest time for event 4 is 5 weeks + week 8 = week 13. Now, activity I cannot start until activities D, H and G are complete thus the earliest event time

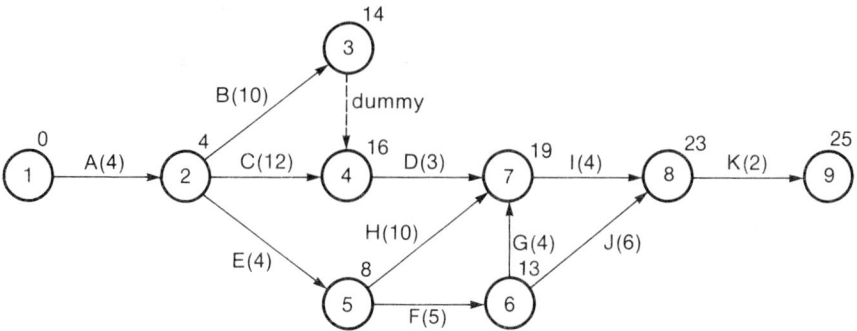

Figure 9.9   Activity network showing earliest event times

for event 7 needs to be considered more closely. The contributing factors to this time are (*i*) activity D added to earliest event 4 time, i.e. 3 weeks + week 16 = week 19, (*ii*) activity H added to earliest event 5 time, i.e. 10 weeks + week 8 = week 18, and (*iii*) activity G added to earliest event 6 time, i.e. 4 weeks + week 13 = week 17. The earliest event time for event 7 is then the greatest of these three times, namely week 19.

Activity J can start as soon as activity F is completed. Activity I can start at the earliest 4 weeks after week 19 (event 7). From this we see that the earliest event time for event 8 is week 23. Activity K can only start once activities I and J are completed. Thus, the time for activity K, 2 weeks, is added to the earliest event time of event 8, i.e. week 23 + 2 weeks = week 25. With activity K completed the earliest event time for event 9 is week 25.

All these earliest event times are added to Figure 9.8 and shown in Figure 9.9. The earliest event times for all nine events have now been identified. There is an additional outcome. The minimum time in which the project can be completed and the Unit open is established at 25 weeks, this being the earliest event time for the last event, event 9.

Stage 2: Latest event times

Completion deadlines are invariably associated with project schedules. This means that a project leader needs to know the latest possible time for starting or finishing an activity while still ensuring that the project deadline is met. Whereas the 'earliest event times' were found from a forward pass through the network, 'latest event times' are found with a backward pass. We refer again to our network.

The last activity K must be started at week 23 for the project to be completed by the deadline. The latest event time for event 8 is thus week 23. The latest event time for event 7 is event 8 latest time minus activity I time, i.e. week 23 − 4 weeks = week 19.

To obtain the latest event time for event 6 we consider the effect of

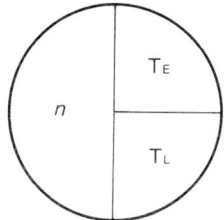

n   —   event number

T_E —   earliest event time

T_L —   latest event time

Figure 9.10   Notation for network analysis

activities G and J on the latest event times of events 7 and 8 respectively. The effect of activity G on the latest event time of event 7 is week $19 - 4$ weeks = week 15, and the effect of activity J on the latest event time of event 8 is week $23 - 6$ weeks = week 17. The smaller of these two times gives the latest event time of event 6, namely week 15.

Further, by adopting this argument the latest event time of event 5 is found to be week 9. The latest event time of event 4 is given by that of event 7 minus the duration of activity D, i.e. week $19 - 3$ weeks = week 16. This time must also apply to event 3 because of the inclusion of the dummy activity.

Adopting the previous argument now with the three activities B, C and

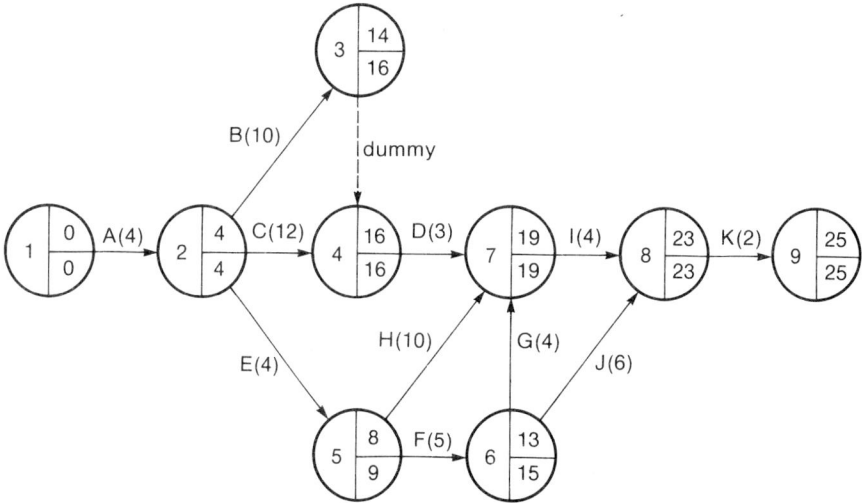

Figure 9.11   Activity network showing earliest and latest event times

E leading back to event 2 from events 3, 4 and 5 respectively, it can be seen that the latest event time of event 2 is week 4. Finally, returning to event 1, its earliest event time is obviously week 0.

It is convenient to combine these latest event times with the earliest event times onto one network diagram. This is done using the notation of Figure 9.10. Using this notation, our network is re-drawn as Figure 9.11.

9.6.2 Critical path

The information shown in the network in Figure 9.11 allows us to determine the critical activities of the project. These are the activities that are connected by events for which the earliest and latest event times are the same. These are shown to be events 1, 2, 4, 7, 8 and 9. The activities connected by these events hence define the *critical path* for the project. These critical activities must be completed on time to ensure that the project is completed in its minimum time. For activities not on the critical path, we observe that any unforeseen delays occurring in these activities may not adversely affect the overall project completion time. Clearly, however, there is a limit to any delay before it affects the overall time. This is analysed both in terms of events and activities.

The 'slack' time of an event is calculated as the difference between the latest and earliest event times. Clearly, the smaller this difference the more critical the event to the point where events on the critical path have zero slack. The slack times for our network are given in Table 9.3.

Activities are analysed by way of the time available to an activity in addition to its estimated duration time. There are two interpretations of this 'floating' time:

(1) Total float = Latest completion time – earliest start time – activity duration, that is the maximum increase in activity duration which is allowable without increasing the overall project time

Table 9.3

Event	Earliest event time	Latest event time	Event slack
1	0	0	0
2	4	4	0
3	14	16	2
4	16	16	0
5	8	9	1
6	13	15	2
7	19	19	0
8	23	23	0
9	25	25	0

Table 9.4

Activity	Duration (in weeks)	Start time Earliest	Start time Latest	Completion time Earliest	Completion time Latest	Total float	Free float
A	4	0	0	4	4	0	0
B	10	4	4	14	16	2	0
C	12	4	4	16	16	0	0
D	3	16	16	19	19	0	0
E	4	4	4	8	9	1	0
F	5	8	9	13	15	2	0
G	4	13	15	19	19	2	2
H	10	8	9	19	19	1	1
I	4	19	19	23	23	0	0
J	6	13	15	23	23	4	4
K	2	23	23	25	25	0	0

(2) Free float = Earliest time of next event – earliest time of preceding event – activity duration, that is the maximum increase in activity duration which is allowable without affecting the floats of following activities.

An analysis of each activity's float times for our network is given in Table 9.4. We note that the activities with zero total float are those on the critical path.

Network analysis also allows us to judge the effect should any of the activities not be completed according to their estimated duration. For instance, suppose in our example the recruitment of new staff, activity H, actually takes twelve weeks and not ten. Looking back to Figure 9.11, we see that the first effect of this change is to alter the earliest event time of event 7 from week 19 to week 20.

The follow-on effects of this change are twofold. One, the minimum time in which the project can be completed is increased by one week to 25 weeks. Two, there will be a new critical path. The reader should verify that the critical activities are now A, E, H, I and K connected by the events 1, 2, 5, 7, 8 and 9. This will also give rise to new earliest and latest event times throughout resulting in revised calculations for the event slack and activity float times.

The network analysis of Example 4 was only concerned with the *times* of the individual activities and events. Often a *resource* analysis on a network is necessary because, should a number of projects be running simultaneously, the same resources, equipment or manpower may be required by more than one project. In such cases, network analysis can be used to balance these resources across the various projects as well as within one project should the same resource be required by different activities.

A *cost* analysis would need to be carried out if the object was to try and minimise the total costs of the project. For instance, with workers doing overtime the overall time of a project could be reduced. But would the costs be reduced as well? The approach taken is similar to that described above, the resulting analysis simply being from a cost point of view.

9.6.3 Solution by computer

There should be available at most computer installations at least one software package which performs a critical path analysis on a network. Even a small package should allow, say, 50 + activities to be analysed; larger packages will allow for many more. There are even some micro-based packages catering for up to 2,500 activities. Packages will receive data in

```
DISPLAY CURRENT NETWORK
------------------------

ACTIVITY   DURATION   RESOURCE
I     J               REQMT.
  1     2      4          0
  2     3     10          0
  2     4     12          0
  4     7      3          0
  2     5      4          0
  5     6      5          0
  6     7      4          0
  5     7     10          0
  7     8      4          0
  6     8      6          0
  8     9      2          0
  3     4      0          0

END OF DISPLAY

                                  OPTION NO.? 6
SOLVE NETWORK & DISPLAY RESULTS
---------------------------------

PLEASE WAIT.....

***** ACTIVITY REPORT *****
ACTIVITY   DURATION   RESOURCE   EARLIEST   LATEST   TOTAL
I     J               REQMT.     START      FINISH   FLOAT
  1     2      4          0          0         4        0   CRITICAL PATH
  2     3     10          0          4        16        2
  2     4     12          0          4        16        0   CRITICAL PATH
  4     7      3          0         16        19        0   CRITICAL PATH
  2     5      4          0          4         9        1
  5     6      5          0          8        15        2
  6     7      4          0         13        19        2
  5     7     10          0          8        19        1
  7     8      4          0         19        23        0   CRITICAL PATH
  6     8      6          0         13        23        4
  8     9      2          0         23        25        0   CRITICAL PATH
  3     4      0          0         14        16        2
```

Figure 9.12 Computer results for Example 4

a set format, typically the preceding event number, the succeeding event number and the duration for each activity, plus resource requirements should they be part of the problem. As well as providing the solution analysis for a network an interactive package will allow a network to be modified and show the resulting effect. Also, most packages will provide a 'resource smoothing' facility whereby the analysis reschedules the activities it can (the non-critical ones) in order to produce a smoother or more level usage of resources.

A standard computer program has been used to analyse, by the critical path method, the network associated with Example 4 above. The printout of the results is shown in Figure 9.12.

Example 5

For the sake of interest we conclude this section on CPM with an example that includes resources (manpower) allocated to each of a project's activities. The same computer program is again used to analyse the data.

The project data is presented in the network format required by the computer program (see Figure 9.13). On running the program the network model is solved, the results displayed and output. These are shown in Figure 9.14.

The results can be used to show how the resources are distributed over the project's life-cycle. At this time, let us suppose that there is no worry concerning the overall availability of manpower and that each activity starts at its earliest start time. A simple twofold resource analysis is possible. First, the activity schedule is mapped out on what is known as a Gantt chart. Secondly, the total resources required over the project's life-cycle are represented in histogram form.

```
DISPLAY CURRENT NETWORK
--------------------------

ACTIVITY   DURATION   RESOURCE
I     J                REQMT.
1     2       2          4
2     3       1          2
2     4       2          2
2     5       2          2
3     6       3          2
3     8       4          2
4     6       1          3
4     8       2          2
5     7       2          3
6     8       2          4
7     8       4          2
8     9       2          4
```

Figure 9.13 Network for Example 5

SOLVE NETWORK & DISPLAY RESULTS

***** ACTIVITY REPORT *****

ACTIVITY		DURATION	RESOURCE REQMT.	EARLIEST START	LATEST FINISH	TOTAL FLOAT	
I	J						
1	2	2	4	0	2	0	CRITICAL PATH
2	3	1	2	2	5	2	
2	4	2	2	2	7	3	
2	5	2	2	2	4	0	CRITICAL PATH
3	6	3	2	3	8	2	
3	8	4	2	3	10	3	
4	6	1	3	4	8	3	
4	8	2	2	4	10	4	
5	7	2	3	4	6	0	CRITICAL PATH
6	8	2	4	6	10	2	
7	8	4	2	6	10	0	CRITICAL PATH
8	9	2	4	10	12	0	CRITICAL PATH

Figure 9.14   Computer results for Example 5

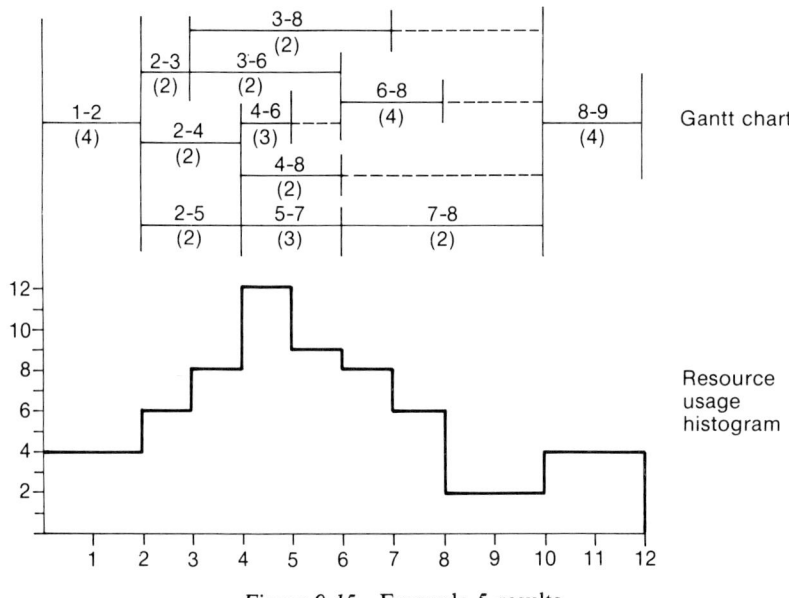

Figure 9.15   Example 5 results

To review the overall situation it is convenient to superimpose both aspects of this twofold analysis onto the same diagram. The effect is seen in Figure 9.15.

9.6.4   Resource smoothing

We look now to see if it is possible to re-schedule the activities in order to 'smooth' the resource usage across the life-cycle of the project. Our

```
***** ACTIVITY REPORT FOR  8 RESOURCES AVAILABLE *****
ACTIVITY   DURATION   RESOURCE   EARLIEST   ACTUAL   ACTUAL
I     J               REQMT.     START      START    FINISH
```

I	J	DURATION	RESOURCE REQMT.	EARLIEST START	ACTUAL START	ACTUAL FINISH	
1	2	2	4	0	0	2	**CRITICAL**
2	3	1	2	2	2	3	
2	4	2	2	2	2	4	
2	5	2	2	2	2	4	**CRITICAL**
3	6	3	2	3	3	6	
3	8	4	2	3	3	7	
4	6	1	3	4	7	8	**CRITICAL**
4	8	2	2	4	6	8	
5	7	2	3	4	4	6	**CRITICAL**
6	8	2	4	6	8	10	**CRITICAL**
7	8	4	2	6	6	10	**CRITICAL**
8	9	2	4	10	10	12	**CRITICAL**

Figure 9.16   Computer results for Example 5 with 'resource smoothing' (project deadline to be met)

computer program has a 'resource smoothing' facility. Using this option interactively the network analysis shows that the same project deadline could be met with a maximum of 8 resources available. The computer output is shown in Figure 9.16. The revised Gantt chart and histogram are shown in Figure 9.17. Gantt charts, as well as showing the network model in a different diagrammatic format, are also used to good effect as an aid to determine how well a project is going once it is in progress.

In some projects, the group of people engaged on the project work as a team. Only the team members have the responsibility of performing all the

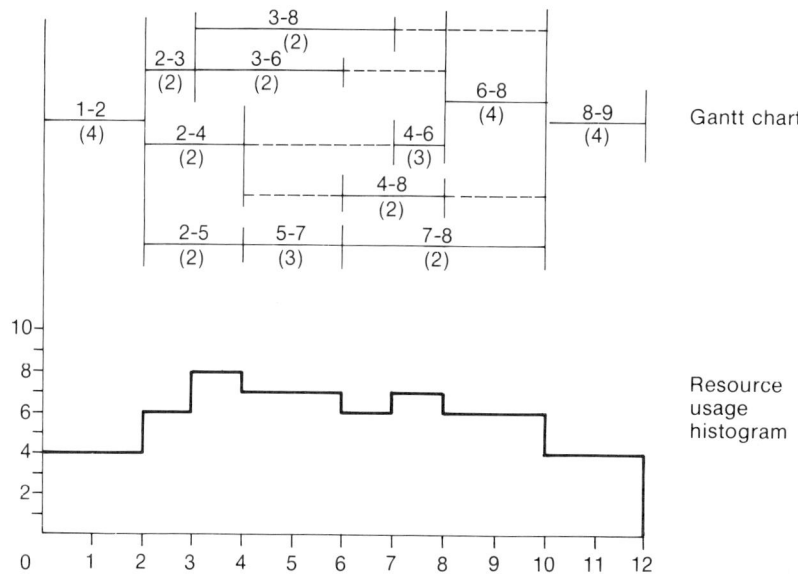

Figure 9.17   Example 5 results with 'resource smoothing'

```
***** ACTIVITY REPORT FOR   4 RESOURCES AVAILABLE *****
ACTIVITY   DURATION   RESOURCE   EARLIEST   ACTUAL   ACTUAL
I     J               REQMT.     START      START    FINISH
1     2        2         4          0          0        2    **CRITICAL**
2     3        1         2          2          2        3
2     4        2         2          2          4        6
2     5        2         2          2          2        4    **CRITICAL**
3     6        3         2          3          3        6
3     8        4         2          3          8       12    **CRITICAL**
4     6        1         3          4         12       13    **CRITICAL**
4     8        2         2          4         15       17    **CRITICAL**
5     7        2         3          4          6        8    **CRITICAL**
6     8        2         4          6         13       15    **CRITICAL**
7     8        4         2          6          8       12    **CRITICAL**
8     9        2         4         10         17       19    **CRITICAL**
```

Figure 9.18   Computer results for Example 5 with 'resource smoothing' (maximum of four resources available)

project's activities. Should this be the case the maximum resource (man-power) available at any one time will be the number of team members. Suppose that in Example 5 this number is four, because it has already been estimated (see Example 5 data) that the maximum resource requirement of any of the project's activities is four. We now need to re-analyse the network to determine a revised project life-cycle based on a maximum of 4 resources available at any time. The results are shown in Figure 9.18 and it is seen that, with this constraint, the minimum life-cycle of the project is 19 time units.

9.7 Summary

This chapter has given the reader an understanding of some of the operational research techniques that are commonly applied to business problems across many different functional areas in all types of organisation.

The basic techniques of linear programming have been covered even though the treatment has been brief. However, enough background information has been included to enable the formulation of simple models as well as the development, perhaps with specialist help, of more complicated models. On the assumption that solutions to linear programming models will be obtained using a computer software package only a brief description of the simplex method has been given.

Linear programming models are widely applied in business. Their most important use is in planning as they are particularly relevant to many types of problem in this area. As the reader gains experience in the use of linear programming models, he or she will naturally need to refer to a more comprehensive coverage of the whole subject.

The critical path method (CPM) for project planning is a very popular technique; it is widely used. One reason is certainly that the technique is relatively simple to understand. Business managers and project leaders are able to familiarise themselves with the techniques of network analysis without the need to become involved with any mathematical abstraction. Also, the procedures are such that they apply equally well to large projects as to small. Clearly, however, the analysis required for a large project is far from trivial even with a computer software package at hand.

Another advantage of CPM is that, once a network model has been constructed and initially analysed, the project leader can consider more closely those activities that have been found to be critical. This is important because the critical activities are the ones that allow no leeway if the project is to be completed on time. Furthermore, the actual construction of a network model for a project planning exercise may bring to light requirements that were at first overlooked.

CPM is a well accepted method for project planning as the information produced by a computerised network analysis provides the means for clear and concise documentation and for good communication of the plans to others.

It should be noted that the CPM network analysis as described in this chapter is based on the assumption that the time for each project activity is a constant, even though it was derived as an estimated value. In practice, some or all of the activity times may be uncertain quantities in that it may only be possible to estimate the time of an activity as lying within a range of values. A variation of CPM, the PERT method standing for *P*rogram (or *P*roject) *E*valuation and *R*eview *T*echnique, takes this uncertainty into account by treating the activity times as random variables. With CPM the most likely estimate of the time of each activity needs to be estimated. With PERT the most optimistic and most pessimistic estimates of activity time also need to be known. Accordingly, many available computer software packages incorporate PERT as well as CPM.

A CPM and/or PERT analysis of a project's activities provides information to a business manager in a useful and understandable manner. It is a form of management information system (MIS) which is 'operations-related'. One part of the system is time-oriented in that it describes in terms of a sequence of activities (or operations) how a project will be performed. The other part of the system is 'resource-orientated' in that it informs the business manager of the resources (manpower/cost) required to accomplish the project. Along with a network-based system there may be other MIS sub-systems, for example cost estimating and accounting. Such sub-systems will interrelate within the overall management information system.

CHAPTER 10

Selecting an information system for computer-based development

10.1 Introduction

The scenario which follows describes a major headache in the life of a data processing manager: how to resolve conflicting demands from users for services from limited resources?

So far in this book we have attempted to show a variety of ways by which we can develop more effective information systems. It is rather hard for the enthusiastic user, therefore, to discover that his need for such a system will be in competition with the needs from other departments and as such he may be assigned a low priority. Frequently, the result of this, as mentioned earlier in Chapter 2, is the development of stand-alone systems in the user departments which not only inhibit central integration throughout the organisation but often fail to address the information needs of the user as comprehensively as they might.

This chapter will explore the issues involved and develop a strategy for the selection, justification and subsequent evaluation of systems for computer-based development.

10.2 An example of the problem

MEMO

TO: J. Barnett, DP Manager, Anyshire County Council

FROM: G. Fall, Director, Administration, Polycollege, Anyshire

SUBJECT: Computerised student enrolment system

I understand that there has been yet again another delay in commencing work on our proposed computer enrolment system. It is now two years since we obtained executive approval for the development of the computer-based system to assist our administrative section in the complex annual task of student enrolments.

Since that time numerous delays have been incurred. First, a delay due to the lack of appropriate hardware facilities. These have, as you know, been acquired at considerable cost and have been available to run the system for over 12 months now.

Further delays have been blamed on the shortage of qualified data processing staff to develop the system but now when a project team has been assigned and the initial investigations, as I understand it, into our user needs are already completed I learn that the project has been dropped in favour of a management information system for the Treasurer's Department using some weird and wonderful new systems technology called 4GL?

I have been assured that this set-back is yet again a temporary delay and that the new systems technology can be used to advantage in our own systems development. After so many false starts, however, I believe we should have been given priority and I request a full explanation and justification for the decision that has been taken (without, I would remind you, any prior consultation with myself) and which has resulted in the abandonment of our system development in favour of the Treasurer's latest hobby horse.

MEMO

TO: J. Barnett, DP Manager, Anyshire County Council

FROM: A. Cauldwell, Chief Librarian, Anyshire Libraries

SUBJECT: Use of VIEWDATA facilities in the public libraries

The local viewdata facilities which you installed for us last year have attracted considerable interest from our patrons and a high level of use. There have been complaints, however, concerning the delay in response time which some of our major users estimate around 60 seconds at peak usage times.

I am sure you will appreciate that there is a highly limited concentration span when undertaking a search for general interest material and as such delays are particularly likely to de-motivate our users. This would be extremely unfortunate as we have attracted a far greater number of schoolchildren into the library with this innovative approach and I would hope that they would soon become committed patrons of our full facilities.

I am therefore writing to request the initiation of a project to enhance our present system. My understanding is that we should be able to achieve a minimum response time, in common with other such systems, of 25 seconds quite easily.

It would be useful if, on completion of this project, we could enter into further discussions regarding the computerisation of the library lending services.

MEMO

TO: J. Barnett, DP Manager, Anyshire County Council

FROM: Trevor Harris, Highways Dept

SUBJECT: Acquisition of database software for the national highways statistical survey analysis

As you will be aware, the Department of Transport and Industry (DTI) require us to complete a two year survey of every transportation route in the county in order to create a national database for use in all future road system planning and developments.

The DTI have made an offer to all highways departments to facilitate the collection of standard data. They are prepared to pay 50% of the cost of a database software package called RAPIDO produced by the software house INFOLOGIC if the authority will then guarantee to use this to store the collected data and to submit a copy to the DTI. The authority would then be allowed free use of the software once the DTI project is completed and can use it for all future in-house developments.

This is obviously too good an opportunity to miss and as such I need you to authorise early acquisition of the package so that we can start to train our people in the use of the system. My understanding is that the full cost of the package is around £40,000 but with discounts from the deal which DTI have negotiated for group purchase and the 50% subsidy we would have to pay only £15k at the most.

We would like work to begin on this as soon as possible so your URGENT attention is requested.

10.3 Strategic planning for information systems development

The memos addressed to J. Barnett are all requests for services which are independent of each other but which must be viewed as competitive demands for resources within the DP department. In order to assess realistically their relative values the department must agree to a method of evaluating each proposal and allocating priorities against the organisational objectives.

The issues to be resolved at strategic level are:

(1) Can this particular project be justified for computer-based systems development and, if so, to what extent does the information system provide additional value?
(2) Given limited resources and a number of viable but competing projects which projects should be selected for immediate development?
(3) What techniques are available which can be meaningfully used to quantify system benefits?
(4) What procedures should we use to cost system developments?
(5) How do we ensure that these methods result in the development of the most effective systems in the most effective manner?

The approach to providing a solution to these questions has changed significantly in recent years, mainly because of the increased emphasis on integrated systems and the development of management information systems to assist in strategic planning. With independent systems designed to replace operational level systems within the organisation, costs and benefits are normally easy to identify. Costs are related directly to the individual hardware and software requirements and to manpower costs based normally on a fairly structured development cycle. In cases where the computer resources were already available then a percentage cost for use of these facilities could be calculated from a standard unit cost per hour figure previously derived within the DP budget.

These costs were then set against benefits in the form of tangible cost savings such as:

● Replacement of clerical staff
● Decrease in stock holdings
● Reduction in shrinkage
● Improved cash flows resulting from faster billing procedures etc.

and occasionally in the form of cost avoidance, such as an increase in sales without the need to increase staff to cope with the additional volume of throughput.

The multi-programming, multi-processing environment of large mainframe computer systems makes projections of processing costs very difficult but the question of whether such costs can be determined at the level of sub-systems within an integrated systems development is even more complex. Undoubtedly there are synergistic benefits which accrue when several systems interrelate which cannot be quantified at individual levels. Moreover, the benefits of such integration are far more likely to be of the 'improved information' type which are much less easy to quantify and often lumped together as 'intangibles'. This is particularly true of systems which are primarily aimed towards strategic level planning within the organisation rather than the operational level.

Experience in forward thinking organisations has shown, however, that the resulting quantifiable effects of such 'intangibles' often greatly outweighs the effects of the more obvious 'tangible' benefits which were used originally to justify the systems development. This leads to the realisation that the wrong systems may be given the priority for development unless a formal approach can be applied to consider the full effects of a system implementation.

To return to the problem which now faces J. Barnett, however, a decision must be reached which will alleviate the problems in the short term but then serious thought must be given to the plan for the long term to ensure that conflicting demands can be resolved within the strategic objectives of the organisation and the agreed data processing policies of the department. Let us examine the short-term situation as it has been presented.

Three user departments require the use of DP resources, and all of them expect to be given immediate access to these facilities. It is obvious that to date there has been no strategic plan for computer-based systems development and, as a result, all of these proposals will require further investigation before any agreement can be reached in the short term. It is also likely that the demands will be found to be in conflict since it is apparent that there is a staff shortage problem, that there have been investments in specific hardware and software resources which may not be compatible, and that there is a set of users whose values are based on their own independent perceptions of needs.

The situation at Polycollege is one which has stemmed directly from the lack of a DP long-term plan and which has led to a complete lack of trust from the user who has already made considerable investment in facilities for future systems developments. It may well be the case that the proposed system could be developed far more efficiently and effectively using the new fourth generation software 4GL. It is also the case that the user is now so frustrated and de-motivated he may look elsewhere for his system needs. As a short-term solution J. Barnett should review the exact user needs against the project work and hardware acquisitions which have already taken place, and if the project still appears feasible then:

(1) Establish a user/DP project team to evaluate the development of the system using the new software as opposed to conventional methods
(2) Prepare a detailed schedule for systems development
(3) Agree the time-table with the user and implement this under strict control

He should also consider, however, the longer-term possibilities for systems development at Polycollege and the viability of the user becoming a systems developer in his own right. The 4GL may well be appropriate for end-users to build into systems and if so then an information centre approach could well be the solution. This will require:

(1) A feasibility study into future system needs
(2) A plan for development and if necessary future resource acquisition
(3) A detailed user training schedule in the use and application of the new software
(4) Re-organisation of the DP department to support an information centre facility.

In the case of the library system we have a situation where a current user expects priority to upgrade an existing system without any evidence of real need and without any quantified expectation of benefit. This illustrates one of the complicating factors in making a cost/benefit decision in that it requires close co-ordination between two disparate groups — the users, in this case the library, and the technicians, the communications and systems experts in the DP department. Users are in the best position to judge the value of information but have often no idea of the inherent cost of providing it. The cost may indeed greatly outweigh the estimate of worth placed on the enhanced information value by the user!

As a short-term measure J. Barnett needs to assign an analyst from his department to examine the feasibility of the request. Ideally this should be someone with a previous involvement in the viewdata system design and a good working relationship with the user. The brief should be:

(1) Examine the current usage of the viewdata system to establish whether there is a real need for an upgraded service.
(2) Evaluate whether an improved service can be provided by a re-scheduling of users on the library system, a re-scheduling of other computer system users and/or an enhancement of the existing software or hardware.

(3) Prepare a cost/benefit justification based on the users' evaluation of worth. This will persuade the user to identify acceptable response times for a certain percentage of transactions (95 per cent confidence level for example) and against these to identify the expected incremental benefits quantified in cost/value terms, for example releasing counter staff to other duties. This would then be matched against an estimate from the DP department as to the cost of meeting these requirements and they can then weigh the incremental costs against the incremental benefits and allow the user to decide whether he can afford to meet the costs of the improved service.

Typical results from this process are shown in Table 10.1. In this way the user could make a decision based on his own perceived view of the value of the enhancement.

In the longer term this approach will prove invaluable for a successful evaluation of future library system developments since it will help to clarify the decision on appropriate processing modes for the new system to adopt.

The case of the Highways Department request specifically highlights the need for a DP policy on compatibility requirements since the user in this case obviously does not realise the difficulties that may be encountered by buying a software package without performing a full evaluation first. There is a further complication, of course, that while the package seems good value there is no mention of maintenance costs or manufacturer support. Given that the department have just acquired a 4GL system it is also likely that they are already committed to a particular database and therefore would not wish to develop the INFOLOGIC system unless it was completely compatible — a most unlikely proposition!

Again there is an urgent need for an investigation into user needs which should include:

(1) A cost/benefit appraisal of the project

Table 10.1

Response time	Incremental benefit	Incremental cost	Net cost
25 seconds (95%)	£2,500	£5,000	£2,500
25 seconds (75%)	£2,000	£4,000	£2,000
30 seconds (75%)	£3,000	£3,500	£500
40 seconds (95%)	£1,500	£3,500	£2,000

(2) An evaluation of the package and its true operational costs
(3) A detailed proposal for the systems development including DP and user department training if required.

These short-term proposals are required because there has obviously been no long-term strategy for DP developments within the organisation and as such there are no criteria which can be used to evaluate system proposals. J. Barnett must now give priority to establishing a 3–5 year strategic plan and to formalising procedures for a cost/benefit analysis approach to the evaluation of system proposals. Once these have been accepted he can then implement a planned schedule of work based on organisational priorities and ensure that a continual monitoring and review process maintains both the time-scale for development and the standard of the final product.

The long-term plan should therefore include:

(1) A definition of the organisation's objectives and strategic plan and, in particular, the policies which should be adopted for the development of information systems within the organisation. This will require a detailed investigation into current and projected information needs to support the decision-making, planning and control functions and operational management of the organisation. The results will be a definition of the key results areas within the organisation which should be given priority for future systems developments.
(2) A definition of data processing policies with regard to projected:
  — Hardware
  — Software
  — DP development strategies and standards
  — Charge-out policies
  — Cost/benefit analysis techniques
  — Priority scheduling of projects
  — Monitoring, review and evaluation procedures
(3) A master development plan which will define specific system projects, rank these and match them against a scheduled time-scale. These projects could be identified by:
  — A review of on-going projects
  — A project set up to investigate the potential for new applications throughout the organisation.
  — Users
  — An evaluation of competitors' or similar organisations' systems (in this case other local authorities or government bodies such as health or water authorities, civil service, nationalised industries, etc.)
  — Discussions with hardware and software suppliers
(4) A complete cycle of planning which will include staged acquisition of:
  — Hardware

— Software
— Communications facilities
— Personnel
— Other resources

and which will be matched against the projected budgets for the department and proposed system developments.

(5) A proposal for DP budgeting policies and an evaluation system to review the impact of the strategic plan

The adoption of the long-term policy will not necessarily resolve all future conflicting proposals but it will act as a yardstick against which such proposals can be measured and against which the real information needs of the organisation can be assessed. It is essential, however, that the strategic plan resolve the issue of future project funding. Too often a DP budget is provided as a result of long-term planning and users then have to interface with the DP department as to how the budget should be spent. This can result in the project becoming an unsatisfactory compromise between the users' perceived ideals and the limited data processing resource capabilities. To ensure user involvement throughout the stages of the system development it is necessary for them to have a specific budget allocation to spend on their information systems project. In this way, the DP departmental budget will be purely for resource provision within that department and as projects are initiated additional funding will flow into the DP department in the form of resources specific to the project and payment for services and facilities for existing resources. Figure 10.1 illustrates this funding flow as

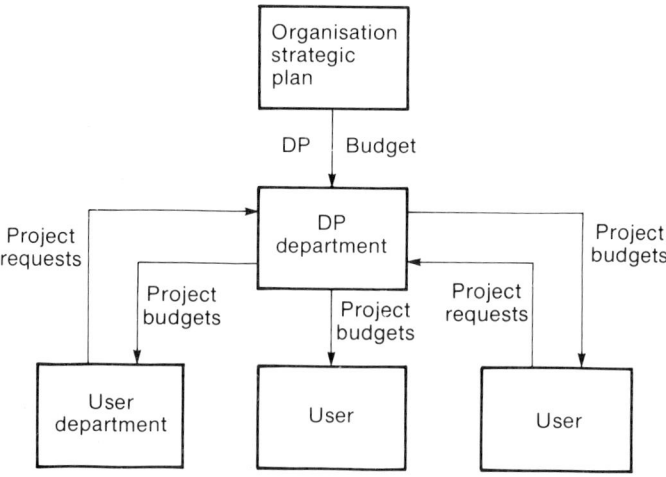

Figure 10.1 Funding flow

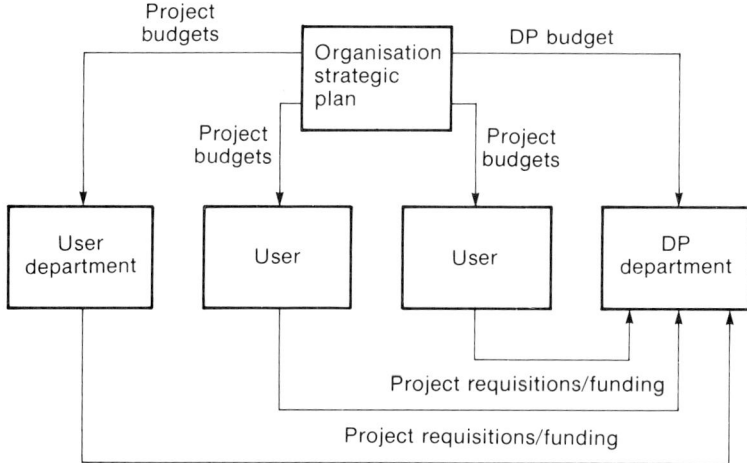

Figure 10.2   Traditional funding flow

opposed to the more traditional funding policy of Figure 10.2. The major difference is the enforced control that results as users pay for the particular services that are required and provided for.

10.4 Defining system benefits and costs

Previously in this chapter we have mentioned tangible and intangible benefits. These terms are normally used to reflect the degree of 'quantifiability' of the benefit. In other words, if we no longer need to employ 10 clerical staff at a cost of £7,000 each per annum then the tangible benefit is a saving to us of £70,000. If, however, we are able to provide management with faster information on which to base decisions we may feel unable to place a monetary value on the effect and so these benefits are declared 'intangible'. In fact, it is not only possible but absolutely essential to quantify these potential benefits since they may represent the true value of the system.

The first step then is to examine the categories into which potential benefits may fall.

10.4.1 Displaced costs (or cost reduction)

The application of these to justify DP systems gives rise to the 'computers replace people' argument which, of course, to some extent is extremely valid. These displaced costs normally occur when we replace operational systems.

10.4.2 Increased productivity (or cost avoidance)

These generally allow fewer people or machines to cope with a greater volume of work so that a projected increase in sales of 30 per cent normally requiring 20 more personnel to cope with the increased volume at a cost of £140,000 but now being processed by a computer system with an additional cost of only £15,000 represents a tangible cost avoidance of £125,000 per annum.

10.4.3 Improved information (or profit improvement)

These should relate directly to management projections of the effects on profit within the organisation given an improved level of information. If the new system can provide a detailed analysis of customer preference the organisation may be able to predict more accurately customer need and hence improve long-term sales. This may lead managers to predict a 50 per cent increase in sales orders' value over the next 3 years. If this represented an increased turnover of £1,000,000 at 15 per cent before tax profit the tangible profit improvement would be £150,000 over 3 years or £50,000 per annum.

It is possible then to quantify all the incremental benefits of a system and Table 10.2 provides a more detailed description of the possible categories in which the benefits may fall.

The costs of the system obviously relate to the actual development costs and also to the operational and maintenance costs for the projected life of the system. Generally, the categories into which these may fall are:

- Manpower
- Hardware
- Software
- Supplies
- Additionals

In addition to development, data capture and conversion (one-time) costs and operational and maintenance (on-going) costs, there may also be an actual cost incurred in displacing the existing system since, for example, equipment may be written off which still had a projected life with the organisation, or 'golden handshakes' may be provided to employees who are no longer required. A possible example of cost categories for the development phase is shown in Table 10.3.

Obviously, therefore, the financial justifications of the system will relate directly to the expected incremental savings derived from a subtraction of the projected costs from the projected benefits. The fact that a system does

Table 10.2 Potential benefits — categories

---

(1) *Displaced costs*
Traditional evaluations technique when tasks, machines, supplies, personnel, etc., are no longer required as a result of the new system, giving.
— Reductions in clerical operations
— Reduction in space required
— Reduction in paperwork
— Reduction in inventory
— Reduction in duplication of files, paperwork and operations
— Reduction in software/hardware maintenance

---

(2) *Increased productivity*
This stems from faster reaction possibilities and improved accuracy — generally allowing fewer people or facilities to do more work:

Reaction:
— Faster processing turnaround time
— Ability to compare alternative courses of action
— Assessment of impact across the organisation's activities
— Larger, more comprehensive database from which to plan and forecast
— Closer monitoring of operations
Accuracy:
— Automation permits more control and less errors
— Shared data between systems
— Improved validation facilities to ensure data integrity
— More information allows more accurate forecasts

---

(3) *Improved information*
This in itself has no value *unless* it is used to make improved decisions and ultimately in the majority of cases to increase income or revenue.
— Management by exception principles allows greater freedom for management
— Capability of developing simulation models
— Automatic decision-making
— Improved performance indications
— Lighter quality information
— Freedom from routine decision-making

---

represent a saving, however, is not in itself sufficient since the saving has to be matched against the expected rate of return for any investment made by the organisation. If the organisation can obtain an interest rate of 20 per cent for cash investments, then placing capital on loan is a preferable investment to the development of a new information system which projects only a 10 per cent return.

The organisation may also have to choose among several projects, all of which offer an acceptable rate of return, and must, therefore, be able to prioritise the systems on their key results value to the organisation and their comparative financial returns.

Table 10.3 Development costs (one-time)

Manpower: salaries and overheads
  Systems analysts
  Programmers
  Technical specialists
  User staff assigned to project
  Secretaries, non-DP staff, administration
  Managers and team leaders
Manpower operating costs
  General cost of labour overheads
  Recruiting costs
  Training
  Accommodation costs
  Expenses, subsistence allowances, etc.
  Fringe benefits etc.
  Incentive bonuses for achievement
External manpower
  Outside consultants
  Other
Hardware
  Machine time for system development
  Computer equipment
  Communication lines
  User equipment
Software
  Purchase or rental of special system software
  Purchase or rental of special applications
  Purchase or rental of special development aids
  On-going maintenance of software during project's lifetime
Supplies
  Data entry for development and testing
  Magnetic file storage for development and testing
  Input forms
  Printer stationery
  Cabinets etc.
Additional costs
  Sub-contracting costs
  Installation, pilot or parallel working
  Additional accommodation and storage
  Printing, stationery, photocopying
  Publicity and marketing costs
  Other

10.5 Standard costing techniques

Once the costs and benefits have been qualified the project can be represented as a long-term investment as shown in Figure 10.3. The questions which still remain to be answered, however, is which of several mutually exclusive investments should be selected, and how many projects in total should be accepted? To this end, three investment appraisal

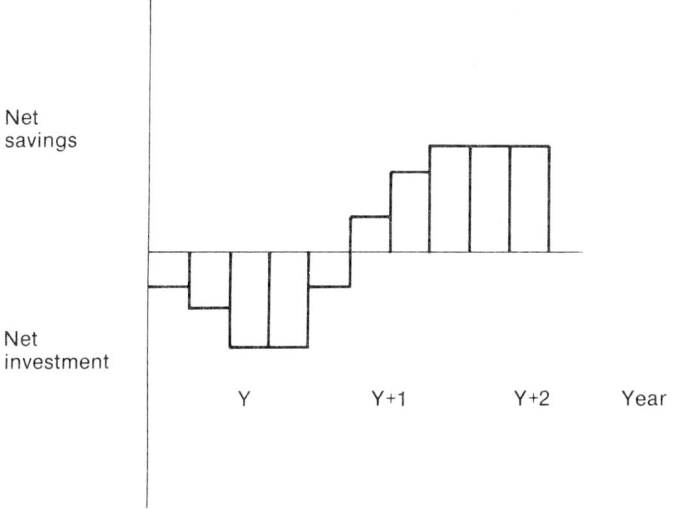

Figure 10.3 Long-term investment

methods are discussed:

(1) *Pay-back method:* number of years required to return the original investment
(2) *Net present value method* (NPV): present value of future returns discounted at the appropriate cost of capital, minus the cost of the investment
(3) *Internal rate of return method* (IRR): interest rate which equates the present value of future returns to the investment outlay.

In conjunction with these a profitability index (PI) may be used to assist ranking.

10.5.1 Pay-back method

Assume that two information systems projects are being considered by a firm, each requiring an investment of £1,000. The firm's marginal cost of capital is 10 per cent. Net cash flows from Projects A and B are:

Year	Project A	Project B
1	£500	£100
2	£400	£200
3	£300	£300
4	£100	£400
5		£500
6		£600

The pay-back period is the number of years it takes a firm to recover its original investment from net cash flow. Therefore, with the cost at £1,000, the pay-back period for A is $2\frac{1}{3}$ years, and the pay-back period for B is 4 years. Thus, if the firm were employing a 3 year pay-back period, A would be accepted and B rejected.

Typical problems which result from use of this method are:

(1) It ignores income beyond the pay-back period and hence if the project matures in later years it can lead to wrong decisions
(2) It fails to take into account the time value of money as shown in the following example.

Projects X and Y each cost £3,000 and each have the following cash flows:

Year	Project X	Project Y
1	£2,000	£1,000
2	£1,000	£2,000
3	£1,000	£1,000

Each has a 2 year pay-back, *but* X with a faster cash flow is more desirable.

The advantages of the method are equally obvious:

(1) It is easy
(2) Returns beyond 3 or 4 years are uncertain and therefore short-term concentration may be adequate
(3) Emphasis is on quick return of funds — a pressing concern for most managers
(4) Faster pay-backs have more favourable effects on earnings per share in the short run
(5) Many firms use pay-back in combination with one of the discounted cash flow procedures — NPV or IRR. Whilst NPV or IRR are used to appraise a project's profitability the pay-back method is used to show how long the initial investment will be at risk.

10.5.2 Net present value (NPV)

To calculate NPV, find the present value of the expected net cash flows of an investment, discounted at the cost of capital, and subtract from it the initial cost outlay of the project. If the NPV is positive the project should be accepted. If the NPV is negative it should be rejected. If the two projects are mutually exclusive the one with the higher NPV should be chosen.

Table 10.4 Present value conversion factors $(1 + r/100)^{-n}$

No. of years (n)	Discount rate (r)									
	1%	2%	3%	4%	5%	6%	7%	8%	9%	10%
1	.9901	.9804	.9709	.9615	.9524	.9434	.9346	.9259	.9174	.9091
2	.9803	.9612	.9426	.9246	.9070	.8900	.8734	.8573	.8417	.8264
3	.9706	.9423	.9151	.8890	.8638	.8396	.8163	.7938	.7722	.7513
4	.9610	.9238	.8885	.8548	.8227	.7921	.7629	.7350	.7084	.6830
5	.9515	.9057	.8626	.8219	.7835	.7473	.7130	.6806	.6499	.6209
6	.9420	.8880	.8375	.7903	.7462	.7050	.6663	.6302	.5963	.5645
7	.9327	.8706	.8131	.7599	.7107	.6651	.6227	.5835	.5470	.5132
8	.9235	.8535	.7894	.7307	.6768	.6274	.5820	.5403	.5019	.4665
9	.9143	.8368	.7664	.7026	.6446	.5919	.5439	.5002	.4604	.4241
10	.9053	.8203	.7441	.6756	.6139	.5584	.5083	.4632	.4224	.3855
11	.8963	.8043	.7224	.6496	.5847	.5268	.4751	.4289	.3875	.3505
12	.8874	.7885	.7014	.6246	.5568	.4970	.4440	.3971	.3555	.3186
13	.8787	.7730	.6810	.6006	.5303	.4688	.4150	.3677	.3262	.2897
14	.8700	.7579	.6611	.5775	.5051	.4423	.3878	.3405	.2992	.2633
15	.8613	.7430	.6419	.5553	.4810	.4173	.3624	.3152	.2745	.2394
16	.8528	.7284	.6232	.5339	.4581	.3936	.3387	.2919	.2519	.2176
17	.8444	.7142	.6050	.5134	.4363	.3714	.3166	.2703	.2311	.1978
18	.8360	.7002	.5874	.4936	.4155	.3503	.2959	.2502	.2120	.1799
19	.8277	.6864	.5703	.4746	.3957	.3305	.2765	.2317	.1945	.1635
20	.8195	.6730	.5537	.4564	.3769	.3118	.2584	.2145	.1784	.1486

No. of years (n)	Discount rate (r)									
	12%	14%	15%	16%	18%	20%	25%	30%	40%	50%
1	.8929	.8772	.8696	.8621	.8475	.8333	.8000	.7692	.7143	.6667
2	.7972	.7695	.7561	.7432	.7182	.6944	.6400	.5917	.5102	.4444
3	.7118	.6750	.6575	.6407	.6086	.5787	.5120	.4552	.3644	.2963
4	.6355	.5921	.5718	.5523	.5158	.4823	.4096	.3501	.2603	.1975
5	.5674	.5194	.4972	.4761	.4371	.4019	.3277	.2693	.1859	.1317
6	.5066	.4556	.4323	.4104	.3704	.3349	.2621	.2072	.1328	.0878
7	.4523	.3996	.3759	.3538	.3139	.2791	.2097	.1594	.0949	.0585
8	.4039	.3506	.3269	.3050	.2660	.2326	.1678	.1226	.0678	.0390
9	.3606	.3075	.2843	.2630	.2255	.1938	.1342	.0943	.0484	.0260
10	.3220	.2697	.2472	.2267	.1911	.1615	.1074	.0725	.0346	.0173
11	.2875	.2366	.2149	.1954	.1619	.1346	.0859	.0558	.0247	.0116
12	.2567	.2076	.1869	.1685	.1372	.1122	.0687	.0429	.0176	.0077
13	.2292	.1821	.1625	.1452	.1163	.0935	.0550	.0330	.0126	.0051
14	.2046	.1597	.1413	.1252	.0985	.0779	.0440	.0254	.0090	.0034
15	.1827	.1401	.1229	.1079	.0835	.0649	.0352	.0195	.0064	.0023
16	.1631	.1229	.1069	.0930	.0708	.0541	.0281	.0150	.0046	.0015
17	.1456	.1078	.0929	.0802	.0600	.0451	.0225	.0116	.0033	.0010
18	.1300	.0946	.0808	.0691	.0508	.0376	.0180	.0089	.0023	.0007
19	.1161	.0829	.0703	.0596	.0431	.0313	.0144	.0068	.0017	.0005
20	.1037	.0728	.0611	.0514	.0365	.0261	.0115	.0053	.0012	.0003

The equation for NPV is as follows:

$$NPV = \left[\frac{F_1}{(1 + K)^1} + \frac{F_2}{(1 + K)^2} + \ldots + \frac{F_N}{(1 + K)^N} \right] - IC$$

where:

F_1, F_2, etc, = Net cash flows (NCF) in year 1, year 2, etc.
K   = Marginal cost of capital = (discount rate)/100 = $r/100$
IC   = Initial cost of project
N   = Project's expected life

that is:

$$NPV = \sum_{i=1}^{i=N} \frac{F_i}{(1 + K)^i} - IC$$

NPV tables are available which simplify this calculation enormously (see Table 10.4).

Example 1

Projects A and B each cost £10,000 with 6 years of net cash flow (NCF). A 10 per cent capital discount rate is taken to determine the present value (PV) cash flows. The present value conversion factors (PVCF) are taken directly from Table 10.4, and the calculation is shown in Tables 10.5 and 10.6.

Project B is preferred to Project A, but which method is preferred using pay-back?

Table 10.5 Calculation of net present value — Project A

Year	NCF	PVCF (10%)	PV cash flow
1	£5,000	0.9091	£4,545.50
2	£4,000	0.8264	£3,305.60
3	£3,000	0.7513	£2,253.90
4	£1,000	0.6830	£683.00
5	£100	0.6209	£62.09
6	£100	0.5645	£56.45
		PV of inflows	£10,906.54
		Less Cost	£10,000.00
		NPV	£906.54

Table 10.6 Calculation of net present value — Project B

Year	NCF	PVCF (10%)	PV cash flow
1	£1,000	0.9091	£909.10
2	£2,000	0.8264	£1,652.80
3	£3,000	0.7513	£2,253.90
4	£4,000	0.6830	£2,732.00
5	£5,000	0.6209	£3,104.50
6	£6,000	0.5645	£3,387.00
		PV of inflows	£14,039.30
		Less Cost	£10,000.00
		NPV	£4,039.30

10.5.3 Internal rate of return (IRR)

IRR is the interest rate that equates the present value of the expected future cash flows to the initial cost outlay. The equation for IRR is:

$$\frac{F_1}{(1 + (r/100))^1} + \frac{F_2}{(1 + (r/100))^2} + \cdots + \frac{F_N}{(1 + (r/100))^N} - IC = 0$$

where IC is initial cost and F_1, F_2, etc., are cash flows, that is:

$$\sum_{i=1}^{i=N} \frac{F_i}{(1 + (r/100))^i} - IC = 0$$

and r is the unknown, a certain value for which will cause the sum of the discounted receipts to equal the initial cost of the project. That value of $r = $ IRR. (This equation is the same as NPV with r the unknown.)

IRR can be found by trial and error as follows:

(1) Compute the present value of cash flows from an investment using arbitrary interest rate (cost of capital is generally in the range 10–15 per cent, therefore 10 per cent is a good starting point).
(2) Compare the PV with the investment cost.
(3) If PV > IC try a higher interest rate until PV ≃ IC. Conversely, when PV < IC try a lower value.
(4) The interest rate which gives equality is the IRR.

Example 2

Project A and Project B each cost £10,000. Six years' cash flows are given below, and the calculation of the IRR is given in Table 10.7

Table 10.7 Calculation of internal rate of return

Year	PVCF (10%)	A	B	PVCF (15%)	A	B	PVCF (20%)	A	B
1	0.9091	£4,545.50	£909.10	0.8696	£4,348.00	£869.60	0.8333	£4,166.50	£833.30
2	0.8264	£3,305.60	£1,652.80	0.7561	£3,024.40	£1,512.20	0.6944	£2,777.60	£1,388.80
3	0.7513	£2,253.90	£2,253.90	0.6575	£1,972.50	£1,972.50	0.5787	£1,736.10	£1,736.10
4	0.6830	£683.00	£2,732.00	0.5718	£571.80	£2,287.20	0.4823	£482.30	£1,929.20
5	0.6209	£62.09	£3,104.50	0.4972	£49.72	£2,486.00	0.4019	£40.19	£2,009.50
6	0.5645	£56.45	£3,387.00	0.4323	£43.23	£2,593.80	0.3349	£33.49	£2,009.40
PV		£10,906.54	£14,039.30		£10,009.65	£11,721.30		£9,236.18	£9,906.30
NPV = PV − IC		£906.54	£4,039.30		£9.65	£1,721.30		£−763.72	£−93.70

Year	Project A	Project B
1	£5,000	£1,000
2	£4,000	£2,000
3	£3,000	£3,000
4	£1,000	£4,000
5	£100	£5,000
6	£100	£6,000

Thus the IRR of Project A is approximately 15 per cent and the IRR of Project B is approximately 20 per cent.

10.5.4 Differences between NPV and IRR and use of a profitability index (PI)

Under certain conditions NPV and IRR methods can rate projects differently, and if mutually exclusive projects are involved or if capital is limited the rankings can be important. These can occur when:

(1) The cost of one project is larger than that of the other.

Example 3

Project S costs £1.00 and yields £1.50 at the end of 1 year. At 10 per cent cost of capital:

$$NPV = £0.36$$
$$IRR = 50\%$$

Project L costs £1 million and yields £1.25m at the end of 1 year. At 10 per cent cost of capital:

$$NPV = £113,625$$
$$IRR = 25\%$$

(2) The timing of the projects' cash flow differs so that the cash flows from one project increase over time while those of the other decrease, or projects may have different expected lives.

Example 4

Projects A and B each cost £1,200 with returns as follows:

Year	Project A	Project B
1	£1,000	£100
2	£500	£600
3	£100	£1,100

Table 10.8 Calculation of IRR — Example 4, Project A

Year	Return	Present value at					
		0%	5%	10%	15%	20%	25%
1	£1,000	£1,000	£952.40	£909.10	£896.60	£833.30	£800.00
2	£500	£500	£453.50	£413.20	£378.05	£347.20	£320.00
3	£100	£100	£86.38	£75.13	£65.75	£57.87	£51.20
Total		£1,600	£1,493.28	£1,397.43	£1,340.40	£1,238.37	£1,171.20
Less Cost		£1,200	£1,200.00	£1,200.00	£1,200.00	£1,200.00	£1,200.00
NPV		£400	£293.28	£197.43	£140.40	£38.37	£ − 28.80

Table 10.9 Calculation of IRR — Example 4, Project B

Year	Return	Present value at				
		0%	5%	10%	15%	20%
1	£100	£100.00	£95.24	£90.91	£86.96	£83.33
2	£600	£600.00	£544.20	£495.84	£453.66	£416.64
3	£1,100	£1,100.00	£950.18	£826.43	£723.25	£636.57
Total		£1,800.00	£1,589.62	£1,413.28	£1,263.87	£1,136.54
Less Cost		£1,200.00	£1,200.00	£1,200.00	£1,200.00	£1,200.00
NPV		£600.00	£389.62	£213.28	£63.87	£ − 63.46

The calculations of IRR are given in Tables 10.8 and 10.9. From these it can be seen that the IRR for Project A is approximately 23 per cent, and for Project B approximately $17\frac{1}{2}$ per cent.

A profitability index (PI) can be useful in ranking situations such as this since it calculates the specific rate of return on the capital investment. The index is given by:

$$PI = PV \text{ benefits}/\text{cost}$$

and shows the relative profitability of any project or the benefits per £1 of cost. For example:

Project X: Let cost = £1,000,000 and NPV = £200,000
Project Y: Let cost =   £300,000 and NPV = £100,000
    PI of X   = 1,200,000/1,000,000 = 1.2
    PI of Y   =   400,000/300,000   = 1.33

Thus, Project Y gives a higher profitability index than Project X.

10.5.5 Other factors

Meaningful use of these techniques can provide a forecast of the project's effect on funds and assist in comparative prioritisation. There may, however, be other factors which should also be taken into consideration.

(1) *Risk:* As many as 70 per cent of projects fail to realise the benefits originally anticipated because the risks involved were not really understood. These largely relate to ill-defined requirements analysis, but it must also be accepted that particular systems are more prone to undefined errors. Systems such as those requiring a large amount of human interaction/customer interface, unusually high reliability or use of unfamiliar technology are all high-risk areas.

(2) *Manageability:* This relates to the amount of experience there is within the organisation in developing this type of system. Possible labour relations problems, changes in organisational structure, and the need to recruit external expertise can all cause project management problems.

(3) *Timespan:* A long timespan for development means less reliable estimates and a greater amount of resources tied up for a longer period.

(4) *Congruence:* It is important to evaluate projects against DP policies and current/planned resources. While no plan should be seen as totally inflexible it is going to cause problems if a project is accepted which does not conform to a general development standard.

Considering all these factors may allow projects to be ranked on a priority scale for future developments. As said previously, however, they all rely on the validity of data input regarding qualified costs and benefits, and so the next section examines the risk potential of analysing benefits and outlines a way of reducing the probabilities of error.

10.6 Risk/benefit analysis techniques

In order to provide realistic data on quantified benefits we have to use probability analysis and ask the user management to predict the probabilities of possible improvements. This applies particularly to those benefits previously classified as 'intangibles'. This technique could be applied as in the following example.

Example 5

In the library system financial benefits would be achieved from the viewdata system if fewer reference books were then required.

Possible decrease in references	Librarians' estimate of probability
5%	80%
10%	15%
15%	5%

The library maintains £100,000 worth of reference books, so:

Decrease	Value	Probability	Expected return
5%	£5,000	0.8	£4,000
10%	£10,000	0.15	£1,500
15%	£15,000	0.05	£750
		1.00	£6,250

Therefore annually the system can achieve a £6,250 reduction in costs.

It would also be possible to add to this figure a further saving on replacement cost if the librarian also calculated a percentage usage of reference books and related this to the average replacement period.

In some cases it is not very easy, of course, to get prediction data, particularly where it involves the clients of the system. In the above example, will the registered patrons of the library use the library more if a computerised lending system is introduced? In order to derive this data, statistical sampling can be used: patrons might be issued with a simple questionnaire designed to determine whether an improved service would result in increased usage.

This type of analysis is related to a student enrolment system in the following examples.

Example 6

First, a cost per student is calculated, based on enrolment numbers and an estimated cost reduction resulting from on-line validation of entry by the computerised system.

Cost reduction:
£0.4 per enrolled student × 10,000 students per year = £4,000
@ 95% probability   = £3,800

The number of students has risen by 10 per cent each year and requires additional clerical staff to process the increased enrolments:

Cost avoidance:
10% increase = 5 additional personnel
5 persons @ £8,000 per year   = £40,000
Less Cost of computer process
    for additional personnel   = £3,000
Cost avoidance   = £37,000
@ 95% probability   = £35,150

Example 7

As a result of the student enrolment system the college is able to build a detailed student database which will be used as the basis for market analysis for the development of future courses to suit demand. The college authorities estimate an expansion over the next 3 years of 30 per. cent over the normal increase. Funding from the grants committee averages £1,500 per student.

Profit improvement:
Projected student number increase   = 3,000
Funding (£1,500 × 3,000/3)   = £1,500,000
Percentage of funding available for staff development = 2%
                             Total = £30,000

Total funding per student head does not increase, but, since costs do not rise in direct proportion to increased numbers, a fixed percentage is available for staff development — the additional capital gain would represent £30,000 of improved staff quality.

In order to present this to senior management at the Polycollege a table could be drawn up, as in Table 10.10, to identify the individual effects of each system and the global effect on the organisation by cumulative implementation of the key results systems.

A very similar form of presentation to that in Table 10.10 is suggested

Table 10.10 Benefits table

KRA systems	Cost reduction	Cost avoidance	Profit improvement	Benefits
Student enrolment	£3,800	£35,150	£30,000	£68,950
Student timetable	£7,000	£12,000	—	£19,000
Student assessment records	£25,000	£15,600	—	£40,600
Total systems				£128,550

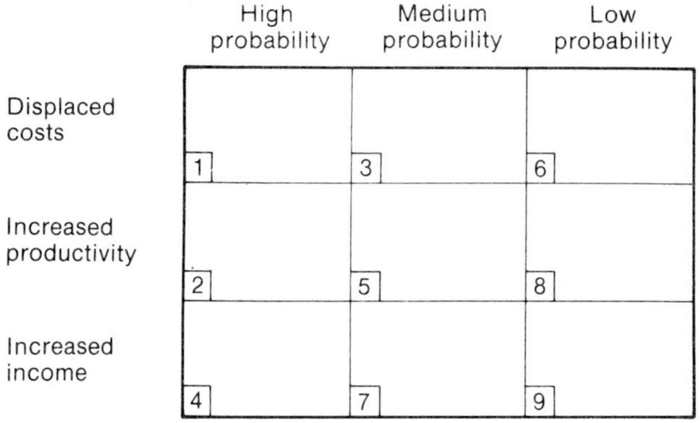

Figure 10.4   Benefits matrix

within the BSP methodology which we have already considered in some detail in Chapter 6. The suggested method is known as risk-potential benefit analysis and uses the benefits matrix as shown in Figure 10.4.

Example 8

Continuing the example of the Polycollege catering inventory control system (Chapter 4), the benefits estimated during the interviews with the Catering Department Head, the Chief Purchasing Officer and the Dining Room Manager might be:

£10,000 reduction in food inventory
£3,000 labour reductions
£4,000 increased production of meals
£6,000 increase in sales

The project team then asks the users to estimate the probability of realisation of the total, such as in the case of inventory reduction. The £10,000 is not achievable immediately but there is:

(1) A high probability of, say, £5,000 savings on dry goods
(2) A moderate probability of, say, £2,000 savings on canned goods
(3) A moderate probability of, say, £3,000 savings on fresh goods

This process is repeated for each estimated potential benefit and then assigned to the matrix as shown in Figure 10.5.

The numbers in the matrix show the likelihood of the potential benefit, and this can be used as input to an expanded table ranking all likely system developments on the basis of their risk levels and return. Table 10.11 is an example of a table where any two systems can be compared within any combination of risk.

One major issue affecting the final decision that has been overlooked so far relates to the quality of information. This forms the subject for discussion in the next section.

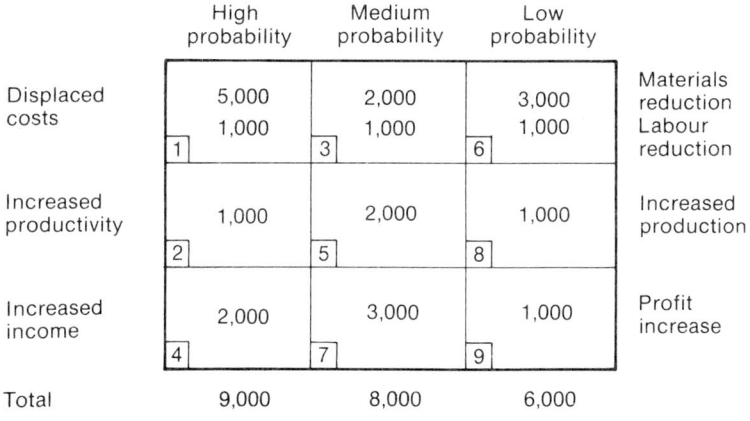

Figure 10.5   Example of a completed benefits matrix

Table 10.11 Benefits comparison table

Subsystem	1	2	3	4	Risk level 5	6	7	8	9	Total
Inventory control	6,000	1,000	3,000	2,000	2,000	4,000	3,000	1,000	1,000	23,000
Purchasing system	...	...	...	...	...	...	...	...	...	...
Sales processing	...	...	...	...	...	...	...	...	...	...
.										
.										
.										

10.7 The value and cost of information

Throughout this book it has been stressed that information has no value unless it can affect a decision. It is also true, however, that while information may have some value, it may not be worth the cost of producing it. This has to be considered very carefully, especially since too much information can be more harmful than too little when it obscures the major issues from the decision maker.

What then is meant by the 'value of information'? A simple concept which nevertheless has major ramifications for the information systems designer is: 'Information has a declining incremental value as its quality increases.' Figure 10.6 shows the effect of this phenomenon and a simple example helps to illustrate it.

Consider a system implemented with a 10 per cent error occurrence in data collections. Suppose the error rate can be reduced from 10 to 5 per cent, providing a 50 per cent error reduction. It may then also be possible to reduce the subsequent 5 per cent error rate to 2.5 per cent, giving again a 50 per cent reduction overall. The effects of the second phase enhancement, however, are far less than the first since fewer errors are in fact removed from the system. There comes a time, therefore, when the analyst and users need to agree on the effectiveness level of the information required and the value that accrues to an improvement in the quality of information.

This is particularly relevant to the evaluation of alternative design specifications, since it may be possible to provide the required quality of information at different levels of cost. The users of the library lending system may identify the need for a catalogue of books which are currently held in the library. Improved quality of information would require an

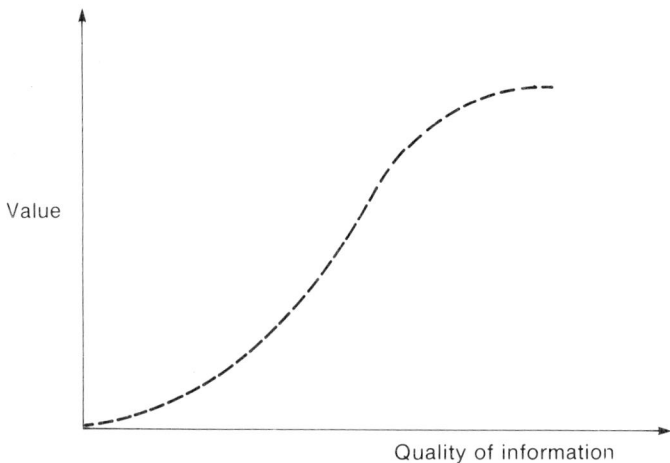

Figure 10.6   Declining incremental value of information

indication of whether the books were currently in stock or on loan. It may be, however, that the value of this information does not require an on-line immediate update on the catalogue but rather a daily catalogue provided from on-line data entry with overnight batch processing. The librarian could then check from the daily transaction list whether any activity had affected a certain book during the day should the library patrons be unable to retrieve it from the shelves. This decision can only be made if there is an agreed definition of the information quality requirements which can then be assigned a value to be weighed against the cost of meeting them.

Obviously, this affects the whole system design. For example:

(1) The allocation of tasks between man and machine:
   - The librarian, in the previous example, is allocated the task of searching the day's to-date transactions at less cost than that of implementing an on-line system but at no great cost to the quality of information which the patrons obtain.
   - For a quick retrieval system for book titles or particular subjects, do we allow 'free word' searches at a very high cost or do we ask the patron to identify the key words from a given list and to work with the librarian using an established efficient search pattern?

(2) The content of the database with respect to the amount of aggregation possible and the desired retention period:
   - Is it important for the librarian to know which patrons borrowed which books over the last year, or rather the number of times a book has been borrowed?
   - Do we need to know the life history of a book or just the previous year's borrowing pattern?

(3) The accuracy of the information obviously affects the quality of decision-making, so it must be related to the requirements of different users:
   - The library patron needs to know if a book is available in order to select and borrow that book or an alternative; the librarian, however, needs only approximate usage over classification groupings to specify budget allocations over the next year.
   - The librarian needs to know when a particular book is overdue, lost or stolen in order to take appropriate action, but a global percentage figure of shrinkage is all that is required to estimate replacement budgets or to evaluate the need for security systems.

(4) The response and retrieval times:
   - As specified earlier, it may not be necessary to have on-line updating and on-line access to the system since current information tends to relate more closely to operational level needs than strategic planning.
   - Fast retrieval must also be assessed with regard to the urgency of system reaction. In the case of the library there is no need to inform

the chief librarian of a lost library membership card immediately it occurs, whereas a credit card system would demand this.

- Similarly, in the viewdata system it may be possible to differentiate between users, allowing some to access on overnight searching only and others to gain advantage from the reduced loading on the system to achieve a 25 second response time.

All of these decisions, of course, relate closely to the way in which the information can then be presented to the user, as discussed in earlier chapters. The important point to be stressed is that the user, in conjunction with the analyst, must define the value of information before the optimum system can be proposed to produce it and before any real decision can be made as to the cost/benefit analysis.

10.8 Summary

This last chapter has considered the issues involved in the selection and justification of information systems for computer-based development and emphasised the need for strategic planning. However, an essential part of this plan is the definition of a Management Information Systems (MIS) plan to meet the long-term needs of the decision makers in the organisation.

For example, in this book we have looked at various functional departments within a typical local authority and examined their need for information. It should be obvious, therefore, that a wide variety of needs exist within this one organisation and this can present a serious problem for centralised decision-making.

Nevertheless, as we have seen, the authority requires to formulate annual budgets based on individual department's requirements but coordinated into an overall strategy for the organisation. This necessitates a definition of information needs at management level, in particular the type of information that will be required to provide meaningful feedback for planning and control in the long term. The ensuing MIS would, therefore, be seen as an integrated user-computer system that provides information to support the operations, management and decision-making functions in an organisation. Such a system would utilise computer hardware and software (including a database), manual procedures and models for analysis, planning, control and decision-making.

In this context MIS is an evolutionary concept as all other information systems within an organisation effectively become sub-systems and must be designed with an MIS orientation. This does not mean, however, that all systems must share all data files or utilise the same hardware. For instance, current technology will allow individual departments to run their systems on micro- or mini-computers with a communications interface to a centralised system permitting users to upload or download data as required.

Decentralisation of facilities such as this enable user departments to have independent control over operational level systems, controlled access to common data for departmental planning systems and the facility to input data to the strategic level system.

The effectiveness, therefore, of the MIS relates directly to the definition of a strategic policy at top management level and the linking of information systems development strategies to this corporate plan. Too often organisations have well-defined corporate strategies but no concomitant information systems strategy, and as a result they seriously under-utilise the effect of computer-based systems within the organisation.

This book has introduced the reader to the analysis of information and related this to the development of effective information systems in this the age of 'Information Technology'. The real power of computer-based information systems, however, lies in their ability to integrate data and so permit the development of organisational models which can then be used to make effective decisions essential to the successful operation of any organisation.

APPENDIX
Selected exercises

Chapter 4

1 Explain the difference between continuous and discrete data items.
  At Anyshire's Polycollege, the percentage marks scored by students in a computing examination are as given in Table A1.

Table A1 Percentage marks scored

68	64	51	68	82	71	76	70	45	43
78	77	71	25	29	79	37	71	80	19
71	56	68	52	32	74	63	12	36	63
75	72	67	81	71	63	70	49	54	64
77	61	73	51	73	63	40	83	40	46
74	73	54	52	58	64	73	79	54	48
42	59	53	71	37	85	43	51	45	63
28	36	42	69	48	50	24	56	47	50
75	44	57	68	64	74	56	54	42	59
55	81	39	50	43	67	59	76	67	74

(a) Organise the data into a suitable frequency distribution table and construct a histogram.
(b) Calculate the arithmetic mean and standard deviation for the grouped data.
(c) The pass, credit and distinction marks for the examination are 40 per cent, 65 per cent and 75 per cent. Draw a pie chart illustrating the breakdown of fails, passes, credits and distinctions for the examination.
(d) Draw a cumulative frequency graph and estimate:
   (i) The percentage of students within one standard deviation of the arithmetic mean. How close is this figure to the true percentage?
   (ii) The interquartile range of marks.

2 Table A2 shows details of the home-help service provided by the four divisions of Anyshire County Council's Social Services Department during last year. For comparison purposes, the figures in brackets relate to the same periods of the previous year.

Prepare suitable graph(s) or chart(s) for presentation of this data to top management.

In addition, write a short report commenting on the significant features of the data.

Table A2 Home-help provision last year (previous year)

	Nature of	Division			
Qtr	*provision*	1	2	3	4
1	Hours/week	2,302(2,146)	9,076(8,539)	3,113(3,050)	5,146(4,674)
	clients/week	853(823)	3,420(3,329)	984(948)	1,866(1,822)
2	Hours/week	2,261(2,090)	8,272(8,002)	2,893(2,854)	4,715(4,092)
	clients/week	853(764)	3,474(3,222)	988(887)	1,935(1,755)
3	Hours/week	2,432(2,463)	9,012(8,847)	3,044(3,158)	5,049(4,968)
	clients/week	859(787)	3,483(3,306)	1,044(941)	1,974(1,793)
4	Hours/week	2,306(2,392)	8,689(8,818)	2,981(3,054)	4,764(5,100)
	clients/week	860(823)	3,479(3,329)	1,014(948)	1,960(1,822)

3 Anyshire County Council is a large employer. It wishes to analyse the effect of the number of work days lost due to illness in recent years. The available data for days lost is set out in Table A3.

Table A3 Work days lost due to illness

	Quarter			
Year	1	2	3	4
y − 3	203	195	221	212
y − 2	221	203	235	238
y − 1	229	219	264	257
y	239	224	268	267

Perform a trend analysis on the data supplied, and estimate any seasonal variations from the calculated trend. What conclusions and/or limitations are indicated by your results?

4 The average weekly earnings of full-time Anyshire County Council employees over a five-year period are set out in Table A4, together with the Retail Price Index (RPI) for the same period.

Table A4 Average weekly earnings

	Average weekly earnings (£)		
Year	Manual	Non-manual	RPI
y − 4	87.50	129.01	119.4
y − 3	91.92	137.42	122.3
y − 2	98.58	151.45	127.7
y − 1	104.43	165.38	136.7
y	112.71	182.04	145.0

Re-form the values in the table with the data for the year y − 4 indexed at 100. What conclusions do you draw from presentation of the data in this form?

Which employee data set correlates the more closely with the RPI over this five-year period?

5 Imagine that you are the course tutor for the BTEC HND in computer studies course at Anyshire Polycollege. You are required to prepare an end-of-year results broadsheet for the first year of the course. The overall mark for each course unit is a combination of in-course and examination marks. The course units and in-course and examination marks weightings are given in Table A5.

Table A5 Examination marks weightings

	Assessment weighting	
Unit	In-course	Examination
Commercial programming	50	50
Programming methodology	50	50
Computer architecture	40	60
Data processing	40	60
Information analysis	40	60

Develop a spreadsheet work file that will accept student in-course and examination marks for each course unit and produce under suitable headings a results broadsheet containing:

(a) The students' in-course, examination and overall marks for each of the course units
(b) Each course unit's average mark
(c) Each student's average mark
(d) The number of 'credits' each student has gained (a credit is gained by achieving a minimum of 50 per cent in both the in-course and examin-

ation components of assessment, together with an overall mark of at least 65 per cent)

Chapters 5 and 6

1 *Anyshire SSD case study*
The outline system has identified three levels of system in the total architecture. For each level define a sample set of three outputs appropriate for use in operational, tactical and strategic planning.
  For each output the specification should include:

- The name of the recipient
- The use to which the output will be put
- The data controls
- The media used
- A format justified with regard to its appropriateness for the intended purpose

Finally, a report of not more than two pages should accompany the sample set addressed to Paul Kent, the Director of Social Services, which outlines typical improvements which could be expected in the information flow as a result of your designs.

2 *Library case study*
As part of Anyshire County Council responsibilities a library lending system is maintained. Using the library in your own institution as a guide and the model developed in the first six chapters of this book, perform a requirements analysis for the development of a library information system.

Chapter 7

1 Discuss, briefly, the following:
  (a) The merits of double-entry accounting systems.
  (b) The different functions of a 'balance sheet' and a 'profit and loss account'.
  (c) The reasons why members of the public might be interested in Anyshire County Council's published accounts.
  (d) The major benefits arising from a budgetary control system.

2 (a) Allocate the following expenditure items to 'Capital' or Revenue':
       — Salaries
       — Rent paid
       — Land purchases

- Minibus acquisition
- Minibus fuel costs
- Minibus depreciation
- Office consumables
- Office furniture

(b) Describe the type of need for the following accounting information within Anyshire County Council:

- Monthly departmental expenditure summaries
- Costs of alternative replacement photocopiers
- Education expenditure per pupil in other counties
- Increase in staff turnover in the data processing department
- Probable effect of not increasing school meal prices

Chapter 8

1 Anyshire County Council Social Services Department runs a number of minibuses. On average the annual operational costs for each minibus have been found to be as follows:

Road tax	£100
Insurance	£300
Servicing and other fixed costs	£240

The minibuses average 20 miles per gallon of petrol and petrol costs £2.00 per gallon. Depreciation is assessed at 0.001 pence times mileage squared.

Formulate a model analysing these costs and hence determine the mileage per year that would minimise the cost per mile of a minibus.

What would be the effect if the depreciation factor were increased from 0.001 to 0.0015 pence?

2 The Printing Services Section of Anyshire County Council is assessing the viability of its A4 copying service to the authority. Based on the charges made to the various departments, the total weekly revenue is given by:

$$R = 16q$$

where q is the weekly production throughput in dozens of reams of A4-size paper. The total weekly production cost is given by:

$$C = 25 + 3q + 0.25q^2$$

Draw the two curves on the same graph and estimate the break-even point. Confirm your answer by finding the break-even point analytically.

The annual usage of A4-size paper is currently 3,000 dozen reams. The unit cost is £1.00 per ream. Storage and other holding costs are estimated at £3.00 per dozen reams per year. The re-order cost is known to be £5.00 per order. Assuming that the inventory policy is based on the 'economic order quantity' model, determine the optimal order quantity. How is the number of orders to be placed during the year affected if the effect of cost of money is included in the calculations? Consider both 5 per cent and 10 per cent costs.

Consider also the following discount options: (a) a 2 per cent discount whenever an order exceeds 100 dozen reams; (b) a 4 per cent discount whenever an order exceeds 200 dozen reams.

3 Set up appropriate models to solve the following:

(a) It is estimated that the amount of statistical information available worldwide is doubling every ten years. What annual growth rate does this represent?
(b) How long will it take £1,000 to increase to £2,000 at 12 per cent annual interest if the interest is added to the capital (i) every year, (ii) every quarter, (iii) every month?
(c) How much should be written off annually for a minicomputer which costs £45,000 and which is expected to be in use for 8 years when it will have an anticipated resale value of £2,000?
(d) A loan of £20,000 is to be paid off by ten equal annual payments with compound interest at $12\frac{1}{2}$ per cent. What is the amount of each payment? How much of the debt will be outstanding after five years?

Chapter 9

1 Solve the following linear programming problems graphically:

(a) Minimise $f = 3x_1 + 2x_2$
subject to $\quad x_1 \geqslant 5$
$x_2 \geqslant 5$
$x_1 + x_2 \geqslant 8$
(b) Maximise $f = 2x_1 + 3x_2$
subject to $3x_1 + x_2 \leqslant 1,200$
$x_1 + x_2 \leqslant 60$
$x_1 + 2x_2 \leqslant 100$
$x_1 \geqslant 0$
$x_2 \geqslant 0$

2 Anyshire County Council wishes to invest a Reserve Fund of £100,000

and has selected three investments. The data currently available is:

Investment	Return
1	$11\frac{1}{2}\%$
2	12%
3	$12\frac{1}{2}\%$

It has been decided that no more than 65 per cent of the Fund is to go into investments 2 and 3. Also, the amount in investment 1 should be at least equal to the amount in investment 3.

Formulate a linear programming model for this problem and solve it if a suitable computer software package is available.

3 Anyshire County Council has tenders for four jobs from four contractors. The bids (£) submitted are as follows:

Job	Contractor A	B	C	D
1	45,000	40,000	35,000	42,500
2	85,000	85,000	80,000	80,000
3	100,000	95,000	85,000	90,000
4	40,000	45,000	40,000	45,000

For speed of job completion, it has been decided that no contractor is to be awarded a contract for more than one job. Determine how the jobs should be assigned to the contractors in order to minimise costs.

4 The activities of a certain project are set out in Table A6.

Table A6 Project activity table

Activity	Duration (weeks)	Precedence relationship
A	5	—
B	10	—
C	8	—
D	6	A
E	12	A
F	7	B,D
G	4	C
H	6	E,F,G
I	10	C

Draw a network diagram for the project. Perform a network analysis that determines:

(a) earliest and latest event times
(b) the slack times of the activities
(c) the critical path
(d) the minimum number of weeks required to complete the project

What is the effect of reducing the duration of activity D from 6 to 3 weeks?

5 Perform a network analysis for a project consisting of the activities shown in Table A7.

Table A7 Project activity data for critical path determination

Activity		Duration	Resource requirement
Start event	Finish event	(days)	(manpower)
0	1	1	2
1	2	2	2
1	4	3	2
2	3	4	2
3	4	14	3
3	5	12	3
3	6	12	2
4	7	10	3
4	8	8	2
4	9	12	4
5	10	0	0
6	10	0	0
7	10	5	2
8	10	6	2
9	10	4	3
10	11	4	3

Determine the critical path(s) and the total duration of the project. Use a suitable computer software package to confirm your results.

How is the duration of the project affected if there are only (a) 7 men, (b) 6 men, (c) 5 men available at any one time?

Chapter 10

1 Use a spreadsheet program to produce in a suitable format:
(a) Compounding tables:

$$(1 + (r/100))^n \text{ for } r = 0.01 \text{ to } r = 0.30, n = 1 \text{ to } 25$$

(b) Discounting tables:

$$(1 + (r/100))^{-n} \text{ for } r = 0.01 \text{ to } r = 0.30, n = 1 \text{ to } 25$$

2 Anyshire County Council is contemplating either purchasing or renting an 'automated office' computer system. The purchase cost is £15,000. The rental cost is £3,000 per year. The anticipated life of the system is 8 years and the current return on capital is 12 per cent. Which is the better investment based on these comparative costs? What other factors might influence the final decision?

3 Anyshire County Council is considering the merits of three investment plans for the introduction of word processing equipment. Each plan costs £36,000. Plan A has estimated savings of £10,000 per year for 5 years; Plan B, savings of £9,000 per year for 6 years; Plan C, savings of £8,000 per year for 7 years. Calculate the net present values of the three plans, and show which is the best investment if the internal rate of return is (a) 8 per cent per year, (b) 10 per cent per year, (c) 12 per cent per year.

Index